The Origin and G ████████████████

'Jaspers has left us a rich and wide-ranging intellectual legacy encompassing psychiatry, intellectual history, and politics as well as philosophy.'
— *Times Literary Supplement*

Karl Jaspers (1883–1969) was a German psychiatrist and philosopher and one of the most original European thinkers of the twentieth century. As a major exponent of existentialism in Germany, he had a strong influence on modern theology, psychiatry and philosophy. He was Hannah Arendt's supervisor before her emigration to the United States in the 1930s and himself experienced the consequences of Nazi persecution. He was removed from his position at the University of Heidelberg in 1937, due to his wife being Jewish.

Published in 1949, the year in which the Federal Republic of Germany was founded, *The Origin and Goal of History* is a vitally important book. It is renowned for Jaspers' theory of an 'Axial Age', running from the 8th to the 3rd century BCE. Jaspers argues that this period witnessed a remarkable flowering of new ways of thinking that appeared in Persia, India, China and the Greco-Roman world, in striking parallel development but without any obvious direct cultural contact between them. Jaspers identifies key thinkers from this age, including Confucius, Buddha, Zarathustra, Homer and Plato, who had a profound influence on the trajectory of future philosophies and religions. For Jaspers, crucially, it is here that we see the flowering of diverse philosophical beliefs such as scepticism, materialism, sophism, nihilism, and debates about good and evil, which taken together demonstrate human beings' shared ability to engage with universal, humanistic questions as opposed to those mired in nationality or authoritarianism.

At a deeper level, *The Origin and Goal of History* provides a crucial philosophical framework for the liberal renewal of German intellectual life after 1945, and indeed of European intellectual life more widely, as a shattered continent attempted to find answers to what had happened in the preceding years.

This Routledge Classics edition includes a new Foreword by Christopher Thornhill.

Karl Jaspers (1883–1969) was a German-born psychiatrist and philosopher and one of the most original, interesting and yet neglected European thinkers of the twentieth century. Initially trained as a psychiatrist before taking up philosophy, his book *General Psychopathology* (1913) remains a classic in psychiatric literature. Never an adherent of any school or movement, his philosophy was shaped by his early encounters with Max Weber, whose family were close friends of Jaspers', and later Martin Heidegger, who had an important influence on Jaspers' own brand of existentialism. Jaspers' thought was also deeply marked by the rise of Nazism in the 1930s. Amongst his best-known works is *The Question of German Guilt* (1946), which examined the culpability of Germany as a whole in the atrocities of Hitler's Third Reich.

Routledge Classics contains the very best of Routledge publishing over the past century or so, books that have, by popular consent, become established as classics in their field. Drawing on a fantastic heritage of innovative writing published by Routledge and its associated imprints, this series makes available in attractive, affordable form some of the most important works of modern times.

For a complete list of titles visit:
https://www.routledge.com/Routledge-Classics/
book-series/SE0585

Karl
Jaspers

The Origin and Goal of History

Translated by Michael Bullock

With a new Foreword by Christopher Thornhill.

 London and New York

First published in Routledge Classics 2021
by Routledge
2 Park Square, Milton Park, Abingdon, Oxon OX14 4RN

and by Routledge
52 Vanderbilt Avenue, New York, NY 10017

Routledge is an imprint of the Taylor & Francis Group, an informa business

First published 1953 by Routledge & Kegan Paul Ltd

British Library Cataloguing-in-Publication Data
A catalogue record for this book is available from the British Library

Library of Congress Cataloging-in-Publication Data
A catalog record has been requested for this book

ISBN: 978-0-367-67987-3 (hbk)
ISBN: 978-0-367-67985-9 (pbk)
ISBN: 978-1-003-13367-4 (ebk)

Typeset in Joanna
by codeMantra

Contents

FOREWORD TO THE ROUTLEDGE CLASSICS EDITION

For a short period after 1945, Karl Jaspers took centre stage as the leading philosopher and political thinker in Germany, before and after the foundation of the Federal Republic of Germany (1949). During this time, Jaspers consciously developed a semi-pedagogic style of reasoning and arguing, designed to provide philosophically founded guidance for the citizens of the re-emergent German polity. His works of this time are clearly conceived both as contributions to philosophical debate and as commentaries on questions of moral-political and educational importance in Germany, intended to accompany and to support the process of re-democratization after 1945.

In this context, Jaspers appeared as the first major philosopher of democracy in German history. To be sure, he had important antecedents in this respect. His thought was suffused by the influence of Kantian political ethics, which clearly informed his democratic commitments. He was also very strongly influenced by Max Weber, whose contribution to the formation of the first full German democracy after 1918 was, although not uncontentious, considerable. However, Jaspers was the first major philosopher in Germany to propose a philosophical framework to understand and legitimate liberal-democratic political life, under a liberal-democratic constitution.

The fact that Jaspers was able to acquire this importance as a public philosopher was linked, in part, to his distinctive intellectual background and trajectory. In the 1920s and early 1930s, he had assumed an intellectual position which, unusually, was relatively unmarked by the patterns of extreme political polarization that characterized the intellectual life of the Weimar Republic. At this time, as one of the leading proponents of existentialist philosophy, his intellectual position was very clearly identifiable as strongly anti-Marxist, belonging, broadly, to the field of phenomenological reflection that was generally reviled by exponents of Marxist dialectics. Despite this, he was rarely drawn into the anti-democratic polemics typical of opponents of the organized political left in Germany in the 1920s. His outlook remained in the liberal-conservative margins of political debate, and his indebtedness to Kantian ethics and to Weberian liberalism ensured that his thought did not move outside the broadly democratic spectrum of political opinion. While notable contemporaries, such as Carl Schmitt and Martin Heidegger, provided emphatic support for the National Socialists after 1933, Jaspers emerged after 1945 as one of the few prominent intellectuals in the Western part of Germany who had not been contaminated by affiliation with the Nazi movement. His credentials were further enhanced by the fact that he had been relieved of his professorial duties by the Nazis, and he was married to a Jewish woman.

From this position, Jaspers began to assert political and theoretical influence in Germany immediately after the German capitulation. At one level, he did this by commenting on the most immediately pressing problems of political ethics in the early post-war years. For example, he published *The Question of German Guilt* in 1946, which formed an ethical-metaphysical reflection on the Nuremberg trials, in which he stressed the moral responsibility of Germans for the holocaust. Less immediately, he did this by promoting an engagement with philosophical questions that he thought likely to direct German society away from its historical propensity for authoritarianism and to establish a philosophical diction to consolidate Germany's democratic future. *Origin and Goal of History*, first published in 1949, the year in which the Federal Republic of Germany was founded, is the main example of this approach. This book is clearly intended to be read on two levels, one philosophical, one moral-political, and it is intended to propose a reflexive framework for the liberal renewal of German intellectual life, and indeed of European intellectual life more widely.

The fact that Jaspers exercised greatest influence in the post-war period has in some ways proved detrimental to his philosophical reputation. In the mirror of intellectual history, he frequently appears as a philosopher of temporary contextual significance, presenting rather outmoded plans for cultural and democratic rebirth in Germany, filling the gap between 1945 and the radicalization of theoretical debate under the influence of the Frankfurt School and other neo-Marxists in the 1960s. His work clearly lacks the sense of intellectual danger that often accompanies extreme political risk taking, as exemplified by Heidegger. However, his thought occupies a very important position in the development of modern European philosophy, and this importance is strongly reflected in this book. His thought illuminates the contours of post-1945 political and philosophical debate very clearly, and it throws unique light on patterns of theoretical redirection at this time. His works show how the lines of philosophical liberalism that became central to European political-philosophical debate emerged originally from multiple, highly varied sources. In particular, his work illuminates the unusual confluences that existed between seemingly opposed theoretical positions during the redrawing of intellectual fault-lines after 1945. It allows us to understand the complexly interlinked premises, attached to quite separate intellectual lineages, around which contemporary German and European philosophy took shape. Most importantly, however, his work is required reading in its own right. Although not usually attributed the same distinction as other exponents of existentialist theory, his impact on political debate proved greater, arguably, than that of other thinkers attached to existentialism, and it is still reflected in political and philosophical discussions today.

From the perspective of intellectual history, this book presents a key position within a series of debates conducted after 1945. It belongs to a small group of works, published in the years after 1945, which endeavoured to address the basic foundations of Western civilization, with a view to analysing the causes of the totalitarian crisis in Germany in the 1930s and the intellectual possibilities of post-war society.

On one hand, most obviously, this book can be read alongside works such as Jean-Paul Sartre's *Existentialism Is a Humanism* (1946) and Heidegger's *Letter on Humanism* (1947), both of which were products of the phenomenological tradition. Like these works, this book seeks to reconstruct existential phenomenology as a philosophical horizon for imagining the conditions of liberty in post-war Europe. At an immediate level, it directs its critical attention to Marxist analyses of history, which – allegedly – impute a totalizing logic to historical development and propose ideological plans for societal organization on the basis of spuriously total knowledge claims. To this degree, it clearly belongs to the context of the early Cold War, and it is not short of invectives against vulgar Marxism. However, the essential question that it poses, regarding the meaning of human existence in history, the nature of human freedom, and the extent to which human being and human knowledge are historically determined, is a question derived, not from Marxism, but from the core of the German phenomenological lineage. The question about the historical sources of human cognition had been posed repeatedly and directly throughout the canon of post-Kantian philosophy in Germany. For example, this question was subject to historicist analysis by Wilhelm Dilthey in *The Formation of the Historical World in the Human Sciences*; it was later subject to phenomenological analysis by Heidegger in *Being and Time*. Each of these works proposed the theory, in diverse fashion, that consciousness of the constitutive historicality of human thought is the primary determinant of authentic knowledge and even of free human life. After 1945, Jaspers returned to these questions. But his political motivation for doing so was quite clear, and he raised the question about human historicality as part of a broader assessment of the ways in which approaches to history might shape cultural and political reorientation. He rephrased this central phenomenological question as a way to elucidate the existential possibilities of post-1945 Europe.

In addressing these questions, Jaspers placed himself in emphatic opposition to constructions of history typical of dialectical materialism, which, he argued, attempt to explain human history in accordance with fixed laws. However, he also opposed earlier historicist interpretations of history, which, he claimed, tended to associate the historical horizon of individual existence with the history of particular nation states. In this regard, he set out a sharp critique of the radical concept of historicity elaborated by Heidegger, who claimed that authentic being is entirely historically constructed, such that all thought occurs as a historical process. At core, Jaspers developed a theory of historicality that claims that human existence is itself intrinsically historical, yet it discloses its historicality by accepting historical contingency, by rejecting certainty about the sense and the goal of history, and by openly disclosing the variable meanings attached to historical phenomena. Underlying these claims is the sense that human freedom is essentially transcendent, and it cannot be limited to or fully appreciated in any historical forms. On this account, authentic understanding of historical forms is a way of understanding that looks for traces of human transcendence within history, and which finds human historical freedom, dialectically, at the limits of history.

In this respect, Jaspers argued for cultural renewal through non-dogmatic, transcendentally uncertain engagement with historical life forms. Between the lines of his argument, he endorsed a reflexive attitude of hermeneutical latitude and tolerance as the new premise for German culture, and German politics.

On the other hand, this book relates closely to two other works that were published in the aftermath of World War II: that is, to *The Dialectic of Enlightenment* (1944/47) by Theodor Adorno and Max Horkheimer, and to *The Origins of Totalitarianism* (1951) by Hannah Arendt. Jaspers had a close personal friendship with Arendt, and he followed the thought processes that shaped her research on totalitarianism before her major work had been published. In different ways, both these works were intended both as diagnoses of the causes of European catastrophe in the 1930s and as indications of the cognitive preconditions required to avoid renewed collapse into extreme authoritarianism. Adorno and Horkheimer are usually seen as antipodes to Jaspers, and their agenda for intellectual reorientation in the Federal Republic, based in a fusion of cultural vitalism and neo-Marxism, is seen as diametrically opposed to the cautious liberalism proposed by Jaspers. However, this book is much less far removed from the Frankfurt School than is typically imagined. It clearly projects a critique of technology which is closely related to the more famous version of the dialectic of Enlightenment, and it immediately mirrors the theories of the early Frankfurt School in analysing technological rationality as an instrumental form of human reason, with partial responsibility for the rise of totalitarianism in the 1930s. The relation between Jaspers and Arendt is visible, in particular, in the fact that both examined the possibility of human freedom through a theory of discursive communication, and both viewed totalitarian thinking as thinking that destroys communication. Jaspers and Arendt both viewed speech, in which participants in dialogue detach themselves from prior cognitive certainties, as the essential prerequisite for political renewal. For Jaspers, human freedom only becomes possible in existentially meaningful communication.

In the context of these debates, Jaspers arrived at a position in which, like Arendt, he attached the question of authentic human historicality very closely to the question of democracy. He implied that an authentic approach to history, reflecting deep uncertainty and lack of dogmatic totalism, is likely to engender democratic practices, such that authentic historicality is always most probable in a democracy. In this respect, to be sure, Jaspers examined democracy in terms that, on occasions, moved close to stock theoretical stances seen in the earlier existential-philosophical canon. Throughout his career, he remained attached to the cultural scepticism of the interwar era, and, after 1945, his thought still echoed more conservative critiques of mass-society and mass-democracy associated with reactionary thinkers in the Weimar Republic. For example, he explained the rise of mass politics and attendant patterns of individualization as processes that undermine human integrity. He also reproduced aspects of Weber's cult of political leadership. Overall, however, this book constitutes an important and unusual position amongst the works promoting moral and intellectual reorientation at this time. It uses a critical debate with historicism to sketch out an attack on Marxism, to outline an interpretive theory of human liberty, and to propose a historical-epistemological underpinning for liberal-democratic politics.

As a result of its position in these debates, second, this book acquires importance because of its subsequent impact. It exerted influence in a number of lines of theoretical inquiry, again straddling the boundaries between a range of different theoretical camps. The influence of the book can be seen in later developments in hermeneutical theory. Its critique of technology and planning was later absorbed in more mainstream German social theory, especially in the institutionalist sociology of Helmut Schelsky and Arnold Gehlen. Most importantly, the impact of this book can be seen in the communication-theoretical approach to democratic legitimacy set out by Jürgen Habermas, especially in *Structural Transformation of the Public Sphere* (1962). Although usually placed in an intellectual context defined by *The Dialectic of Enlightenment*, the earlier work of Habermas clearly built on Arendt and Jaspers. Indeed, the essential precondition of his theory of democracy – that is, the claim that legitimacy arises from open communication not subject to coercive or instrumental planning and not pre-defined by cognitive certainty – expressed a strong debt to Jaspers.

Most strikingly, third, the importance of this book is reflected in the fact that it articulates a series of principles and impulses that cannot be attached to a particular school of thought or to a particular theorist, yet which have become parts of the common repertoire of progressive reflection in Europe. Despite its awkward fusion of liberalism and elitism, certain tropes appear in this book that possessed a certain radicality when first expressed, and which now belong to a broad canon of liberal thinking. As mentioned, for example, the book argues strongly in favour of mental or cultural renewal as the basis for democracy, implying that democracy can only be consolidated after an ethical-attitudinal transformation has taken place amongst the people expected to act as citizens. It proposes an analysis of the cognitive ethics required for democracy, stressing free discourse and deep tolerance as essential elements of such ethics. In this respect, the book insists on reflexive individualism as the precondition of democracy, and it argues that democracy can only result from the ethical decisions of citizens, closely linked to their historical self-construction. Perhaps most importantly, this book argues very strongly for a universal conception of history and historical consciousness. Jaspers presented an account of human history in which he claimed that history can only be seen as the history of all people, to which all people are heirs, so that all people are implicated in the same cognitive and existential communities and the same cognitive and existential obligations. This understanding of history was underpinned by his renowned theory of the *Axial Age*, in which he claimed that, in the period lasting from approximately 800 to 200 BCE, a number of thinkers had emerged in different parts of the globe, who brought human consciousness to a common state of reflexivity and defined the fundamental, enduring parameters of human thinking. On this basis, strikingly for the post-war context, Jaspers appears as an early cosmopolitan theorist, clearly moving towards a planetary theory of world culture, which also provided the basis for a theory of world law and cosmopolitan democracy.

Chris Thornhill

2020

PART 1

WORLD HISTORY

INTRODUCTION

The Structure of World History

By virtue of the extent and depth to which it has transformed human life, our age is of the most incisive significance. It requires the whole history of mankind to furnish us with standards by which to measure the meaning of what is happening at the present time.

A glance at the history of mankind leads us, however, into the mystery of our humanity. The fact that we possess a history at all, that history has made us what we are and that the duration of this history up to now has been comparatively short prompts us to ask: Where does it come from? Where does it lead? What does it mean?

Since the earliest times man has attempted to picture the whole to himself: first in mythical images (in theogonies and cosmogonies, in which man had his appointed place), then in the image of divine activity operating through the decisive events of world politics (the historical vision of the prophets), then as a process of revelation running through the whole course of history, from the creation of the world and the fall of man to the end of the world and the last judgement (St. Augustine).

The historical consciousness is fundamentally altered when it bases itself on empirical foundations and on these alone. The accounts of a natural genesis of civilisation, such as were devised everywhere, from China to the West, though still in fact legendary, were already empirical in intent. Today the real horizon has become immensely wider. Temporal limitations—such, for example, as the Biblical belief in a world 6,000 years old—have been broken through. Something endless opens up into the past and into the future. Within it research adheres to historical remains, documents and monuments of the past.

Confronted by limitless multiplicity, this empirical conception of history must either restrict itself to the demonstration of single regularities and never-ending descriptions of the manifold: the same happenings repeat themselves; the analogous recurs within the diverse; there are orders of power-politics in typical series of forms, and there are chaos and confusion; there are regular sequences of styles in the realm of the spirit, and there is levelling-down into that which endures without any regular pattern.

Or the endeavour is made to achieve a unified and integrating overall view of the history of mankind: the factual cycles of civilisation are seen in their development and decline—first in isolation and then in mutual interaction; the common element underlying the problems of meaning and mutual comprehensibility is apprehended and leads finally to the concept of a single meaningful pattern, in which all diversities have their appointed place (Hegel).[1]

Whoever turns to history involuntarily adopts one of these universal viewpoints, which reduce the whole of history to a unity. These viewpoints may be accepted uncritically, may even remain unconscious and therefore unquestioned. In the modes of historical thought they are usually taken as self-evident presuppositions.

Thus in the nineteenth century world history was regarded as that which, after its preliminary stages in Egypt and Mesopotamia, really began in Greece and Palestine and led up to ourselves. Everything else came under the heading of ethnology and lay outside the province of history proper. World history was the history of the West (Ranke).

As against this view nineteenth-century positivism aimed at according equal rights to all men. Where there are men there is history. World history embraces, in time and space, the entire globe. It is arranged geographically on the basis of its distribution in space (Helmolt). It took place everywhere on earth. Battles between negroes in the Sudan were on the same historical plane as Marathon and Salamis—or were even, by virtue of the greater numbers involved, of superior importance.

Hierarchy and structure seemed once more to be perceptible in history as a result of the conception of integral cultures.[2] From the undifferentiated mass of mere primitive existence, cultures—so it was thought—develop like organisms, as independent life-forms having a beginning and an end, being of no concern to one another but capable of meeting and interfering with each other. Spengler recognises eight such historical organisms, Toynbee twenty-one. Spengler ascribes to them a life-span of one thousand years, Toynbee an indefinite one. Spengler sees the necessity for a mysterious total process to be accomplished by any given culture-organism: a metamorphosis governed by natural laws which he claims to perceive morphologically, from analogies between the phases of the various organisms. In his physiognomic conception everything assumes the character of a symbol. Toynbee undertakes a multiple causal analysis from sociological points of view. Beyond that he finds room for the free decisions of individuals, but in such a way that, in his view too, the whole appears in the guise of a currently necessary process. Both, therefore, make predictions for the future on the basis of their overall conceptions.[3]

In our time, apart from Spengler and Toynbee, Alfred Weber has evolved a great independent conception of history. In spite of his disposition to make the totalities of cultures the object of knowledge, his universal conception of history—his sociology of civilisation—remains, in fact, remarkably open. Guided by his clear-sighted historical intuition and gifted with an unerring feeling for the status of spiritual creations, he adumbrates the historical process in such a manner that neither dispersal into unrelated culture-organisms nor the unity of human history as such becomes a principle. In fact, however, he finds himself confronted by the shape of a universal historical process, which divides itself up into primary civilisations, secondary cultures at the first and second stage, and so on down to the history of the expanding West after 1500.

I shall not devote any further time to the discussion of these conceptions, but shall attempt, in my turn, to outline the schema of a total conception.

My outline is based on an article of faith: that mankind has one single origin and one goal. Origin and goal are unknown to us, utterly unknown by any kind of knowledge. They can only be felt in the glimmer of ambiguous symbols. Our actual existence moves between these two poles; in philosophical reflection we may endeavour to draw closer to both origin and goal.

All men are related in Adam, originate from the hand of God and are created after His image.

In the beginning was the manifestness of Being in a present without consciousness. The fall set us on the path leading through knowledge and finite practical activity with temporal objectives, to the lucidity of the consciously manifest.

With the consummation of the end we shall attain concord of souls, shall view one another in a loving present and in boundless understanding, members of a single realm of everlasting spirits.

All these are symbols, not realities. The meaning of universal history, so far as it is empirically accessible—whether it possesses such a meaning, or whether human beings only attribute one to it—we can only grasp when guided by the idea of the unity of the whole of history. We shall examine empirical facts in order to see to what extent they are in accordance with such an idea of unity, or how far they absolutely contradict it.

In so doing we shall evolve a conception of history which ascribes historical significance to that which, firstly, stands unmistakably in its place within one single overall process of human history, as a unique event, and which, secondly, possesses the qualities of reality and indispensability in the communication or continuity of humanity.

We shall now proceed, by an analysis of the structure of world history, to adumbrate our schema, whose aim is the greatest inclusiveness and the most categoric unity of human history.

NOTES

1   (Page 4): Of imperishable importance to the philosophy of history are the relevant writings of Vico, Montesquieu, Lessing, Kant, Herder, Fichte, Hegel, Marx, Max Weber. A general view is given by: Johannes Thyssen, *Geschichte der Geschichtsphilosophie*, Berlin 1936. R. Rocholl, *Die Philosophie der Geschichte*, Band I, Göttingen 1878.

2   (Page 4): O. Spengler, *Der Untergang des Abendlandes*, 1918. Alfred Weber, *Kulturgeschichte als Kultursoziologie*, Leiden 1935. *Das Tragische und die Geschichte*, Hamburg 1943. *Abschied von der bisherigen Geschichte*, Hamburg 1946. Toynbee, *A Study of History*, London 1935 ff.

3   (Page 5): Toynbee is careful about this. He breaks through or arches over his conception with a Christian outlook. In his view it is fundamentally possible for a culture to continue to exist without going under. It is not subject to the blind necessity of biological old age and death. What will happen is also dependent upon human freedom. And God may help.

Spengler claims that he—the first to do so in his opinion—formulates an historical prognosis methodologically with the certitude of an astronomer. He predicts the decline of the West. Many people found in his book the corroboration of a state of mind which they brought with them to the reading of it.

Two insights are, in principle, to be set in opposition to the dictatorial certitude of his brilliant conception of the play of relationships, which fluctuates between arbitrariness and plausibility: Firstly, Spengler's interpretation

in comparisons and analogies is frequently appropriate to the characterisation of a 'spirit', of an atmosphere, but it pertains to the nature of all
physiognomic definition that it involves not the methodological recognition of a reality, but an interpretation extending to the infinite in terms of
possibilities. In the process, the imperious idea of the 'necessity' of events
becomes confused. Morphological form-sequences are construed causally,
the evidence of the senses as a real necessity of events. Spengler is methodologically untenable where he gives more than a characterisation of phenomena. If real problems very often lie hidden in his analogies, they come
to light only when it becomes possible to test his statements causally and
particularly by investigation, and not simply in the physiognomic view as
such. The playful approach, which, in the particular, always supposes itself
to have the total within reach, must be transmuted into definiteness and
demonstrability; this calls for renunciation of insight into the whole.

The substantialisation or hypostasisation of cultural totalities will then
cease. There will then be only ideas of a relative spiritual whole and schemata of such ideas in ideal-typical constructions. These are able to bring a
great multiformity of phenomena into context through the application of
principles. But they always remain within the comprehensive whole; they
are not capable of taking a total grip of any such whole, as though it were a
circumscribed body.

Secondly, in opposition to Spengler's absolute separation of cultures
standing side by side without relations, we must point to the empirically
demonstrable contacts, transferences, adaptations (Buddhism in China,
Christianity in the West), which for Spengler lead only to disturbances and
pseudomorphoses, but are in fact indications of a common fundament.

What this fundamental unity is, remains for us a task both of cognition
and of practical implementation. No definitely construed unity—such as biological make-up, the universally valid thinking of the intelligence, common
attributes of humanity—is unity *per se*. The presupposition that man is the
potentiality for being the same everywhere, is just as correct as the contradictory assumption that man is everywhere disparate, differentiated down
to the particularity of the individual.

In any case, the capacity for understanding pertains to unity. Spengler
denies this capacity: the various cultural realms are irreconcilably diverse,
incomprehensible to one another. We, for example, do not understand the
Ancient Greeks.

This side by side coexistence of the everlastingly alien is contradicted by
the possibility, and the partial reality, of understanding and adoption. Whatever men think, do and create concerns the rest; ultimately it somehow or
other involves the same thing.

1

THE AXIAL PERIOD

In the Western World the philosophy of history was founded in the Christian faith. In a grandiose sequence of works ranging from St. Augustine to Hegel this faith visualised the movement of God through history. God's acts of revelation represent the decisive dividing lines. Thus Hegel could still say: All history goes toward and comes from Christ. The appearance of the Son of God is the axis of world history. Our chronology bears daily witness to this Christian structure of history.

But the Christian faith is only one faith, not the faith of mankind. This view of universal history therefore suffers from the defect that it can only be valid for believing Christians. But even in the West, Christians have not tied their empirical conceptions of history to their faith. An article of faith is not an article of empirical insight into the real course of history. For Christians sacred history was separated from profane history, as being different in its meaning. Even the believing Christian was able to examine the Christian tradition itself in the same way as other empirical objects of research.

An axis of world history, if such a thing exists, would have to be discovered *empirically*, as a fact capable of being accepted as such by all men, Christians included. This axis would be situated at the point in history which gave birth to everything which, since then, man has been able to be, the point most overwhelmingly fruitful in fashioning humanity; its character would have to be, if not empirically cogent and evident, yet so convincing to empirical insight as to give rise to a common frame of historical self-comprehension for all peoples—for the West, for Asia, and for all men on earth, without regard to particular articles of faith. It would seem that this axis of history is to be found in the period around 500 B.C., in the spiritual process that occurred between 800 and 200 B.C. It is there that we meet with the most deepcut dividing line in history. Man, as we know him today, came into being. For short we may style this the 'Axial Period'.

A. CHARACTERISATION OF THE AXIAL PERIOD

The most extraordinary events are concentrated in this period. Confucius and Lao-tse were living in China, all the schools of Chinese philosophy came into being, including those of Mo-ti, Chuang-tse, Lieh-tsu and a host of others; India produced the Upanishads and Buddha and, like China, ran the whole gamut of philosophical possibilities down to scepticism, to materialism, sophism and nihilism; in Iran Zarathustra taught a challenging view of the world as a struggle between good and evil; in Palestine the prophets made their appearance, from Elijah, by way of Isaiah and Jeremiah to Deutero-Isaiah; Greece witnessed the appearance of Homer, of the philosophers—Parmenides, Heraclitus and Plato—of the tragedians, Thucydides and Archimedes. Everything implied by these names developed during these few centuries almost simultaneously in China, India, and the West, without any one of these regions knowing of the others.

What is new about this age, in all three areas of the world, is that man becomes conscious of Being as a whole, of himself and his limitations. He experiences the terror of the world and his own powerlessness. He asks radical questions. Face to face with the void he strives for liberation and redemption. By consciously recognising his limits he sets himself the highest goals. He experiences absoluteness in the depths of selfhood and in the lucidity of transcendence.

All this took place in reflection. Consciousness became once more conscious of itself, thinking became its own object. Spiritual conflicts arose, accompanied by attempts to convince others through the communication of thoughts, reasons and experiences. The most contradictory possibilities were essayed. Discussion, the formation of parties and the division of the spiritual realm into opposites which nonetheless remained related to one another, created unrest and movement to the very brink of spiritual chaos.

In this age were born the fundamental categories within which we still think today, and the beginnings of the world religions, by which human beings still live, were created. The step into universality was taken in every sense.

As a result of this process, hitherto unconsciously accepted ideas, customs and conditions were subjected to examination, questioned and liquidated. Everything was swept into the vortex. In so far as the traditional substance still possessed vitality and reality, its manifestations were clarified and thereby transmuted.

The *Mythical Age*, with its tranquillity and self-evidence, was at an end. The Greek, Indian and Chinese philosophers were unmythical in their decisive insights, as were the prophets in their ideas of God. Rationality and rationally clarified experience launched a struggle against the myth (*logos* against *mythos*); a further struggle developed for the transcendence of the One God against non-existent demons, and finally an ethical rebellion took place against the unreal figures of the gods. Religion was rendered ethical, and the majesty of the deity thereby increased. The myth, on the other hand, became the material of a language which expressed by it something very different from what it had originally signified: it was turned into parable. Myths were remoulded, were understood at a new depth during this transition, which was myth-creating after a new fashion, at the very moment when the myth as a whole was destroyed. The old mythical world slowly sank into oblivion, but remained as a background to the whole through the continued belief of the mass of the people (and was subsequently able to gain the upper hand over wide areas).

This overall modification of humanity may be termed *spiritualisation*. The unquestioned grasp on life is loosened, the calm of polarities becomes the disquiet of opposites and antinomies. Man is no longer enclosed within himself. He becomes uncertain of himself and thereby open to new and boundless possibilities. He can hear and understand what no one had hitherto asked or proclaimed. The unheard-of becomes manifest. Together with his world and his own self, Being becomes sensible to man, but not with finality: the question remains.

For the first time *philosophers* appeared. Human beings dared to rely on themselves as individuals. Hermits and wandering thinkers in China, ascetics in India, philosophers in Greece and prophets in Israel all belong together, however much they may differ from each other in their beliefs, the contents of their thought and their inner dispositions. Man proved capable of contrasting himself inwardly with the entire universe. He discovered within himself the origin from which to raise himself above his own self and the world.

In *speculative thought* he lifts himself up towards Being itelf, which is apprehended without duality in the disappearance of subject and object, in the
coincidence of opposites. That which is experienced in the loftiest flights of
the spirit as a coming-to-oneself within Being, or as *unio mystica*, as becoming
one with the Godhead, or as becoming a tool for the will of God is expressed
in an ambiguous and easily misunderstood form in objectifying speculative
thought.

It is the *specifically human in man* which, bound to and concealed within the
body, fettered by instincts and only dimly aware of himself, longs for liberation
and redemption and is able to attain to them already in this world—in soaring
toward the idea, in the resignation of ataraxia, in the absorption of meditation,
in the knowledge of his self and the world as *atman*, in the experience of *nirvana*,
in concord with the *tao*, or in surrender to the will of God. These paths are
widely divergent in their conviction and dogma, but common to all of them
is man's reaching out beyond himself by growing aware of himself within the
whole of Being and the fact that he can tread them only as an individual on
his own. He may renounce all worldly goods, may withdraw into the desert,
into the forest or the mountains, may discover as a hermit the creative power
of solitude, and may then return into the world as the possessor of knowledge,
as a sage or as a prophet. What was later called reason and personality was
revealed for the first time during the Axial Period.

What the individual achieves is by no means passed on to all. The gap
between the peaks of human potentiality and the crowd became exceptionally great at that time. Nonetheless, what the individual becomes indirectly
changes all. The whole of humanity took a forward leap.

Corresponding to this new spiritual world, we find a *sociological* situation
showing analogies in all three regions. There were a multitude of small States
and cities, a struggle of all against all, which to begin with nevertheless
permitted an astonishing prosperity, an unfolding of vigour and wealth. In
China the small States and cities had achieved sovereign life under the powerless imperial rulers of the Chou dynasty; the political process consisted of
the enlargement of small units through the subjection of other small units.
In Hellas and the Near East small territorial units—even, to some extent,
those subjected by Persia—enjoyed an independent existence. In India there
were many States and free cities.

Reciprocal intercourse set a spiritual movement circulating within each of these
three regions. The Chinese philosophers—Confucius, Mo-ti and others—
wandered about the country and met in places of renown favourable to the

spiritual life, founding schools which are termed academies by sinologists: the sophists and philosophers of Hellas travelled about in similar fashion and Buddha passed his entire life in wandering from place to place.

In the past, spiritual conditions had been comparatively enduring; despite catastrophes everything had repeated itself, confined within the horizons of a still, very slow spiritual movement that did not enter consciousness and was therefore not apprehended. Now, on the contrary, tension increases and causes a movement of torrential swiftness.

This movement reaches consciousness. Human existence becomes the object of meditation, as history. Men feel and know that something extraordinary is beginning in their own present. But this very realisation also makes men aware of the fact that this present was preceded by an infinite past. At the very commencement of this awakening of the specifically human spirit, man is sustained by memory and is conscious of belonging to a late or even a decadent age.

Men see themselves faced by catastrophe and feel the desire to help through insight, education and reform. The endeavour is made to dominate the course of events by planning, right conditions are to be re-established or brought about for the first time. History as a whole is seen as a sequence of shapes assumed by the world, either as a process of continual decline, or as a circular motion, or as an ascent. Thought is devoted to the manner in which human beings may best live together, may best be governed and administered. Practical activity is dominated by ideas of reform. Philosophers travel from State to State, become advisers and teachers, are scorned or sought after, enter into discussions and compete with one another. A sociological parallel can be drawn between Confucius' failure at the court of Wei and Plato's failure at Syracuse, between the school of Confucius, which trained future statesmen, and the academy of Plato, which served the same purpose.

The age that saw all these developments, which spanned several centuries, cannot be regarded as a simple upward movement. It was an age of simultaneous destruction and creation. No final consummation was attained. The highest potentialities of thought and practical expression realised in individuals did not become common property, because the majority of men were unable to follow in their footsteps. What began as freedom of motion finally became anarchy. When the age lost its creativeness, a process of dogmatic fixation and levelling-down took place in all three cultural realms. Out of a disorder that was growing intolerable arose a striving after new ties, through the re-establishment of enduring conditions.

The *conclusion* is at first of a political character. Mighty empires, made great by conquest, arose almost simultaneously in China (Tsin Shi hwang-ti), in India (Maurya dynasty) and in the West (the Hellenistic empires and the Im-*perium Romanum*). Everywhere the first outcome of the collapse was an order of technological and organisational planning.

But the *relation to the spirit of what had gone before* remained everywhere. It became a model and an object of veneration. Its achievements and great personalities stood clearly in view and provided the content of schooling and education (Confucianism was evolved under the Han dynasty, Buddhism by Asoka, and the age of Augustus consciously established Graeco-Roman cultural education).

The universal empires which came into being at the end of the Axial Period considered themselves founded for eternity. But their stability was only apparent. Even though these empires lasted for a long time by comparison with the State-formations of the Axial Period, in the end they all decayed and fell to pieces. Subsequent millennia produced an extraordinary amount of change. From one point of view the disintegration and re-establishment of great empires has constituted history ever since the end of the Axial Period, as it had constituted it through the millennia during which the ancient civilisations were flourishing. During these millennia, however, it had possessed a different significance: it had lacked that spiritual tension which was first felt during the Axial Period and has been at work ever since, questioning all human activity and conferring upon it a new meaning.

B. THE STRUCTURE OF WORLD HISTORY SINCE THE AXIAL PERIOD

Reference to a few facts, such as I have made, does not suffice in itself to bring about complete conviction as to the truth of a particular view of history. Portrayal of the full wealth of historical material can alone cause the thesis either to appear in ever greater clarity or to be rejected. Such a portrayal is beyond the scope of a short book. The facts to which I have referred should be looked upon as a question and a challenge to put the thesis to the test.

Assuming this view of the Axial Period to be correct, it would seem to throw a light upon the entire history of the world, in such a way as to reveal something like a structure of world history. Let me endeavour to adumbrate this structure:

(1) The *thousands of years old ancient civilisations* are everywhere brought to an end by the Axial Period, which melts them down, assimilates them or causes them to sink from view, irrespective of whether it was the same peoples or others that became the bearers of the new cultural forms. Pre-Axial cultures, like those of Babylon, Egypt, the Indus valley and the aboriginal culture of China, may have been magnificent in their own way, but they appear in some manner unawakened. The ancient cultures only persist in those elements which enter into the Axial Period and become part of the new beginning. Measured against the lucid humanity of the Axial Period, a strange veil seems to lie over the most ancient cultures preceding it, as though man had not yet really come to himself. This fact is not obscured by isolated beginnings, moving in themselves, but without effect on the whole or on what followed (such as the Egyptian discourse of a man tired of life with his soul, the Babylonian psalms of repentance and the Gilgamesh). The monumental element in religion and religious art, and the extensive State-formations and juridical creations corresponding to it, are objects of awe and admiration to the consciousness of the Axial Period; they are even taken as models (by Confucius and Plato, for instance), but they are seen in a new light that transmutes their meaning.

Thus the imperial idea, which gains new force toward the end of the Axial Period and terminates this era in the political domain, was a heritage from the ancient civilisations. But whereas it originally constituted a culture-creating principle, it now becomes the means by which a declining culture is stabilised by being laid in its coffin. It is as though the principle that once bore mankind upward, despite its factually despotic nature, had broken through afresh in the form of conscious despotism, but this time merely to preserve a culture in icy rigidity.

(2) *Until today* mankind has lived by what happened during the Axial Period, by what was thought and created during that period. In each new upward flight it returns in recollection to this period and is fired anew by it. Ever since then it has been the case that recollections and

reawakenings of the potentialities of the Axial Period—renaissances—afford a spiritual impetus. Return to this beginning is the ever-recurrent event in China, India and the West.

(3) The Axial Period commenced within spatial limitations, but *it became historically all-embracing*. Any people that attained no part in the Axial Period remained 'primitive', continued to live that unhistorical life which had been going on for tens or even hundreds of thousands of years. Men living outside the three regions of the Axial Period either remained apart or came into contact with one of these three centres of spiritual radiation. In the latter event they were drawn into history. In the West this happened, for example, to the Germanic and Slav peoples, in the East to the Japanese, Malays and Siamese. For many primitive peoples this contact resulted in their extinction. All human beings living after the Axial Period either remained in a primitive state or took part in the new course of events, now the only one of fundamental significance. Once history had come into being, the primitive peoples represented the residue of prehistory, which occupied a continually shrinking space and has only now reached its final end.

(4) Between these three realms a *profound mutual comprehension was possible* from the moment they met. At the first encounter they recognised that they were concerned with the same problems. Despite the distance that separated them they at once became involved in one another. To be sure, they were not bound by the common possession of a single, objective truth (such a truth is only to be found in science which, methodologically conscious and compelling general assent to its propositions, is capable of spreading over the entire globe without undergoing any metamorphosis as a result and has a claim on the collaboration of all); but the authentically and absolutely true, which is lived by mankind historically from diverse origins, was seen and heard reciprocally in this encounter.

To sum up: The conception of the Axial Period furnishes the questions and standards with which to approach all preceding and subsequent developments. The outlines of the preceding civilisations dissolve. The peoples that bore them vanish from sight as they join in the movement of the Axial Period. The prehistoric peoples remain prehistoric until they merge into the historical movement that proceeds from the Axial Period, or die out.

The Axial Period assimilates everything that remains. From it world history receives the only structure and unity that has endured—at least until our own time.

C. EXAMINATION OF THE AXIAL PERIOD THESIS

1. Does it exist as a fact?

The earliest discussion of the facts of the Axial Period known to me is to be found in the works of Lasaulx and Viktor von Strauss.

Lasaulx (*Neuer Versuch einer Philosophie der Geschichte*, Munich, 1856, p. 115) writes: 'It cannot possibly be an accident that, six hundred years before Christ, Zarathustra in Persia, Gautama Buddha in India, Confucius in China, the prophets in Israel, King Numa in Rome and the first philosophers— Ionians, Dorians and Eleatics—in Hellas, all made their appearance pretty well simultaneously as reformers of the national religion.'

Viktor von Strauss, in his wonderful Lao-tse commentary, p. lxiv (1870), says: 'During the centuries when Lao-tse and Confucius were living in China, a strange movement of the spirit passed through all civilised peoples. In Israel Jeremiah, Habakkuk, Daniel and Ezekiel were prophesying and in a renewed generation (521–516) the second temple was erected in Jeru- salem. Among the Greeks Thales was still living, Anaximander, Pythagoras, Heraclitus and Xenophanes appeared and Parmenides was born. In Persia an important reformation of Zarathustra's ancient teaching seems to have been carried through, and India produced Sakyamuni, the founder of Buddhism.'

Since then these facts have now and then been noted, but only marginally. As far as I am aware, they have never been grasped as a whole, with the aim of demonstrating the universal parallels obtaining for the entire spiritual being of the humanity of that time. Let us consider possible objections to this view.

(1) One objection might be that the common element is only apparent. The differences—differences of language and race, differences as to the types of empire and in the mode of historical recollection—are so great that, by comparison, the common element strikes us as no more than a series of coincidences. Every clear-cut formulation of the common element as a whole is refuted by the facts. Or, it is argued, it amounts to no more than the trivial maxim that fundamentally everything can

be found everywhere amongst men, either as a beginning or as a potentiality. In the realisation of common human possibilities it is the
differences which are essential, distinctive and historical; the whole can
never be apprehended as a unity, except in the unhistorical, universal
characteristics of human existence.

The answer to this is: What is involved in the Axial Period is precisely the
common element in an overall historical picture, the break-through to the
principles which, right up to our own time, have been operative for humanity in borderline situations. The essential thing here is this common element,
which does not stem from all over the earth, wherever man as such exists,
but historically speaking solely from these three origins and the narrow
area they occupy. The question is whether increasing knowledge will prove
this common element to go even deeper than appeared at first, despite the
differences that still remain. In that event, the temporal coincidence would
become a fact, all the more astonishing the more clearly it is visualised. To
demonstrate it thus convincingly would, however, demand a broader canvas.

(2) A further possible objection would be: The Axial Period is not a fact at
all, but the product of a judgement of value. It is on the basis of a preconceived
opinion that the achievements of this period are appraised so inordinately highly.

The answer to this is: In matters of the spirit, a fact can only be apprehended through the understanding of meaning. Understanding, however,
is by its nature valuation. Though it rests empirically upon an accumulation
of separate data, an historical construction never comes into being through
these alone. Only through understanding do we arrive at our view of the
Axial Period, as of the spirit of any historical period. And this view involves
understanding and valuation at the same time; it includes the fact that we
are emotionally moved, because we feel ourselves touched by it, because it
concerns us as our own history and not merely as a past of which we can
trace the effects, but as the past whose wider, more original effect, which is
continually beginning afresh, is incalculable.

For this reason the whole man is the organon of historical research. 'Every
man sees that which he bears within his own heart.' The source of understanding is our own present, the here and now, our sole reality. Thus the
higher we ourselves ascend, the more clearly do we see the Axial Period.

If the hierarchy of the contents of history can only be grasped in the subjectivity of human existence, this subjectivity is not extinguished in the objectivity of something purely factual, but in the objectivity of communal perception—perception on the part of a community which man seeks after if he does not find himself already within it; for truth is that which links us to one another.

It is my thesis that in common understanding, which is inseparably bound up with valuation, we shall realise the significance of the Axial Period. This thesis is not, by the nature of the matter, susceptible of final proof; it can, however, be substantiated through a widening and deepening of the conception.

(3) A further objection may be: *This parallel is not historical in character.* For that which has no contact in spiritual intercourse does not share a common history.

This objection was already put forward against Hegel, who brought together China, India and the West as stages in the dialectical sequence of the development of the spirit. It was argued that here no real contact led from one stage to the next, as it did between the various stages in the development of the history of the West.

Our thesis, however, involves something altogether different. It is precisely this series of stages from China to Greece whose reality we deny; there is no such series, either in time or in meaning. The true situation was rather one of contemporaneous, side by side existence without contact. To begin with, several roads seem to lead from disparate origins toward the same goal. There is a multiplicity of the same in three shapes. There are three independent roots of one history, which later—after isolated and interrupted contacts, finally only a few centuries ago and properly speaking not until our own day—become a single unity.

The question at issue is, therefore, the nature of the parallelism involved.

2. What is the nature of the parallelism asserted?

The facts of the Axial Period might represent nothing more than a number of synchronistic curiosities devoid of historical significance. Numerous strange synchronisms can be pointed to in world history. For example:

In the sixteenth century the Jesuits discovered in Japan a Buddhist sect which had flourished there since the thirteenth century. It seemed to bear (and actually did bear) an astonishing resemblance to Protestantism. According to the description given by the Japanologist Florenz (in the textbook by Chantepie de la Saussaye) their teaching was somewhat as follows: Man's own efforts contribute nothing toward his salvation. Everything depends upon faith, faith in Amida's loving kindness and aid. There are no meritorious good works. Prayer is not an achievement, but only an expression of gratitude for the redemption granted by Amida. 'If even the good shall enter into eternal life, how much more so shall sinners', said Shinran, the founder of the sect. As against traditional Buddhism it demanded: no works, no magical formulae or conjurations, no amulets, pilgrimages, atonements, fasts or other forms of asceticism. The layman has the same prospects of salvation as the priest and monk. The priests are only a body of teachers to the laity. There is no more need for them to differ from the laity in their way of life and they wear the same clothes. Celibacy is abolished. The family is regarded as the best sphere of action for the religious life. Members of the sect are counselled to 'preserve order, obey the laws of the State and, as good citizens, to care for the wellbeing of their country'.

This example of synchronicity, which extends to identity with the basic doctrines of Lutheranism, is astonishing. Numerous other parallels occur throughout the centuries, from China to Europe. They have been tabulated on synchronistic charts.

The answer to this is:

Firstly: It can be said of many parallels in history, whether they are synchronistic or not, that they manifest a rule which holds good for single phenomena. Only in the Axial Period do we encounter a parallelism that follows no general law, but constitutes rather a specifically historical, unique fact of an all-embracing character which includes within itself all spiritual phenomena. The Axial Period is the only one that represents a total universal parallelism on the plane of world history, and not merely the chance concurrence of particular phenomena. Single phenomena or series of phenomena do not suffice to establish the kind of parallelism with which we are dealing in the Axial Period.

Secondly, the three parallel movements are close to each other only during those centuries. The attempt to prolong the parallels beyond the Axial Period—in synchronistic tables spanning millennia—becomes increasingly artificial. The lines of subsequent development do not run parallel, but rather diverge. Though originally they appeared like three roads directed toward the same goal, they finally became deeply estranged from one another. But the farther back we go toward the Axial Period, the closer our relationship becomes, the closer we feel to one another.

It seems to me continually more unlikely that this overall aspect of the Axial Period should be no more than an illusion created by historical coincidence. It seems rather to be the manifestation of some profound common element, the one primal source of humanity. What followed later in the course of increasing divergence produces occasional analogies, marks of a common origin, but never again in toto that real, original community of meaning.

The only comparable world historical parallelism occurs at the commencement of the ancient civilisations in Egypt, Mesopotamia, the Indus valley and China.

Within this temporal coincidence, however, there are differences of millennia. The beginnings stretch from 5000 to 3000 B.C. (Mesopotamia and Egypt; the earliest discoveries on Crete and at Troy date from the same period). The beginnings of the Chinese and Indus civilisations fall within the third millennium B.C.

Comparable to these ancient civilisations are those of Mexico and Peru, which are conjectured to have arisen during the first millennium A.D.

Their common properties are highly developed organisation and a high level of technical achievement. In Egypt, Mesopotamia, the Indus valley and in China along the banks of the Hwang-ho, analogous civilisations sprung up in the river valleys characterised by the central administration of a highly evolved mechanism for satisfying the needs of the community.

They also have in common a magical religion destitute of philosophical enlightenment, devoid of any quest for salvation and lacking any breakthrough into liberty in the face of extreme situations, as well as a singular apathy accompanying extraordinary stylistic achievements in art; especially, in the case of some of these civilisations, in architecture and sculpture.

However, this parallelism does not exhibit the same synchronism as does that of the Axial Period. Moreover it consists only of the similarity of an established type, not of a spiritual movement. It involves strangely stable conditions which, after destructive catastrophe, tend to reconstitute themselves in their old form. It is a world between prehistory, which is almost a closed book to us, and history proper which no longer permits things to remain constant in the realm of the spirit. It is a world which furnished the basis for the Axial Period, but was submerged in and by the latter.

3. What caused the facts of the Axial Period?

If the facts of the Axial Period are beyond dispute, we must now ask ourselves what caused them. Why did the same thing happen at three mutually independent points? The fact that these three regions were originally unknown to each other seems, at first, to be entirely extraneous—but it is an historical mystery which progressive research into the facts of the situation renders increasingly great. The Axial Period, with its overwhelming plenitude of spiritual creations, which has determined all human history down to the present day, is accompanied by the enigma of the occurrence, in these three mutually independent regions, of an analogous and inseparably connected process.

Apart from the Axial Period, the mystery of simultaneity applies, as we have shown, to perhaps only one other situation in the whole of world history: the genesis of the ancient civilisations. The question is, why did the development from the general condition of prehistoric peoples to the ancient civilisations take place more or less simultaneously—despite intervals of up to two millennia—in the river valleys of the Nile, of Mesopotamia, the Indus, and the Hwang-ho?

The usual answer is that analogous tasks (provision of irrigation and the fight against floods) had similar consequences. But in that case, why simultaneously? Why only in respect of these particular rivers? Why much later and under different conditions in America?

Commercial and cultural exchanges might have had a releasing effect. At all times civilising achievements of a craft character have slowly made their way across the earth, or at least the entire Eurasian continent. The invention of writing may possibly have taken place at a single spot and spread from there; without it the tasks of administration, and especially of river-control, would have been insuperable. But these are only possibilities. Such exchanges can be proved to have occurred in the third millennium between the Sumerian culture of Mesopotamia and the culture of the Indus valley; they existed between Egypt and Babylonia in early times, being very active during the second millennium.

But the multiple developments leading up to the ancient civilisations of the early millennia cannot be explained in terms of diffusion from a single source. E. Meyer (*Geschichte des Altertums*, I, 2, p. 935) therefore remarks: 'We must assume that around 5000 B.C. the genus *homo* had reached a stage in his evolution that opened up to all human groups or peoples, whose inherent aptitudes (i.e. the spiritual forces latent with them) rendered them capable of rising above this level at all, the way toward the genesis of a culture which would thereafter continue to advance.' The parallel phenomena would, in that event, have to be regarded as simultaneous developments in the biological evolution of human beings who are members of a similarly endowed humanity. That which, by virtue of a common origin, is dormant in all of them, manifests itself simultaneously and independently—as happens during the life-span of identical twins who have been separated from one another.

But this idea is a mere figure of speech which explains nothing. It is empty because it provides no basis for further research. The 'evolution of the genus *homo*' is not a reality that can be apprehended as such or serve as an explanation of anything. And, above all, this 'biological evolution' would only have been accomplished by a small, scattered section of mankind, not by mankind as a whole.

The mystery of the simultaneous inception of the Axial Period appears to me to be situated at a much deeper level than the problem of the birth of the ancient civilisations. In the first place, the simultaneity is much more exact and, in the second, it relates to spiritual-historical developments in the whole conscious, thinking aspect of humanity. The three regions which, from the beginnings of the ancient civilisations onward, were possessed of a unique character, brought forth creations during the millennium before Christ upon which the entire history of the human spirit has rested ever since.

These developments were originally independent of one another. Real communications and stimuli must be ruled out. Only after the penetration of Buddhism into China, which took place at the end of the Axial Period, did a profound spiritual communication between India and China come into being. Though there had always been relations between India and the Alest, these only became extensive during Roman times, *via* Alexandria. But the origin of these developments is not affected at all by the relations between India and the West, their further course not visibly so.

Let us see how this mystery has been explained:

Lasaulx writes: 'This strange concurrence can only be founded on the inner unity of substance in the life of mankind and the life of peoples, on a vibration of the total life of humanity which passed through all peoples, and not on the particular efflorescence of the spirit of any one people.' But that is not an explanation, it is merely a paraphrase of the mystery.

V. von Strauss talks of a hidden law: 'This phenomenon, for which there is no lack of parallels in history, and from which very mysterious laws may be inferred, probably has its roots, on the one hand, in the total organism of mankind, by virtue of its homogeneous origin, while on the other it presupposes the influence of a higher spiritual power, in the same way that the urge to florescence in nature only arrives at the unfolding of its magnificence through the vivifying rays of the returning sun.' But, as with Lasaulx, such figures of speech only paraphrase the mystery. In addition they make the mistake of levelling down the uniqueness of the historical fact of the parallels of the Axial Period in the name of supposedly similar instances of shared development throughout history.

Keyserling says (*Buch vom Ursprung*, p. 151): 'From generation to generation men seem to change in the same fashion and in the same direction, and at turning-points of history a similar change embraces enormous areas and peoples who are complete strangers to one another.' But this again is simply a paraphrase of the mystery, and a bad one at that, because it sinks down completely into the realm of biology without there being the slightest basis for approaching the problem from a biological standpoint.

All these explanations overlook the clear fact that it was not mankind, not all men, who by that time had occupied the entire planet, but only a few, relatively very few, who took this step forward at three points. As in the case of the ancient civilisations not mankind as such, but only a small section was involved.

Instead, therefore, of taking as a basis a biology of mankind, something falsely supposed to be held in common and valid for the whole of humanity, the attempt has been made to trace back the few peoples amongst whom this revolution occurred to a *common historical origin* within mankind. This origin is admittedly unknown to us. It would have to be assumed to lie in prehistoric Central Asia. With their source in such a common origin the parallel developments could perhaps be considered related. But this hypothesis has so far eluded all possibility of verification. It is improbable because it would have to prove a common origin for such disparate racial groups as the Chinese, the Indo-Europeans and the Semites; furthermore, this common origin would have to be taken as only a few millennia prior to the period at which the inception of these peoples' history becomes visible to us—biologically speaking a very short space of time and hardly sufficient to allow profound racial differentiations to take place.

In response to the question, why this simultaneity? only one methodologically arguable hypothesis has so far been advanced, that put forward by Alfred
Weber. The penetration of the nations of charioteers and horsemen from Central Asia—which did, in fact, reach China, India and the West and introduced
the horse to the ancient civilisations—had, so he argues, analogous consequences in all three regions. The men of these equestrian peoples came to
experience, thanks to the horse, the limitless vastness of the world. They took
over the ancient civilisations by conquest. In hazards and disasters they experienced the problematic character of existence, as master-peoples they developed an heroico-tragic consciousness that found expression in the epic.

This turning-point of history was brought about by the Indo-European
nations of horsemen. By the end of the third millennium they had reached
Europe and the Mediterranean. A great new thrust carried them as far as Iran
and India round about 1200. In the same way, other nations of horsemen
reached China by the end of the second millennium.

Before, from Europe to China, there had been the ancient civilisations
reaching back into the depths of the past and characterised variously as matriarchal, as civilisations of settled cattle-breeders, or simply as the population masses flourishing in closed self-sufficiency in the fertile regions of the
belt of civilisation extending from China to Europe.

History became a conflict between these two forces: the old, stable, unawakened matriarchal powers against the new, mobile, liberating tendencies
of the equestrian peoples which were rising into consciousness.

Alfred Weber's thesis demonstrates the existence of a real uniformity
within the Eurasian bloc; how far the appearance of the equestrian peoples
was decisive is difficult to determine, however. Geographical situations and
historical constellations may have given rise to the preconditions; but what
set the work of creation in motion remains the great enigma.

Weber's thesis possesses a singular power of illumination arising out of its
simple, causal explanation based on the human character of the life of the
horseman. But it still applies at most to a precondition. The contents of the
Axial Period are so remarkable and all-embracing that one hesitates to derive
them from such a cause, even if it be regarded as only a necessary precondition. Counter-evidence is afforded, for example, by China, which produced
the rich contents of the Axial Period, but neither the tragic consciousness
nor the epic (in China nothing comparable to the epic appears until the
centuries after Christ, during the period of long-drawn-out struggles against

new peoples, corresponding to our migration of the peoples). A further contradictory instance is Palestine, whose population experienced no mingling
with equestrian peoples and yet, through the prophets, produced an essential factor in the spiritual creation of the Axial Period.

The credibility of the hypothesis is further impaired by the fact that movements, migrations and conquests had been precipitating themselves upon
the ancient civilisations for millennia; to this is added the further fact that
the period of incubation between the Indo-European invasions—themselves
distributed over a period of more than a thousand years—and the inception of the spiritual development of the Axial Period was very long, while
this inception, when it took place, did so with such astonishingly exact
simultaneity.

That it is necessary to enquire after the historical reason for the events of
the Axial Period is due to the fact that it is a question of a new departure
within mankind—involving small areas only—and not of a development
shared by the whole of humanity. The Axial Period does not represent a universal stage in human evolution, but a singular ramified historical process.

Whereas Alfred Weber has given an ingenious and clear-cut reply to this
question, that can be put to the test and rendered fruitful by further discussion, the mystery of the lack of contact between the three independent
origins has usually been veiled by the vague assertion of a general Eurasian
interrelationship. Perhaps, so it is meaninglessly said, influences no longer
apparent to us were at work. The unity of the history of the whole Eurasian
bloc, determined by constantly renewed advances, migrations and conquests
from Central Asia, is pointed to, as well as the demonstrable parallels that
can be observed in archaeological finds of a technological and ornamental
character. These finds go back to early prehistory and permit a perpetual cultural exchange over the entire major continent to be inferred. Against this,
however, it must be said that the spiritual movement of the Axial Period, in
its simultaneity and the sublimity of its content, cannot be accounted for in
terms of such migrations and exchanges.

In the end, the simplest explanation of the phenomena of the Axial Period
seems to lie in common sociological preconditions favourable to spiritual
creativeness: many small States and small towns; a politically divided age
engaged in incessant conflicts; the misery caused by wars and revolutions
accompanied by simultaneous prosperity elsewhere, since destruction was
neither universal nor radical; questioning of previously existing conditions.

These are sociological considerations which are meaningful and lead to methodical investigation, but ultimately they merely illuminate the facts and do not provide a causal explanation of them. For these conditions form part of the total spiritual phenomenon of the Axial Period. They are preconditions of which the creative result is not a necessary sequel; as part of the overall pattern their own origin remains in question.

No one can adequately comprehend what occurred here and became the axis of world history! The facts of this break-through must be seen from all sides, their many aspects must be fixed in the mind and their meaning interpreted, in order to gain a provisional conception of the Axial Period, which grows more mysterious the more closely we examine it.

It might seem as though I were out to prove direct intervention on the part of the deity, without saying so openly. By no means. For that would not only be a *salto mortale* of cognition into pseudo-knowledge, but also an importunity against the deity. I want rather to prevent the comfortable and empty conception of history as a comprehensible and necessary movement of humanity; I should like to maintain awareness of the dependence of our cognition upon current standpoints, methods and facts and, thereby, of the particularity of all cognition; I should like to hold the question open and leave room for possible new starting-points in the search for knowledge, which we cannot imagine in advance at all.

Wonder at the mystery is itself a fruitful act of understanding, in that it affords a point of departure for further research. It may even be the very goal of all understanding, since it means penetrating through the greatest possible amount of knowledge to authentic nescience, instead of allowing Being to disappear by absolutising it away into a self-enclosed object of cognition.

4. The meaning of the Axial Period

The problem of the meaning of the Axial Period is something quite different from that of its cause.

The fact of the threefold manifestation of the Axial Period is in the nature of a miracle, in so far as no really adequate explanation is possible within the limits of our present knowledge. The hidden meaning of this fact, however, cannot be discovered empirically at all, as a meaning somewhere intended by someone. In enquiring after it we are really only putting our own interpretation on the facts and causing something to grow out of them for us.

If, in the process, we make use of terms which seem to indicate that we have in mind some plan of providence, these are only metaphors.

(a)   Really to visualise the facts of the Axial Period and to make them the basis of our universal conception of history is to gain possession of something common to all mankind, beyond all differences of creed. It is one thing to see the unity of history from one's own ground and in the light of one's own faith, another to think of it in communication with every other human ground, linking one's own consciousness to the alien consciousness. In this sense, it can be said of the centuries between 800 and 200 B.C. that they are the empirically evident axis of world history for all men.

The transcendental history of the revealed Christian faith is made up out of the creation, the fall, stages of revelation, prophecies, the appearance of the Son of God, redemption and the last judgement. As the contents of the faith of an historical human group it remains untouched. That which binds all men together, however, cannot be revelation but must be experience. Revelation is the form taken by particular historical creeds, experience is accessible to man as man. We—all men—can share the knowledge of the reality of this universal transformation of mankind during the Axial Period. Although confined to China, India and the West, and though there was to begin with no contact between these three worlds, the Axial Period nonetheless founded universal history and, spiritually, drew all men into itself.

(b)   The fact of the threefold historical modification effected by the step we call the Axial Period acts as a challenge to boundless communication. To see and understand others helps in the achievement of clarity about oneself, in overcoming the potential narrowness of all self-enclosed historicity, and in taking the leap into expanding reality. This venture into boundless communication is once again the secret of becoming-human, not as it occurred in the inaccessible prehistoric past, but as it takes place within ourselves.

This demand for communication—made by the historical fact of the threefold origin—is the best remedy against the erroneous claim to exclusive possession of truth by any one creed. For a creed can only be absolute in its historical existence, not universally valid for all in its predications, like scientific truth. The claim to exclusive possession of truth, that tool of fanaticism, of human arrogance and self-deception through the will to power, that disaster for the West—most intensely so in its secularised forms, such as the dogmatic philosophies and the so-called scientific ideologies—can be vanquished by the very fact that God has manifested himself historically in several fashions and has opened up many ways toward Himself. It is as though the deity were issuing a warning, through the language of universal history, against the claim to exclusiveness in the possession of truth.

(c)   If the Axial Period gains in importance with the degree to which we immerse ourselves in it, the question arises: Is this period, are its creations, the yardstick for all that follows? If we do not consider the quantitative aspect of its effect, nor the extent of the areas involved in its political processes, nor the pre-eminence accorded to spiritual phenomena throughout the centuries, is it still true that the austere grandeur, the creative lucidity, the depth of meaning and the extent of the leap toward new spiritual worlds contained in the phenomena of the Axial Period are to be regarded as the spiritual peak of all history up to the present? Do later manifestations, in spite of the heights to which they attained and in spite of having become irreplaceable in their turn, pale before the earlier—Virgil before Homer, Augustus before Solon, Jesus before Jeremiah?

It would certainly be wrong to answer this question with a mechanical affirmative. The later manifestation invariably possesses a value of its own, which was not present in the earlier one: a maturity of its own, a sublime costliness, a depth of soul, especially in the case of the 'exception'. It is quite impossible to arrange history in a hierarchy of values following automatically from one universally applicable conception. But the manner in which this question is formulated—and also, perhaps, a prejudice against the later—does result from an understanding of the Axial Period. This in turn illumines what is specifically new and great after a different fashion and does not belong to the Axial Period. For example: Anyone studying philosophy is likely to find that after months with the Greek philosophers, St. Augustine affects him like a liberation from coldness and impersonality into questions of conscience, which have remained with us ever since the time of

St. Augustine but were alien to the Greeks. Conversely, however, after spending some time on St. Augustine, he will experience an increasing desire to return to the Greeks and cleanse himself of the feeling of impurity that seems to grow with the pursuit of this type of thinking, to regain his health by immersion in the pellucid waters of Greek thought. Nowhere on earth can we find final truth, authentic salvation.

The Axial Period too ended in failure. History went on.

Only this much seems certain to me: Our present-day historical consciousness, as well as our consciousness of our present situation, is determined, down to consequences I have only been able to hint at, by the conception of the Axial Period, irrespective of whether this thesis is accepted or rejected. It is a question of the manner in which the unity of mankind becomes a concrete reality for us.

2

SCHEMA OF WORLD HISTORY

To ascertain the basis of our existence we look at the globe. We cannot consider too frequently, by examining the revolving globe, the information made available to us by geographers and historians concerning the major features of the division between land and sea, the shapes of continents and countries and the geographical positions of the earliest cultures:

(1) A single great sweep of mainland extends from the western coasts of Europe and Africa to the farthest east of America, that is, from the Atlantic Ocean to the Atlantic Ocean. Unlike the Pacific, the Atlantic, until the time of Columbus, was the great natural cleavage point of mankind, whereas everywhere else throughout prehistory migrations took place toward east and west (the landing of Northmen in North America was an exception devoid of consequences).

(2) The *races*: White, Negroes, Mongols and Red Indians, until more recent times, were distributed over the face of the earth in fairly closed regions of settlement, though with racial transitions at the edges.

(3) Wherever it is possible to live at all, man has *settled*. We see the vast territories of Northern Asia, Africa and America, which were inhabited by men but saw the birth of nothing of importance to the history of the spirit. We see the outermost regions in the north and south, where

displaced populations demonstrate in their ways of life what man is capable of under pressure.

The principal *types of landscape* and their importance for civilisation appear to the eye: river valleys, Mediterranean coastlines, oceanic coastlines, archipelagos, plains, steppes and deserts.

(4) The *American* continent was populated from north to south by the same race, the Red Indians. It has not been the scene of any discoveries of bones of a pre-human or early human character. The continent must have been populated from north to south at a relatively late date by migrants from Asia.

(5) The *area within which civilisation came into being* extends, when compared with the total surface of the earth, like a narrow *strip of land* from the Atlantic to the Pacific, from Europe *via* North Africa and Asia Minor to India and China. This strip—in length about a quarter, in width less than a twelfth of the circumference of the earth—contains fertile land scattered amongst deserts, steppes and mountain ranges. The places of origin of the higher forms of civilisation are all situated within this strip. To begin with, they were independent of one another, their creations spread, touched and lost contact again. Continuous intercourse, even within this belt, was only established relatively late and was constantly interrupted; in its full extent, it was only established a few centuries ago, by Europeans.

Within the vast expanses of human settlement, the area in which civilisation first arose is very small. It is the same in regard to time.

History in the restricted sense can be pictured in the following *schema*:

From the dark world of a prehistory lasting for hundreds of thousands of years and from the life of human beings similar to ourselves, which had gone on for tens of thousands of years, the ancient civilisations emerged, thousands of years before Christ, in Mesopotamia, Egypt, the Indus valley and along the banks of the Hwang-ho.

In comparison with the globe as a whole, these were islands of light amidst the broad mass of the rest of humanity, in the midst of the world of primitive peoples, which was all-embracing until close to our own time.

From the midst of the ancient civilisations, or from within their orbit, during the Axial Period from 800 to 200 B.C., the spiritual foundation of mankind arose in three mutually independent places, in the West—polarised in Orient and Occident—in India, and in China.

Since the end of the Middle Ages the West has produced in Europe modern science and with it, after the end of the eighteenth century, the age of technology—the first entirely new development in the spiritual or material sphere since the Axial Period.

From Europe, America was populated and provided with spiritual foundations; from Europe, Russia—which has its roots in Eastern Christianity—was decisively shaped in the spheres of rationality and technology, while in her turn Russia colonised the whole of Northern Asia down to the Pacific Ocean.

The contemporary world, with its great American and Russian blocs, with Europe, India and China, Asia Minor, South America and all the other regions of the earth, has in the course of a slow process dating from the sixteenth century become a *de facto* single unit of communications, in consequence of the development of technology. Despite all conflict and division, the fact that the world is now a single unit of communications gives rise to a growing drive toward political unification, either by force in a despotic world-empire or through mutual agreement in a world order based on the rule of law.

It is possible to claim that there has been no world history until now, but only an aggregate of local histories.

What we call history, and what in the old sense is now at an end, was an interim period of five thousand years' duration between the settlement of the globe, which went on throughout the hundreds of thousands of years of prehistory, and the beginning of world history properly so called, in our own time. Before history, all that happened in the isolation of human groups unaware of their interrelatedness was an entirely repetitive continuance of living, still closely allied to the processes of nature. Our subsequent brief history, however, was like a meeting and gathering of men for the action of world history; it was the spiritual and technical acquisition of the equipment necessary for the journey. We are just setting out.

It is always a gross simplification to give history a structure by dividing it up into a few periods, but the purpose of such simplifications is to indicate the essentials. Let us formulate the schema of world history once again, so that it shall not petrify into a false singleness of meaning:

Four times man seems, as it were, to have started out *from a new basis:*

First from prehistory, from the Promethean Age that is scarcely accessible to us (genesis of speech, of tools and of the use of fire), through which he first became man.

Secondly, from the establishment of the ancient civilisations.

Thirdly, from the Axial Period through which, spiritually, he unfolded his full human potentialities.

Fourthly, from the scientific-technological age, whose remoulding effects we are experiencing in ourselves.

In accordance with this division, our historical insight is confronted by four separate groups of questions, which today appear the fundamental questions of world history:

(1) Which steps taken in prehistory were decisive in their effect on humanity?
(2) How did the first civilisations come into being after 5000 B.C.?
(3) What is the essential nature of the Axial Period and how did it come about?
(4) How are we to understand the rise of science and technology? How did the 'Age of Technology' come about?

This schema suffers from the disability that it describes four stages in world history which, though all of exceptional importance, are heterogeneous in their significance: the Promethean Age, the age of the ancient civilisations, the age in which were laid the spiritual foundations of our humanity as it stands today, and the age of technology.

More significantly, but anticipating the future, the schema might be formulated like this: The history of mankind visible to us took, so to speak, two breaths.

The first led from the Promethean Age *via* the ancient civilisations to the Axial Period and its consequences.

The second started with the scientific-technological, the new Promethean Age and may lead, through constructions that will be analogous to the organisation and planning of the ancient civilisations, into a new, second Axial Period, to the final process of becoming-human, which is still remote and invisible to us.

There are, however, essential differences between these two breaths. From the second breath, which we are just beginning to take, we can know the first, that is we possess the experience of history. The second essential difference is this: whereas the first breath was, as it were, split up into several parallel ones, the second breath is being taken by mankind as a whole.

During the first breath every event, even in the shape of the mightiest of empires, was local and nowhere decisive for the whole. This made possible the special character of the West and the departure that took its rise there, when the other movements that had issued from the Axial Period seemed to be declining further and further, without producing, as far as can be seen at the moment, any great new possibilities.

What happens in the future, however, will be universal and all-embracing; there can be no more limitation to China, Europe or America. Decisive events will be of a total, and therefore also quite unprecedentedly fateful, character.

The developments issuing from the first breath in their manifold conformation look to us as though, as a whole, they would have come to naught if something new had not arisen in the West. The question now is whether the coming course of historical evolution will remain open and lead, through terrible sufferings, distortions and horrifying abysses, to the specifically human. As to how this might happen we can form no idea.

The one origin of mankind at the beginning of prehistory is as obscure as the future world of humanity dominating the globe, when it has entered into the unity of its legally ordered existence, whose spiritual and material horizons are infinite.

Between the origin (which we simply cannot imagine or conceive) and the goal (of which we cannot formulate any adequate concrete image) our actual history is taking place.

But origin and goal are interrelated: as I think of the one, so I think of the other. Symbols make manifest that which cannot attain any convincing perceptual shape as a reality: in the 'Creation of Man'—the origin—and in the 'Everlasting Realm of Spirits'—the goal.

The following chapters deal with the basic problems and topics of history—of this happening *between* origin and goal—in so far as it is past. The course of world history is summarised in the following simple schema (to be read from the bottom upwards):

THE ONE WORLD OF MANKIND ON THE EARTH

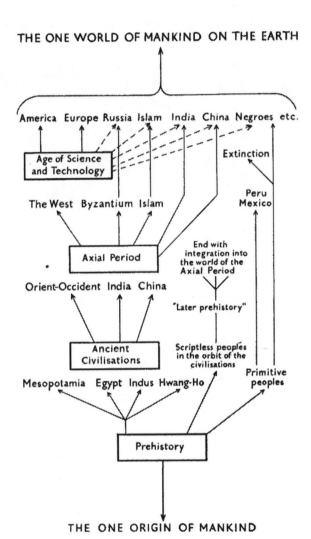

THE ONE ORIGIN OF MANKIND

3

PREHISTORY

A. HISTORY AND PREHISTORY

History extends as far back as linguistic evidence. It is as though we feel solid ground under our feet wherever a word reaches us. All non-verbal artifacts from prehistoric excavations seem to us lifeless in their dumb silence. It takes the element of language to communicate to man the intimate meaning of a work, its atmosphere and the impulses that gave it birth, with any vividness. Nowhere does linguistic evidence extend further back than 3000 B.C. History has therefore lasted about 5,000 years.

No doubt prehistory, objectively speaking, was a flux of perpetual change; but spiritually it does not attain to the status of history, in so far as history only exists where there is also knowledge of history, where there are historical remains and documentation, consciousness of origins and of contemporary events. It is a preconceived notion that where there are no remains there nevertheless may, and indeed must, have been the thing itself—history.

History is that section of the past which, at any given time, is clearly visible to man; it is the sector of things past which he can make his own, it is consciousness of origins. Prehistory is that section of the past which, although it is in fact the foundation of all that comes after, is itself unknown.

The evolution of man in prehistory is the development of the basic elements constituting humanity. His evolution in history is an unfolding of inherited contents of a spiritual and technical nature. The basic constitution took an immeasurable period of time in which to develop; by contrast, historical evolution has the appearance of something taking temporary shape in works, notions, thoughts and spiritual configurations on the broad and deep foundation of humanity, which was evolved in prehistory and is still real today.

Prehistory and history, therefore, one after the other, created the two fundaments of our humanity. Prehistoric becoming, that process of the growth of man's basic structure, with its elemental impulses and characteristics, with all the unconscious part of our make-up, formed the basic stock of our being. The historical process, in which man consciously took over the past and built up on it, which shows us what man was capable of and what is the fountainhead of our education, our belief, knowledge and ability and their contents—this second fundament is like a thin skin stretched over the heart of the volcano that is man. It may seem possible for this skin to be cast off, whereas the basic stock of man's being as formed during prehistoric ages can never be cast off. We may feel the threat of becoming Stone Age men once more, because beneath the surface we are so all the time. Our weapons would be aeroplanes instead of stone axes, but everything else would be the same as it was then, as though all the millennia of history had been blotted out of memory. With the dissolution of history man would fall into the condition in which he was—when still and already human—thousands of years ago; without knowledge or awareness of his cultural heritage.

We know nothing of the soul of the man of 20,000 years ago. But we do know that during the course of the short period of known history at least, man as a whole has not changed biologically or psycho-physically, that there has been no demonstrable modification in his elemental, unconscious impulses (after all, only some hundred generations are involved).

The outcome of the prehistoric process of becoming is something biologically inheritable, and to this extent something whose continuance through all historical catastrophes is assured. The acquisitions of history, on the other hand, have to be consciously passed on and may get lost. Everything which was planted in the human kingdom in the sudden burst of creation, and has stamped and altered the appearance of man through entering into the cultural heritage, is so closely bound up with this heritage that without it, because it is not biologically inheritable, it might die out entirely: we should be back with the bare fundamental constitution.

Historical consciousness is now confronted by the major question of man's basic stock as inherited from the ages before history, of this universal fundament of humanity. Man is alive with subterranean forces from the ages during which he received his characteristic stamp. Prehistory was the time during which this human nature came into being. If we could know prehistory we should gain an insight into one of the fundamental substances of humanity, by watching it come into existence, by seeing the conditions and situations that made it what it is.

The questions to which prehistory, if it could be reached empirically, might provide an answer are:

What are man's primary motives, what are his vital impulses? Which remain constant throughout the ages, which undergo modification? Are they still capable of transformation? Are they invariably veiled? Have these impulses only been held in check since the beginning of history, or were they already curbed by the social orders of prehistory? Do they break out from time to time or in certain situations and tear through the veil? When and how has this happened? Will they break out with greater violence than ever before if all our beliefs and our cultural heritage break down? What becomes of them when they are moulded? How can they be moulded? What becomes of them when they are deprived of speech and every means of direct expression, when they are so thickly veiled as to be paralysed by conceptional schemata, interpretations of the world, established values and outright violation?

What little we know of prehistory, together with the picture that we are able to form with the aid of ethnography, ethnology and history, and of which we make use in visualising psychologically the primal human impulses, combine to give us a mirror of our inner being. This mirror shows us what we often prefer to conceal, under certain circumstances forget, and what may then take us by surprise as a reality signifying disaster.

But none of the pictures we form of man, of his basic constitution and his elemental impulses, are absolute representations of something that really exists as we see it. These pictures are rather instances of our own motivating, illuminating and impelling self-awareness. This self-awareness contains that which is empirically inevitable, whose factuality demands recognition, indissolubly linked with the freedom that bestows the quality of attraction or repulsion on the pictures seen.

B. OUR ATTITUDE TO PREHISTORY

By comparison with the history of the earth (in the region of two thousand million years)—by comparison with the much shorter history of life on the earth (in the region of five hundred million years)—by comparison with the hundreds of thousands of years during which, as is proved by skeletal remains, there were humans living on earth—the history of mankind that is known to us and in which man was conscious of himself as history was—let us repeat—of ephemeral duration. Temporally this history is like the first minute of a new happening. It has just started. This fundamental fact cannot be too emphatically brought to mind. Seen within this horizon the whole of history becomes a small, still germinal world in the life of mankind, dwindling almost to nothing in immeasurable space and unending time. We ask:

What does this beginning mean?

Why has man, ever since this cultural heritage began to be handed on, which means since the beginning of history, always felt himself to have reached an end—whether this end was one of culmination or decline?

Is it a mere passing moment, condemned to utter disappearance and oblivion? If so, what does it mean?

How did man become what he is before history began? What trials did he pass through, what potentialities did he unfold, what did he achieve and discover before the dawn of transmitted history?

The demand made on our cognition by prehistory is contained in the almost unanswerable questions: Where do we come from? What were we when we started history? What can possibly have gone before history? Through what incisive processes that took place in those times did man become man and capable of having a history? What forgotten depths were there, what 'primal revelation', what lucidity that is concealed from us? How did languages arise and myths, that exist complete at the very dawn of history?

In the face of these questions, the phantasy of a romanticism in whose eyes the whole course of history is merely a downward path is as erroneous as the sobriety that sees in prehistory nothing but dull facts, which it interprets by analogies with natural history. Yet almost all answers are hypotheses.

Prehistory, sinking into the unfathomable depths of time, has for us, because of our lack of knowledge, the appearance of calm, of distance, of inapprehensibly profound significance. The moment we catch a glimpse of it, it exerts over us a power of attraction that seems to give promise of something extraordinary. Prehistory casts a spell from which we can never escape, no matter how often we are disappointed.

(1)   We can see the attitude which, from the very first moment of history, men have adopted toward prehistory; how they claimed a knowledge of it which they expressed in myths and images that entered into the fabric of their lives; how they found in it a lost paradise, immense crises—like that of the Tower of Babel—a golden age and disasters; how they mingled the natural with the supernatural, made gods walk the earth and told tales of inspiration and instruction from above. Such myths contain no core of tenable knowledge of the remote past, no basis of factual tradition. But the whole mass of them presents a grandiose image of the necessity which man felt, as he still feels, to relate himself to his foundations in the depths of the prehistoric age.

(2)   Today we seek to investigate that which can be known. Within modest limits we are able to ascertain what man already possessed at the dawn of history, and hence what must have developed and been acquired during prehistory; language, tools, myths, social orders. We can gain only external knowledge of prehistory itself, to the extent to which we are able to unearth relics of prehistoric man (in the shape of bone remains) and his artifacts. Up to now such finds have been considerable in number, but very meagre as to the information they can give us regarding the soul, inner attitude, beliefs and spiritual motion of prehistoric man, of which they afford at best a very hazy picture. Even burial places, buildings, ornaments and the celebrated cave-paintings only bring us a lively grasp of an occasional detail; we are unable to understand it in the context of its world, of which we can form no total image. Nothing can be known with certainty but the purposes of the implements. For this reason, we hear a great deal that is hypothetical from prehistorians. They interpret. But their interpretations rarely contain any element of

cogency; they never cause vanished imports to become vividly manifest as do the linguistic documents of history. It is therefore a wise principle for historians who want to hold fast to that which has perceptible, comprehensible form, not to have too much to do with the beginnings. What we know about prehistory is far from being nothing, but in the empty ages and spaces there are a multitude of objective facts with very little meaning.

Visualisation of prehistory brings us no satisfactory positive information. The clarity of the facts shows us the existence of prehistory. But to questions concerning the humanity that we ourselves are, knowledge of prehistory gives no adequate reply.

(3) Quite a different path of penetration into prehistory is laid down by the permanent element in man's spiritual make-up from the dawn of history down to later ages and the present day. This permanent element is understood as an unconsciously preserved heritage from prehistory. Here primal insights into the main features of humanity are essayed through creative visions. These visions are then employed in the same manner as hypotheses, to see how far they render the factual heritage and the factual processes of history comprehensible. But it is the essence of these insights that they reveal imports which can never be lost, of which, even if they are empirically undemonstrable, something remains. The visions of Bachofen are the prime example. Through them we learn to see. There is no meagreness of material. But at the same time there is no proven insight into a prehistory now factually laid bare. There is only a wide area of vivid and meaningful possibility in respect of forms of life and their inner implications, which is opened up, not by archaeological finds, nor through positivistic construction, but by the seeing comprehension of historically existent behaviour, of the customs and practices, of the symbols and thought-patterns of men.

To try out all these different attitudes to prehistory increases awareness of the immense potentialities that prehistory contains: here something happened which, by giving humanity its characteristic stamp, has, so to speak, decided the whole ensuing course of history in advance.

C. A TEMPORAL SCHEMA OF PREHISTORY

With regard to the remains of human skeletons, two facts appear to be of essential significance:

(1) The skeletal finds in Java, China, Africa and Europe—not, so far, in America—cannot be fitted into any real sequence of the genesis of the human form: all attempts to make them fit any such sequence are arbitrary, ideal constructions in which unconnected findings are linked on the principle that such a manifoldness of phenomena is inconceivable and incomprehensible except as arising through derivation and evolution.

(2) All these finds, even those which, judged by the geological strata in which they lay, must be the earliest, show a skull with a brain-weight approaching the present-day average—and greater by more than double that of the most highly evolved anthropoid apes. Biologically, therefore, they are all of them already human. Individual features, such as the absence of chin, supra-orbital ridges and shallowness of the skull, are not of universal occurrence. It is nowhere possible to tell which finds represent a major race, which a lateral branch and which the ancestral stock: their real genealogical relationship to contemporary man is completely unknown.

These findings defy the establishment of an evolutionary sequence. Only the geological strata in which the finds were made permit the formulation of a temporal sequence which does coincide, in some measure, with the order of age conjectured from the nature of the finds themselves. Worked out in a rough schema:

Diluvium is the term used to designate the final phase of the earth's history with its series of ice ages and inter-ice ages. Alluvium designates the years subsequent to the last ice age; its duration has not yet reached that of an inter-ice age and amounts to perhaps 15,000 years. The diluvium must span a million years.

Finds have proved the existence of man during the diluvium in the later ice ages and inter-ice ages. Not until the last ice age—in other words about 20,000 years ago—did the man of the Cromagnon race appear, who is anthropologically no different from ourselves. It was the Cromagnon race which, toward the end of the last ice age, produced the amazing paintings in the caves of Spain and France. This is called the Palaeolithic Period after the method used in the primitive manufacture of stone implements.

The Neolithic Period (the age of polished stones) is dated from eight or five thousand years B.C. The earliest phases of the cultures in Egypt and Mesopotamia, on the banks of the Indus and in China also fall within the Neolithic Period.

It is in no sense a matter of a straight line of advancing development, however, but of manifold spheres of culture simultaneous with and succeeding one another. At the same time, certain technical advances, such as the working of stone, ran through them as they were diffused by a slow process of transmission from one culture to another.

Temporally, two groups of prehistory are to be distinguished:

Absolute prehistory, prior to the inception of the great early cultures after 4000 B.C. And *relative* prehistory, which went on simultaneously with the course of these cultures that left documentary evidence of themselves, in part in the neighbourhood and under the influence of the latter and in part remote from and almost without contact with them. This relative prehistory was partly the prehistory of later civilised peoples, such as the Germano-Romance and Slav worlds, and partly led on to the peoples which have remained primitive down to the present day and constitute a permanent prehistory.

D. WHAT HAPPENED IN PREHISTORY?

At bottom, the vast stretches of time during which humans already existed are an enigma to us. They represent an age of historical silence in which, nonetheless, something of vital importance must have taken place.

The moment of *becoming completely human* is the deepest enigma of all, up to now utterly impenetrable and beyond all comprehension. Such figures of speech as 'a gradual process of transition' merely serve to obscure it. We can evolve phantasies of the genesis of man. But even these phantasies break down; whenever we try to picture man coming into being, our imagination sees him already there.

On top of this, we cannot even give a definitive and satisfactory answer to the question: What is man? We can give no complete answer to the question of what man is. The very fact that we do not know what man really is, is an essential part of our humanity. Visualisation of the problem of man's becoming in prehistory and history means, at the same time, visualising the question of the essential nature of humanity.

Prehistory contains two elements, the biological evolution of man, and his historical evolution, which took place in prehistory, and, even without writing, created a cultural heritage. It would seem necessary to begin by separating these two elements, both in their reality and as to the method of investigating them:

Biological evolution brings inheritable characteristics, historical evolution only a cultural heritage. That which is biologically inheritable is permanent; the cultural heritage can be destroyed and forgotten in a very short space of time. Biological reality can be apprehended in the structure, function and psycho-physical characteristics of the body; the reality of the cultural heritage can be apprehended in language, behaviour-patterns and works.

In the process of becoming human, going on through long millennia, the fundamental features of humanity must have been fixed as inheritable biological qualities that are still present. In historical times, on the other hand, man has not undergone any demonstrable biological metamorphosis. We 'have not the slightest indication that during the historical period susceptible of scientific control the inherited predisposition of the newborn child has undergone any modification' (Portmann).

The two modes of approach and the realities corresponding to them—the biological and the historical—do not coincide. It looks on the surface as though the one, the evolution of human history, is a sequel to the other, the biological evolution culminating in the genesis of man as such. What we call history has, it seems, nothing to do with biological evolution.

Humanity, however, consists of that in which the biological and the historical are, in fact, indissolubly combined. Immediately we have made the conceptual division we are confronted by the question: What biological consequences did the phenomenon of history have?—What biological realities may have been the causes of historical potentialities?

Even the biology of man, if we once succeed in grasping it, may perhaps prove different in some way from all other biology.

But the manner in which biological evolution and historical metamorphosis interact upon one another is, once again, a closed book to us as a totality. We know of remarkable facts in history, in our own present, in prehistory and amongst primitive peoples, on the basis of which we can endeavour to formulate hypotheses concerning the paths that led up to them. Such endeavours raise questions that are well-founded, but the answers that have been given to them up to now are, in all probability, entirely erroneous.

Let us see which of the characteristics of man strike us in the light of this conception of a dual prehistory.

1. Biological characteristics of man

What is the difference between man and animal? The answer is: The upright carriage, the great brain-weight, the skull structure corresponding to it and the lofty brow—the development of the hand—his nakedness—man alone can laugh and weep, etc. Although as a structure man falls, morphologically, into the category of zoological life-forms, he is perhaps unique even from a physical point of view. His body is the expression of his soul. The human body has its own specific beauty. But the uniqueness of the human body has not hitherto been recognised as a cogent and conceptually clearly demonstrable fact, at least not as an overall principle, but only in respect of individual phenomena which, as such, have no bearing on the total judgement.

The most valid general criterion is this: Every animal, without exception, develops organs adapted to particular tasks in connexion with the special circumstances obtaining in the particular environment by which its life is confined. This specialisation of organs results in every animal being superior to man at some point, in terms of particular abilities. But this very superiority means, at the same time, a narrowing down of its potentialities. Man has avoided all such specialisations of his organs. Hence the fact that though he is inferior in each individual organ, he remains superior in the potentialities he has kept alive by non-specialisation. He is compelled by his inferiority and enabled by his superiority, through the medium of his consciousness, to follow paths quite different from those taken by animals in bringing his existence to realisation. It is this, and not his body, that renders him capable of adapting himself to all climates and all zones, to all situations and all environments.

If man must have been, from the very first, a creature that avoided all definitive fixation, then even in his weakness he enjoyed a superiority over the animals deriving from his spirit and his power of thought. Thanks to the absence of organ specialisation, he remained open to possibilities for the fashioning of his environment, in which his organs were replaced by implements. Man's very weaknesses (in comparison with the animals) give him the freedom to enter upon a course of spiritual self-transformation, the culmination of whose upward path is beyond our ken. Instead of endlessly repeating the natural and constant cycle of life, as do the animals, he became capable of creating history. Nature possesses history only in the form of an unconscious, by human standards infinitely slow, irreversible process of becoming different. Man achieves history, on the foundation of the purely repetitive function of natural life, which he shares with everything living (and which has remained constant throughout the period visible to the historical eye), as a conscious, rapid transformation through the free acts and creations of his spirit.

Biologically we can observe facts which, though they seem to differentiate man from the animals, nevertheless remain on the plane of that which is not specifically human, e.g.:

There are morbid biological predispositions, such as the psychoses, that only occur in man, but in all races of men.

There are qualities of character, such as a peculiar malignancy, which is by no means common to all animals, but is possessed by many apes. Amongst chimpanzees such, so to speak, biological characteristics as good-nature, the urge to inflict pain, intelligence and stupidity and, above all, humanness can be observed. Perhaps there is a humanness which, in this sense, is also biological. Our subterranean store of instincts and propensities reaches deep down into the realm of biology; on occasion it may confront us within ourselves as an alien force that terrifies us.

All this is not specifically human. Portmann was the first to attempt to penetrate, along biological paths, to a radical conception of the element specific to humanity![1]

For example, he draws attention to the following: The newborn human is different from all other mammals: His sense organs are developed, his brain- and body-weight are much higher than is the case with the apes—and yet, by comparison, he is a premature birth in the sense of being completely helpless. The first year of life in the human requires the maturing of functions which, in other mammals, mature *before* birth. Man lives his first year in the world, although—measured against the newborn animal—he ought to be continuing his intra-uterine growth. For instance, his spine acquires its S-shape through sitting up and standing. How does this come about? As the result of an instinctive urge and the imitation of adults, fostered by the latter's interest and encouragement; in every case, the historically deter-mined environment is a co-factor in inducing the first step toward physical maturity. The spirit is already operative, even in the biological realm itself. In all probability, the experiences undergone during the first year of life, the year in which those primary biological functions mature that are acquired by animals whilst still in the embryonic stage, are of such great importance as to lend a decisive stamp to the individual's whole ensuing life.

In short: 'In contradistinction to all the higher animals, man acquires his specific life-form "in the open", in a free and rich relationship to colours and shapes, to living creatures and, above all, to other human beings', whereas the animal is born with his life-form complete.

Hence, for Portmann, the peculiar nature of man does not lie in palpable morphological and physiological characteristics of the body. To define man it is not enough to trace the line of evolution that leads from the receding jaw of the ape, by way of the facial angle of early and Neanderthal man, to the projecting chin of modern man.

The essential factor is rather man's mode of life in its entirety. 'We find in man a form of life which is peculiar in every respect. Notwithstanding the extent of his resemblance to the animal in body structure and behaviour, man's whole make-up is as dissimilar to the animal's as it is akin. Every limb of our bodies, every one of our motions, is an expression of this peculiar character, to which we give no name, but which we are at pains to advertise in all the phenomena of human existence.'

If we seek to grasp the biological element in man, we find that it ceases to be merely biological. It is certainly impossible to apprehend man in toto through the medium of biology—yet he is, at the same time, a biological reality down to the smallest detail and capable of being apprehended bio-logically, i.e. by means of the categories in which all life, in animals and plants, is investigated. In the case of man, however, 'biologically' has a wider signification, since it includes that which distinguishes man from all other living creatures, that element of difference in man which contrasts with the innumerable biological identities and analogies.

Since it thus proves impossible to separate biological from spiritual reality in man, we are bound to say: Man cannot be conceived of as a zoological spe-cies, capable of evolution, to which spirit was one day added as a new acqui-sition. Within the biological sphere man must have been, from the very start, something different, even in a biological sense, from all other forms of life.

Attempts have been made to interpret man's biological peculiarity as the product of domestication, on the analogy of animals, which change their essential nature as the result of the domestication inflicted on them by man. It is not man who has created culture, but culture that has created man. Quite apart from the question of where culture comes from in this case, from a purely biological standpoint the universal consequences of domestication are not found. Portmann has drawn attention to the decisive points:

(1) In man the brain-weight is increased—in contradistinction to the normal rule of domestication, which is that a reduced brain-weight is always found in domesticated animals.

(2) In man the process leading to sexual maturity is greatly delayed—in domesticated animals early sexual maturity is the rule.

(3) The disappearance of the annual rutting-season normal to animals is taken to be a sign of domestication in the human. But this phenomenon also occurs in primates in a wild state. 'Here we may well be confronted with a characteristic of the primates, which is more likely to be a precondition for the development of culture than its consequence.'

(4) Man's nakedness. This, however, is not merely a negative absence of the hair coat, but a positive increase in the sensory performance of the skin.

In particular, though men do exhibit certain effects of domestication (e.g. dental caries), these do not determine the specific quality of humanity.

Far back in prehistory stands the compelling question of the differentiation of the basic constitution of man into the major *races*—whites, negroes and the yellow race.

All the races are in themselves mixtures, forms of humanity that are mobile in selection and mutation. But from the very beginning there have been interminglings between the major races as well. Intermingling between the white and the yellow races went so far in India that pure descendants of the once immigrant whites are now hardly to be found. In antiquity, interbreeding between whites and negroes was rare; during the last three centuries it has become more frequent. Interbreeding between whites and Red Indians led to a numerous population.

Pure races are never more than ideal types. The existence of firmly closed, immutable, unmixed races at any period of time has not been demonstrated as a reality. It is an extreme notion presupposing isolated pure races.

Moreover, prehistory seems to bear witness to races that no longer exist. It does not show one primal race, from which all others evolved, nor does it show several primary races which, in their diversity, would provide a tangible starting-point for the whole evolution of man. We look into a seething ocean of forms, in which clear-cut divisions only exist in the foreground, in seeming, for a moment—not absolutely and for ever. But the real descent and movement of man in immeasureable prehistory is known to none. In all probability it never will be known.

2. Historical acquisitions

We have no information concerning the historical moments of creation, none concerning the spiritual steps that made up the course of becoming; what we know relates only to their results. The rest must be inferred from these results. We enquire after the essential factors which, in prehistory, caused man to become man in his world; we look to see what sort of inventions his fear and courage led him to achieve in situations of danger and conflict, how the relation of the sexes and the attitude to birth and death, to mother and father, took shape. Amongst the essential factors we may perhaps number the following: •

(1) The *use of fire and implements*. A creature destitute of these two would hardly seem human to us.

(2) The *formation of language*. The radical difference from animal communication through unpurposed expression lies in the conjectured meaning of the world of objects, which becomes conscious and communicable to man alone and to which his thinking and speaking refers.

(3) The characteristic ways in which man *does violence to himself e.g.* through tabus. It is the nature of man to be incapable of being solely nature and to bring himself to realisation through art. The nature of man is his artificiality.

(4) The *formation of groups and communities*. Human community is something different to its very roots from the instinctively automatic insect States. In contrast to the group formations and the circumstances of superior and subordinate status in the higher animals, human community is founded on conscious meaning.

In the human, social life, right up to the formation of States, seems to be based on an additional phenomenon which is peculiar to him alone: the conquest of sexual jealousy through masculine solidarity. Amongst animals, there occur either herd-formations that are purely temporary and split apart at every rutting-season, or else permanent formations made possible by the asexuality of the majority. The human alone was able, without giving up his sexuality, to bring forth an organisation of masculine comradeship whose wealth of tensions has made historical life possible.

(5) Life through *myths*. How the images contained in myths first lent their stamp to life and came to exercise a predominant influence over the whole business of living, over the family, society, work and warfare is beyond our ken. These images are susceptible of infinite interpretation and infinitely heightened meaning, yet they simply bear the awareness of Being and the self and give security and certitude. At the dawn of history and thenceforth man lived in their world. Bachofen's visions may be historically dubious in respect of the evidence on which they are based, they may prove untenable as documentary tradition, nevertheless they capture vital truths, both in their general outline and also, probably, in much of their contents.

E. THE OVERALL ASPECT OF PREHISTORY

During incalculable ages and spaces of time man spread over the globe; within this diffuse happening, endlessly fragmented in limited regions, something of an embracing and integral character took place: the great, slow, processes of the imperceptible breeding of races, of the formation of languages and myths, the silent spread of technical inventions and the migrations. All these events were unconscious and, although already human, still closely attached to nature.

Associations of human beings took place with their eyes on other associations of human beings. Men knew of one another and looked at one another. Diffusion gradually drew together in conflict and made its way to the formation of more inclusive units. This was the transition to history, which began definitively with writing.

Prehistory is a gigantic reality—for in it man made his appearance—yet it is a reality of which we are fundamentally ignorant. But if we seek an answer to the question of what we humans really are through the knowledge of whence we come, we cannot plunge deep enough into the enigma of prehistory. This obscurity possesses a power of attraction which rightly lures us on—and causes us perpetual disappointments through our ignorance.

F. DO ALL MEN FORM PART OF A SINGLE WHOLE?

Prehistory might help to provide an answer to the question of whether men as men form part of a single whole, and in what way, by providing us with a decision between the *monophyletic* or the *polyphyletic* origin of man.

Man exists in the multiplicity of races. Are these races branches of a single stem, or are they independent developments from pre-human life, implying that man came into being on several different occasions? All the facts speak for the monophyletic as against the polyphyletic origin of man.

First there is the pointer given by the fact that no earlier human relics have been found in America. America must have been settled from the north across the Bering Straits by emigrants from Asia in late prehistoric times. At all events, no human race appears to have had its origin in this continent, although the Red Indian races bear a strongly individual stamp.

Then there is the biological argument for a monophyletic origin provided by the ability of all races to beget progeny through interbreeding who are in their turn capable of reproduction. To this is added the spiritual unison of the main features of their being, when they are compared with animals. The distance that separates man from the animal is immeasurably greater than the distance that separates men of the most alien races from each other. In comparison with the distance that separates them from the animal, the closest affinity exists between all men. The immense divergences between us, the differences of character, the remoteness that goes as far as non-comprehension, our outbreaks of mortal enmity, the horrifyingly silent disintegration that takes place in mental illness or in the reality of national-socialist concentration camps—all this is the torment of authentic affinity, which has been forgotten or can no longer find a path to realisation.

An empirical verdict as to the monophyletic or polyphyletic origin of man is impossible, since we know nothing whatsoever about the biological origin of man. Hence the unity of human origin is an idea and not a reality open to experience.

To all such arguments the reply is: Interrelationship between men does not consist essentially in their zoological structure, but in the fact that they can understand each other, that they are all made up of consciousness, thought and spirit. Here there is an intimate affinity between men, whereas an abyss divides them from even the closest of the animals.

Hence we cannot deduce the unity of mankind and the existence of human solidarity from empirical investigations, even though these give us some pointers; nor can we refute this unity and solidarity by empirical investigations. Whether man's origin was monophyletic or polyphyletic is, in the last analysis, not decisive. What we are dealing with here is the belief in the unity of mankind which has grown, in the course of history, into an integral part of the human make-up; the abyss separating man from the animal is its presupposition.

Concomitant with this belief in human solidarity is the will to make it a reality. To the extent to which man becomes aware of himself, he ceases to see his fellow-man as merely nature, merely a means. He experiences his own inner being as a duty. This feeling of duty penetrates so deep into his reality as to become a second nature. But it lacks altogether the reliability of a natural law. Cannibalism has come to an end, yet it is capable of breaking out again at any moment. Genocide took place in history and now, after coming to be looked upon as an impossibility, it has happened again on an unprecedented scale. One of the preconditions of humanity is human solidarity, illumined by natural and human law, continually betrayed and for ever presenting its demands afresh.

This is the reason for the peculiarly human satisfaction to be obtained from achieving understanding with those remote from us—and the demand to see man as man, as Rembrandt paints a negro or, as Kant puts it: A human being must never be looked upon or treated as merely a means, but always as an end in himself.

NOTE

1   (Page 46): Adolf Portmann, *Biologische Fragments zu einer Lehre vom Menschen*, Basle 1944. *Vom Ursprung des Menschen*, Basle 1944. From my book *Der Philosophische Glaube*, Munich 1948, Zurich 1948 (English translation by Ralph Mannheim, *The Perennial Scope of Philosophy*, Routledge & Kegan Paul, 1950), the third lecture: 'Man'.

4

THE ANCIENT HISTORICAL CIVILISATIONS

A. SUMMARY

At only approximately the same time the three earliest civilisations arose in three regions of the earth: firstly the Sumero-Babylonian, Egyptian, Aegean world from 4000 B.C.; secondly the pre-Aryan Indus culture of the third millennium, which initial excavations are just bringing to light and which had some connexions with the Sumerians; thirdly the ancient, archaic Chinese world of the second millennium B.C. (probably even earlier), of which only a glimpse can be caught in the recollections of its successors and in a few tangible relics.

At one stroke the whole atmosphere becomes different from that of prehistory. Silence no longer reigns; men speak to one another in written documents, and thereby to us once we have learned to understand their script and their language; they speak in buildings, which presuppose organisation and the existence of a State, and in works of art which conceal a meaning that is strange to us in forms that are nonetheless eloquent.

Yet these civilisations are destitute of the spiritual revolution which we have outlined in our picture of the Axial Period and which laid the foundations for a new humanity, our humanity. The American cultures in Mexico are comparable to them, though they blossomed thousands of years later. They too are devoid of everything which the Axial Period brought with it—although it preceded them in time. They vanished before the mere presence of Western culture deriving from the Axial Period.

In the desert belt that stretches from the Atlantic Ocean through Africa by way of Arabia deep into Asia, apart from many small oases, there are two great river valleys, the land of the Nile and the land of the two rivers, Mesopotamia. In both these regions the history of man can be traced back, in an unbroken sequence of documents and monuments, further than anywhere else on earth. Here we can see what existed some 3000 years B.C. and can deduce from relics what existed even further back than that. In China we cannot see much beyond the second millennium, while clear and comprehensive records are only available from the first millennium. Excavations in India reveal cities at a high level of civilisation in the third millennium—but they still stand in isolation and, at the moment, show hardly any connexion with the later India, which begins toward the end of the second millennium. In America everything is much later, without exception subsequent to the start of the Christian era. Europe gives evidence, through excavations, of a prehistoric existence amounting to an autonomous culture going back to the third millennium; but it does not carry the weight of a physiognomy of its own capable of affecting us strongly today. Only because this is the site of our own prehistory do we feel our interest caught and held by it.

The later stages of the Egyptian and Babylonian culture were known to the Greeks and the Jews—who lived within their orbit—and the recollection of them became part of the Western tradition; but it is only today that excavations and the deciphering of their languages have brought them really vividly before us in their passage through thousands of years. Finally the Indus culture has become known to us through excavations, but only in the course of the last few decades; it had vanished completely from the memory of the present population of India (its written characters have not yet been deciphered). The Chinese cultural heritage idealises its own foundations as laid in the second millennium and earlier. Excavations have brought to light only a few relics.

B. WHAT EVENTS USHERED IN HISTORY?

We ask: With what tangible events did history begin? Perhaps the following are the most essential:

(1) The task of *organising* river-control and irrigation on the Nile, the Euphrates and Tigris and the Hwang-ho enforced centralisation, a civil service and the formation of a State.

(2) The discovery of *writing*—a necessary precondition for this organisation—was made (according to Hrozny) around 3300 by the Sumerians, around 3000 in Egypt and around 2000 in China (the alphabetic script was only discovered during the last millennium B.C. by the Phoenicians). There remains the question of whether the discovery can be traced back to one single source (the Sumerians), or whether it was made independently at several places. The indispensability of writing to administration led to the acquisition of a dominant social position by the scribes, who formed an intellectual aristocracy.

(3) The genesis of *peoples* who feel themselves a unity with a common *language*, a common *culture* and a common body of *myths*.

(4) Later on the *world-empires*, beginning with Mesopotamia. Their origin was the task of preventing the perpetual attacks of nomads on the civilised country, by achieving dominion over all surrounding countries and over the nomads themselves. The first world-empires to arise were those of the Assyrians and Egyptians, followed in a new shape by that of the Persians; after this the Indians founded their empire, perhaps with the Persian empire as a model; last of all the Chinese empire came into being.

(5) The introduction of the *horse*—after these civilisations had already developed and as a factor in their transformation—employed either for drawing war-chariots or for riding. The horse set man free from the soil and gave him distance and liberty; it furnished him with a new and superior battle-technique and brought with it a spirit of mastery that is bound up with the taming and curbing of the horse, the courage of the rider and conqueror and the feeling for the beauty of the animal.

These events that open up history lead on to the deeper question: What came over man that he stepped out of unhistoricity into history? What is the specific factor in his being that leads to history? What are the basic characteristics of the historical process as compared to prehistory? We should like to derive an answer from the inner core of man's being. It is not the outward occurrences, but the inward transformation of man that we should like to know.

Prior to history a process of becoming and self-transformation went on, a process which man very largely shares with nature. The leap from this mere happening into history was perhaps characterised:

(1) by consciousness and recollection, by the handing on of spiritual acquisitions—this set man free from the mere present;

(2) by rationalisation, in varying senses and to varying degrees, by technology—this set man free from dependence on his immediate environment for the satisfaction and safeguarding of his vital needs;

(3) the emergence of men to be emulated, in the shape of rulers and sages, whose deeds, achievements and destinies were in full view of the masses—this was the first step toward setting men free from the apathy of self-awareness and the fear of demons.

The outcome of history was an unceasing change in conditions, knowledge and the manifestation of the inner implications of life; but in such a manner that the relationship of everything to everything, the inter-connexion of all aspects of the cultural heritage and universal communication was felt to be possible and indeed demanded.

For what reason did man take the leap? When he took it he neither desired nor knew what came over him as he did so. All other living creatures are at once confined and consummate in their peculiar structure, but man is boundlessly open in his potentialities, his being has not attained consummate shape and never can do so. Everything dormant in man from his inception, everything that must already have been at work in prehistory as the seed of history, broke forcefully through when history began.

This leap made by humanity which resulted in history, may be conceived of as a disaster that overtook mankind; something incomprehensible happened, the fall of man, the intrusion of an alien power; history is a process of annihilation in the cycle of a firework that may be magnificent, but is short-lived; that which took place at the outset may be reversed again; in the end man will return to the blissful state of his prehistoric existence.

Or else the leap was humanity's great gift and the fact that man made it is his high destiny, his path to unprecedented experiences and to an ascent that drives him forward out of his inconsummate state. Through history man has become the being that strives to rise above itself. Not until history commenced did he take up his high task. No one knows whither it will lead him. Even disaster and misery can serve to give it momentum. Only with the beginning of history did man become truly human:

(a) From his beginnings flows the stream of *potentialities given him as part of his substance*. But these only become full, rich, manifest by entering into the movement of history, where they are illumined, verified, enhanced, where they get lost, are remembered and rise up afresh. They have need of rationalisation, which is itself not the primary factor, but the medium through which the origins and final aims are made manifest.

(b) With the leap to history *transitoriness becomes conscious*. Everything in the world has its appointed time and must pass away. Man alone knows of his own death. In the recoil from this terminal situation he experiences eternity in time, historicity as a phenomenon of being, in time the effacement of time. His historical consciousness becomes identical with his consciousness of eternity.

(c) History is a continual thrusting forward on the part of *single individuals*. They call to the rest to follow them. Whoever hears and understands them joins them in the forward movement. But history remains *at the same time mere happening*, a continual going-with-the-tide in which these calls are vain and the lead is not followed. An immense gravitational pull seems again and again to paralyse every upward sweep. The tremendous forces of the masses, with their attributes of mediocrity, suffocate whatever is not in line with them. Anything in their midst which does not win the right to exist through its significance as a realisation of that which is inherent in the mass, and anything that does not arouse their belief, must perish. History is the great question—which is still undecided and never can be decided by thought, but only by reality itself—as to whether history in its upward sweep is a mere interlude between unhistorical conditions, or whether it is the break-through into the depths. If it is the latter it will lead in its entirety, even in the guise of boundless disaster and to the accompaniment of danger and ever-renewed failure, to Being becoming manifest through man and to man himself, in an upward sweep whose limits we cannot foresee, laying hold of potentialities of which we can have no foreknowledge.

C. ANALOGIES AND DIVERSITIES BETWEEN THE ANCIENT CIVILISATIONS

The analogous basic features—large-scale organisations, writing, the dominant social position of the scribe class—gave rise to a type of human who, despite his more refined civilisation, has something unawakened about him. A specific form of technological rationalisation corresponds to this unawakenedness devoid of authentic reflection.

In the great communities everything is bogged down by perceptual images of existence, held fast in unquestioned orders. Living expresses and is patterned upon unproblematic acceptance of things as they are. The fundamental human problems are embedded in sacred knowledge of a magical character, not broken open in the restlessness of search—apart from a few profoundly moving first steps (these traces of awakening do not come to fruition). A vigorous start was made in the ideas concerning justice evolved in Egypt, and particularly in Babylonia. But the problem of meaning was not expressly posed. It is as though the answer were there before the question.

The resemblance between the conditions and developments sets us looking for a common ground. At all periods implements and ideas spread slowly over the face of the earth. Any new discovery causes us to search for the centre from which its diffusion proceeds. This led to the hypothesis of the fundamental and universal importance of the Sumerians on the banks of the Euphrates, from whom decisive influences radiated out to Egypt and as far as China. But far more significance is attributed to this influence than can be proved. The dubious hypothesis of a centre of culture in Asia—somewhere round Western Kurdistan and the Caspian Sea—is put forward. It is supposed that this was a flourishing province of culture while the surface of the earth was moister, and that when it dried up there was a general migration in all directions. This migration resulted in the founding of cultures all over the Eurasian continent, from China to Egypt. But if we gaze into the chasm of prehistory we come upon no ground for this supposition that is confirmed by compelling empirical evidence.

However, the divergences between the various ancient civilisations are also considerable. We feel within each the presence of its own peculiar spirit. In China there are only the rudiments of myths, a limited number of *a priori* notions of a cosmic order, and a living view of nature combined with a natural humanity. In Mesopotamia there is a hardness and vigour, a dramatic quality, and, in the early Gilgamesh epos, a touch of tragedy. In Egypt there is a serene joy in the intimate aspects of life, coupled with a veiling of life by the levelling compulsion of labour, and a lofty feeling for a style of solemn magnitude.

The diversity of language reaches down to the very roots of the spirit. The Chinese language is so radically disparate from the languages to the west of it, not only in its roots, but also in its structure, that its derivation from a common primal language is hardly conceivable. If there were such a primal language, the process leading to such disparity must have gone on for so long as to make it very unlikely that the common source could have been a Central Asiatic culture existing on the verge of prehistory.

The relationship of these civilisations to their successors is also totally diverse. To the Greeks and the Jews they were something different and alien, they knew them and retained them in memory, they saw them at first with awe and wonder and then with contempt as well. The later Indians knew nothing of the ancient cultures, which had completely vanished from recollection. The later Chinese of the Axial Period saw in the old civilisation their own past in a continuous, unbroken line of succession; they had no sense of living in a new age (unless it were one of decadence); they saw the past, in an idealised shape that was taking on the character of a myth, as a model that was unfolded in creative phantasy.

Nevertheless, these ancient civilisations were destitute of any specifically historical movement. After remarkable initial creations, the millennia passed with comparatively little spiritual movement; they were a period of constantly recurring migrations from Central Asia, of conquests and revolutions, of the extermination and mingling of peoples—and the continual re-establishment of the old culture, which catastrophes merely interrupted.

Hence the account of the history of these millennia is eventful in the extreme, and yet its events do not bear the character of historical decisions vital to humanity.

5

THE AXIAL PERIOD AND ITS CONSEQUENCES

We began this book by anticipating the characterisation of the Axial Period, because an understanding of this period seems to us of central importance for the whole conception of universal history.

If we are concerned with the history of philosophy, the Axial Period affords the most rewarding field of study and the one most fruitful in respect of our own thought.

It may be called an interregnum between two ages of great empires, a pause for liberty, a deep breath bringing the most lucid consciousness.

A. THE STRUCTURING OF WORLD HISTORY BY THE AXIAL PERIOD

The Axial Period becomes a ferment that draws humanity into the single context of world history. It becomes, for us, a yardstick with whose aid we measure the historical significance of the various peoples to mankind as a whole.

A deep division falls between the peoples according to the manner in which they react to the break-through. We can distinguish:

(1) *The Axial peoples.*—These are the peoples which accomplished the leap as a direct continuation of their own pasts. To them it was a second birth,

so to speak, and through it they laid the foundations of man's spiritual being and his history properly so called. The Axial peoples are the Chinese, Indians, Iranians, Jews and Greeks.

(2) *The peoples without the break-through.*—Although the break-through was decisive for universal history, it was not a universal occurrence. There were the great peoples of the ancient civilisations, who lived before and even concurrently with the break-through, but had no part in it and, despite their temporal concurrence, remained inwardly unaffected by it.

During the Axial Period the Egyptian and Babylonian cultures were still flourishing, although in a palpably later shape. Both of them were destitute of that quality of reflection which transformed mankind; they underwent no metamorphoses under the influence of the Axial peoples; they no longer reacted to the break-through that had taken place outside their orbit. To begin with they remained what they had been earlier, as the predecessors of the Axial Period: magnificent in the organisation of public and social life, in architecture, in sculpture and painting, in the fashioning of their magical religion. But now they came slowly to an end. Outwardly subjected by the new powers, they also lost inwardly their old culture, which flowed out into Persian, afterwards Sasanian culture and Islam (in Mesopotamia) or into the Roman world and Christendom (which in Egypt subsequently became part of Islam).

Both of them are of significance to universal history, because the Jews and Greeks, who created the basis of the Western World, grew up in sight of them, learning from them, drawing away from them and striving to outdo them. Then these ancient cultures were almost forgotten, until they were rediscovered in our own time.

We are gripped by their magnificence but feel somehow remote from them, in consequence of the gulf created by their lack of everything that went with the break-through. We are infinitely closer to the Chinese and the Indians than to the Egyptians and the Babylonians. The grandeur of the Egyptian and Babylonian world is unique. But that which is familiar to us only starts with the new age of the break-through. In evanescent beginnings we see an anticipation of what comes later that excites our wonder; it is as though the break-through were about to commence and then came to nothing, particularly in Egypt.

There is one *fundamental question* that is crucial for our conception of human history: Are China and India to be set alongside Egypt and Babylonia and really only distinguished from them by the fact that they have survived until today—or did India and China, through their share in the creation of the Axial Period itself, take that great step which carries them right past those ancient civilisations? I will repeat what I have already said: Egypt and Babylonia may be set alongside early China and alongside the Indus culture of the third millennium, but not alongside China and India in their entirety. China and India occupy a position beside the West, not only because they lived on, but also because they accomplished the break-through. We will look briefly at the pros and cons of this view:

It is an old thesis that, compared with the West, China and India had no proper history. For history implies movement, changes of inner nature, new beginnings. In the West there are a succession of totally diverse cultures; first the ancient culture of Hither Asia, then the Graeco-Roman, then the Teuto-Romance. There is a constant change of geographical centres, areas and peoples. In Asia, on the other hand, a constant situation persists; it modifies its manifestations, it founders in catastrophes and reestablishes itself on the one and only basis as that which is constantly the same. This view gives rise to a conception that pictures unhistorical stability east of the Indus and the Hindu-Kush, to the west of them historical movement. Accordingly the deepest division between the great provinces of culture lies between Persia and India. The European might believe himself still in Europe till he reaches the Indus, said Lord Elphinstone (who is quoted by Hegel).[1]

This view seems to me to have its origins in the historical situation of China and India in the eighteenth century. Lord Elphinstone saw the circumstances of his own time and failed altogether to discern China and India in their overall import. At that time they had both reached an advanced stage in their downward path.

Is not the recession that has taken place in India and China since the seventeenth century like a great symbol of what may happen to the whole of mankind? Is not the problem of our destiny to avoid sinking back into the Asiatic matrix from which China and India had also raised themselves up?

(3) *The peoples that came after.*—All the peoples were divided into those which had their foundations in the world of the break-through and those which remained apart. The former were the historical peoples, the latter the primitives.

The peoples responsible for the political construction of the new great empires were the Macedonians and the Romans. Their spiritual poverty consisted in the fact that the experiences of the break-through failed to touch the inner core of their souls. For this reason they were able, in the historical world, to conquer, to govern, to organise, to acquire and preserve the forms of civilisation, to safeguard the continuity of the cultural heritage, but not to carry forward or deepen experience.

It was different with the Nordics. To be sure, the great spiritual revolution no more took place in the North than it did in Babylonia or Egypt. The Nordic peoples lay in the slumber of primitivity, but when the Axial Period reached them they had attained, with the essence of their psychic attitude which it is so difficult for us to apprehend objectively (Hegel calls it the Northern soul), to an autonomous substance.

B. WORLD HISTORY AFTER THE BREAK-THROUGH

Two thousand years have passed since the Axial Period. The consolidation in world-empires was not definitive. The empires collapsed; in all three regions there was a succession of ages of warfare between States, ages of confusion, of the migration of peoples, of ephemeral conquests and fresh moments of the highest cultural productiveness which rapidly vanished in their turn. New peoples entered the three great spheres of culture, in the West the Teutons and Slavs, in Eastern Asia the Japanese, Malays and Siamese; all of them for their part brought forth new cultural configurations. But they did so in a process of coming to terms with the civilisation transmitted to them, by appropriating and refashioning it.

The Teutons only began their spiritual world-mission at the moment when they achieved a share in that revolution of humanity which had started a thousand years earlier. The instant they related themselves to this world, they began a new movement in the midst of which, as the Teuto-Romance world of Europe, they still stand today. One more historically unique phenomenon commenced. That which Antiquity had no longer been capable of achieving now took place. The most extreme tensions of humanity, the luminosity of extreme situations, everything which had begun in the period of the break-through, but had almost foundered in late Antiquity, was accomplished afresh at the same depth and in perhaps greater extension; on this occasion it was not accomplished for the first time and not by the Nordic peoples out of their own resources, but originally as a result of the meeting with an alien tradition which they now felt to be their own. A fresh trial was begun of what is possible to man.

In comparison with China and India, there seem to be far more dramatic fresh starts in the West. Side by side with a spiritual continuity, which became very attentuated at times, there appeared a series of totally dissimilar spiritual worlds. The pyramids, the Parthenon, Gothic cathedrals—China and India can show no such diverse phenomena as these appearing in historical succession.

Yet there can be no question of stability in Asia. In China and India there were silent centuries, like our period of the migration of the peoples, during which everything seems to disappear in chaos, only to reappear and give birth to a new culture. In Asia, too—in India and China—there were shifts in the geographical position of cultural pinnacles and political centres; the peoples bearing the movement of history alternate. The dissimilarity to Europe is not a radical one. The great analogy remains: the creative epoch of the Axial Period followed by revolutions and renaissances; until A.D. 1500, when Europe takes its unprecedented step, whereas China and India, at precisely the same moment, enter into cultural decline.

Once the break-through of the Axial Period had taken place, once the spirit that grew up in it had been communicated, through ideas, works and constructs, to all who were capable of hearing and understanding, once its infinite possibilities had become perceptible, all the peoples that come after were historical by virtue of the intensity with which they laid hold of that break-through and the depth at which they felt themselves spoken to by it.

The great break-through was like an initiation of humanity. Every later contact with it is like a fresh initiation. Subsequent to it, only initiated individuals and peoples are within the course of history proper. But this initiation is no hidden, anxiously guarded arcanum. Rather has it stepped out into the brightness of day, filled with a boundless desire for communication, laying itself open to every test and verification, showing itself to all, and yet an 'open secret' in so far as he alone can discern it who is ready for it, he who, transformed by it, comes to himself.

The fresh initiation takes place in interpretation and assimilation. Conscious transmission, authoritative writings and study become an indispensable element of life.

C. THE SIGNIFICANCE OF THE INDO-GERMANIC PEOPLES

From time immemorial peoples have streamed out of Asia toward the south. The Sumerians themselves came from the north. From about 2000 B.C.

peoples with Indo-Germanic languages moved into India and Iran and then into Greece and Italy; the Celts and Teutons who, during the last millennium B.C., again disturbed the cultural worlds of the south and were for a time held at bay by the Roman Empire—as the nomadic Mongols were for a time by China—were also Indo-Germanic peoples. After that it was the Teutonic and Slavonic peoples of the period of the migration of the peoples, then the Turkish peoples, then the Mongols. This incessant movement of wandering peoples toward the regions of culture only came to a stop a few centuries ago. Its final conclusion was the cessation of the nomadic way of life. From the eighteenth century until today Chinese peasants from the south have peacefully settled Mongolia. From the north the last of the nomads were compelled to settle by the Soviets.

Amongst these wandering peoples who, throughout the millennia, have determined the course of events, we are wont to give historical precedence to the bearers of the Indo-Germanic languages—with justice, but with limited justice.

At no point were the ancient civilisations Indo-Germanic. The linguistic type of the Hittites, which shows clear Indo-Germanic influence, was not accompanied by any tangible spiritual distinctiveness.

It is true that the past of the Indo-Europeans, contemporary with the ancient civilisations, exhibits no organised world comparable to the latter, with writing, State power and cultural tradition. But there must have been a world of more than simply linguistic community. Profound spiritual contents may be inferred—such, for example, as the idea of a Father-God and the peculiar closeness to nature.

There runs through history a periodicity of times in which the past is neglected, forgotten and allowed to sink out of sight, alternating with times in which it is recognised afresh, recalled to mind, re-established and repeated. Ever since then renaissances have run through history at all points (the Augustan age, the Carolingian, the Ottonian renaissance, the Renaissance so called in a narrower sense, the German humanist movement from 1770 to 1830, the Sanskrit renaissance in the twelfth century—the Confucianism of the Han period, the neo-Confucianism of the Sung period).

For the Axial Period and for the ensuing millennia of the West, however, the cultures founded by the Indo-Germanic peoples were of paramount importance. These peoples—Indians, Greeks, Teutons, as well as Celts, Slavs and the later Persians—have one thing in common: They gave birth to the heroic saga and the epic, they discovered, shaped and evolved the tragic spirit. Comparable creations on the part of other peoples—the Babylonians' Gilgamesh, the account of the battle of Kadesh written by the Egyptians, the Chinese San-kwo tshi—are quite different in feeling. The Indo-Germanic peoples played a part in determining the mode of the Axial Period in India, Persia and Greece. But peoples such as the Jews and Chinese, who were so essential to the Axial Period, are not Indo-Germanic at all. Moreover, everything founded by the Indo-Germanic peoples was based on the higher cultures that preceded them and developed through mixture with the previous population and assimilation of the alien heritage.

In Europe there awoke out of the Nordic peoples, after they had come into contact with the Axial Period in the first millennium A.D., a hitherto unreflected substance, which—vague as such notions are bound to be—is akin to the forces partially manifested in the Axial Period itself. It needed this much later contact to enable the content of impulses, which were perhaps uncomprehended by themselves, to attain sublimation in the Nordic peoples. In new creations of the spirit there developed qualities that progressed from intractable obstinacy to a movement of spiritual rebellion and then of questioning and seeking, or from the unshakable ego to the free personality founded on existence as an autonomous individual. With resolution every tension is pushed to the extreme and in tension itself Northern man learns the significance of mankind, of life on earth, of Being itself; in tension he becomes cognisant of transcendence.

D. HISTORY OF THE WEST

(1) *Overall aspect.*—The history of China and India does not fall into such clear-cut divisions as that of the West, it does not contain the same clarity of opposites, nor the lucidity of spiritual conflict in which the various inner forces and religious trends displace one another. The West possesses the polarity of Orient and Occident not only in the distinction between itself and the other world outside it, but also as a polarity within itself.

The history of the West may be divided into epochs as follows:

Three thousand years of Babylonia and Egypt up to about the middle of the last millennium B.C.

One thousand years, based on the break-through of the Axis, of the history of the Jews, Persians, Greeks, and Romans, in the course of which the

West was consciously constituted; this lasted from the middle of the last millennium B.C. to the middle of the first millennium A.D.

Following the division into East and West round about the middle of the first century A.D., there grew up in the West, after an interval of some five hundred years, the new history of the Western World of the Romance-Teutonic peoples; this began in about the tenth century A.D. and has now lasted approximately one thousand years. In the East the empire and culture of Constantinople persisted in unbroken continuity into the fifteenth century. There the present-day Orient of Hither Asia was formed by Islam, in constant touch with both Europe and India.

In this passage through the millennia the Western World made its way with decisive steps, not shrinking from sharp breaks and sudden bounds and introducing radicality into the world, in a measure unknown to China or India. The differentiation into a multiplicity of languages and peoples is perhaps no less in India and China. But there this differentiation does not become, in the course of struggle, the foundation for a three-dimensional contrast between the various forms taken by social and cultural reality, it does not become the historical structure of a world in which the particular configurations develop an energy and consistency that threaten to burst asunder the whole mass.

(2) *The significance of the Christian axis.*—For the consciousness of the West, Christ is the axis of history. Christianity, in the shape of the Christian Church, is perhaps the greatest and highest organisational form yet evolved by the human spirit. Its religious impulses and premises stem from the Jews (from an historical viewpoint Jesus was the last in the series of Jewish prophets and stood in conscious continuity to them); its philosophic breadth and the illuminative power of its ideas stem from the Greeks, its organisational energy and its wisdom in the mastery of reality from the Romans. These elements combine to make a whole which no one planned as such and which, on the one hand, is a remarkably complex end-product in the syncretistic world of the Roman Empire, while on the other, it is set in motion by new religious and philosophic conceptions (the most important representative of which is St. Augustine). This Church proved capable of compelling contradictory elements into union, of absorbing the highest ideals formulated up to that time and of protecting its acquisitions in a dependable tradition.

Historically, however, Christianity, in respect of its contents and in its reality, is a late product. The fact that this was taken as the matrix and origin of the time to come led to a shift in the perspective of the Western view of history in favour of a late-Antique phenomenon—analogous shifts took place in India and China. Throughout the whole of the Middle Ages Caesar and Augustus were esteemed more highly than Solon and Pericles, Virgil than Homer, Dionysius the Areopagite and St. Augustine than Heraclitus and Plato. The later return to the real and original axis never took place as a whole, but only fragmentarily in various rediscoveries, such as the appraisal of Aristotle and Plato already during the Middle Ages, the renewal of the profundity of the prophetic religion by Protestant movements and the re-experiencing of the Greek spirit by German Humanism at the end of the eighteenth century.

The ways of Western Christianity became decisive for Europe not only spiritually, but also politically. This is disclosed by a comparative view. The great dogmatic religions, after the third century A.D., became factors of political unity. The Iranian religion became the bearer of the Sasanian Empire from 224 onward, the Christian religion the bearer of the Roman Empire from the time of Constantine, Islam the bearer of the Arab Empire from the seventh century. In contrast to the world of relatively free cultural exchanges in Antiquity, that world of humanity, the chasm now yawned. Wars became religious wars at the same time—between Byzantium and the Sasanids, between Byzantium and the Arabs, later on the wars of the Western States with the Arabs and after that the wars of the Crusades. In this world, transformed Christianity in Byzantium was not very different from all the other dogmatic religions. It was a more or less theocratic State. Things were different in the West. Here the demands of the Church were just the same. But because they were not fulfilled the Church fought; here it not only unfolded the spiritual life, but became a factor of liberty against worldly power. Here Christianity fostered liberty even in the very foes of the Church. The great statesmen were pious. The force of their wills not only to the accomplishment of the passing designs of power politics, but also as they operated to fill the forms of life and of the State with ethos and with religion, was one of the major wellsprings of Western liberty after the Middle Ages.

(3) *The cultural continuity of the West.*—The cultural continuity of the West was never lost, notwithstanding extraordinary ruptures, destructions and apparently total decay. There are at least certain conceptional forms and

schemata, words and formulae which have persisted through millennia. And where conscious references to the past ceased, some degree of factual continuity remained and was consciously linked up with past tradition again later.

China and India always lived in continuity with their own pasts; Greece, on the other hand, lived beyond its own past in continuity with an alien, Oriental past; the Nordic peoples lived in continuity with the culture of the Mediterranean world which, to begin with, was foreign to them. The West is characterised by the manner in which, at a given moment, it introduced its own originality into a continuity taken over from a foreign source, which it appropriated, worked over and transmuted.

The West founded itself on Christianity and Antiquity, both of them to begin with in the form in which late-Antiquity transmitted them to the Germanic peoples; it then thrust back step by step into the origins both of the Biblical religion and of the essential spirit of Greece.

Since the times of the Scipios, Humanism has been a form of the cultural consciousness which, in varying inflections, has run through Western history right up to the present.

The West created for itself the universal crystallisations from which the continuity of culture drew its life: the *Imperium Romanum* and the Catholic Church. Both of them went to make up the basis of the European consciousness which, though it is continually threatening to disintegrate, has always been constituted afresh—though not reliably—in the great undertakings against the menacing stranger (as at the time of the Crusades, and of the Mongol and the Turkish threats).

The tendency to unitary forms of culture did not, however, lead to static mummification of the spiritual life, as very largely took place in the Confucianism of China. There were continual break-throughs, in which the various European peoples in turn had their creative epochs, from which the whole of Europe then drew its life.

The period following the Italian Renaissance conceived of itself as a renewal of Antiquity, that following the German Reformation as the re-establishment of Christianity. In the sequel both of them, in fact, became the most penetrating recognition of the axis of world history. Both of them, however, were also and above all original creations of the new Western World, which had already set in with growing vigour before that recognition. The period of world history from 1500 to 1830, which in the West is distinguished by its wealth of exceptional personalities, by its imperishable works of poetry and art, by the most profound impulses of religion and finally by its creations in the fields of science and technology, is the immediate presupposition of our own spiritual life.

NOTE

1   (Page 62): A similar conception was formulated by Alfred Weber. He places the ancient civilisations of Egypt and Babylonia alongside the still surviving cultures of China and India as belonging to the same type of primary culture that remains unhistorical and bound to magic, with which he contrasts the secondary cultures that have arisen solely in the West.

We find this differentiation to be particularly inapplicable to the variation between China and India on the one hand, and the West on the other. Once we have become aware of the spiritual compass and depth of the Axial Period, we cannot retain the parallel: Egypt, Babylonia, India, China—In contrast to all of which the West, with its Graeco-Jewish foundations, is to be considered the only new culture. On the contrary, the Axial Period very definitely has a place in the Indian and Chinese worlds as well.

The India and China that we know were born from the Axial Period, not primary but secondary; spiritually they penetrated to the same depth as the West, which happened neither in Egypt and Babylonia, nor in the aboriginal cultures of India and China (the existence of these latter is attested by a few archaeological finds, which, however, are not sufficient to enable us to form a broad picture of them, as we can of Egypt and Babylonia). Hence China and India as a whole are not to be set alongside Egypt and Babylonia as primary cultures. At the earliest stages of their development they were comparable to the primary cultures; but following the break-through of the Axial Period they became parallels to the secondary cultures of the West. The parallel between Egypt and Mesopotamia, and India and China, holds good only in respect of their *de facto* synchronicity. From the Axial Period onward China and India can no longer be thought of as parallels to the ancient civilisations; they can be reasonably compared only to the Axial Period of the West. Egypt and Babylonia did not give birth to any Axial Period.

Alfred Weber's historical edifice is buttressed by the principle: 'In the framework of a consideration of the total process we must depict the growth and dissolution of closed cultural wholes.' Hence he expressly repudiates operation with world epochs, which he regards as 'empty perspectives'. But his undogmatic approach and his perspicacious historical vision see the same facts as we do. Like a fragment out of another historical edifice, we find in his work a passage that might be cited as chief witness for our interpretation. With him it remains parenthetic and without sequel:

'From the ninth to the sixth century B.C. the three cultural spheres of the world, which had formed in the meantime—the Hither Asiatic-Greek, the Indian, and the Chinese—came, with remarkable simultaneity and apparently independently of one another, to a religious and philosophic quest, enquiry and decision directed toward universals. From this starting-point, in a synchronistic world epoch dating from Zoroaster, the Jewish prophets, the Greek philosophers, from Buddha, from Lao-tse, they evolved those religious and philosophic interpretations of the world and those attitudes of mind which, developed and recast, merged, reborn, or transformed and reformed under mutual spiritual influence, constitute mankind's criteria of faith in the world religions and its criteria of philosophic interpretation, to the religious side of which nothing fundamentally new has been added since the end of this period, i.e. since the sixteenth century.'

Alfred Weber's interpretation of the effect of the equestrian peoples points to a reason for the genesis of the secondary cultures in the West (which we call the Axial Period); it was at the same time, however, the reason for the spiritual upheavals in China and India, which he nevertheless leaves in the category of primary cultures.

Alfred Weber does in fact portray the deep dividing-lines in India and China, which, at the outset, represented changes of essence as in the West: the original Buddhism in India, the transmutation of the magico-metaphysical into ethicism by Jainism and by Buddha—and in China the transmutation by Buddhism. He deems it of crucial significance, however, that the magical was re-established, that it is a matter not of a 'fundamental', but of a 'superficial' transmutation of the eternal and immutable fabric in which China as well as India was enveloped. The dominion of a supreme immutable is supposed to distinguish Asia from the West.

Is there really a radical difference here? Is there not rather here too a common factor, which may be termed the constant peril to us all, namely the risk that having ascended into the unmagical, human, rational, above the demons to God, we may in the end sink back again into the magical and demonological?

6

THE SPECIFIC QUALITY OF
THE WEST

In earlier centuries the historical consciousness of Europe disparaged everything pre-Greek and pre-Jewish as alien to it and a mere introduction to history; it placed all men living on the globe, outside its own spiritual world, in the broad province of ethnology and collected their creations in ethnological museums. This blindness, which has long ago been corrected, does in fact contain a truth.

The differences are already present in the Axial Period—the time at which the greatest similarity existed between the various cultural zones from China to the West, before divergent lines of development carried them apart. Notwithstanding this subsequent parting of the ways, a resemblance between the great provinces of culture can be perceived until as late as A.D. 1500.

During the last few centuries, however, a single phenomenon that is intrinsically new in all respects has made its appearance: science with its consequences in technology. It has revolutionised the world inwardly and outwardly as no other event since the dawn of recorded history. It has brought with it unprecedented opportunities and hazards. The technological age, in which we have been living for a bare century and a half, has only achieved full dominion during the last few decades; this dominion is now being intensified to a degree whose limits cannot be foreseen. We are, as yet, only partially aware of the prodigious consequences. New foundations for the whole of existence have now been inescapably laid.

The origin of science and technology lay with the Teuto-Romance peoples. With it these peoples accomplished a break in history. They began the really universal, the planetary history of mankind. Only those peoples who make Western science and technology their own, and thereby take upon themselves the dangers to humanity which are bound up with this Western knowledge and skill, are still capable of playing an active part in determining the destiny of man.

If science and technology were created by the West, we are faced with the question: Why did this happen in the West and not in the two other great cultural zones? Can some peculiar element have already been present in the West during the Axial Period, which has only had these effects in the course of the last few centuries? Did that which finally manifested itself in science already exist in embryo during the Axial Period? Is there some quality specific to the West? The sole entirely new and radically transforming development that took place in the West must have its roots in some more comprehensive principle. This principle cannot be apprehended. But there may perhaps be certain pointers to the nature of the quality specific to the West.

(1) *Geographically* alone there is a vast difference. *Vis-à-vis* the closed continental territories of China and India, the West is characterised by an extraordinary variety in its geographical elements. The manifold richness of its division into peninsulas, islands, areas of desert interspersed with oases, into regions with a Mediterranean climate and the alpine regions of the north, together with its comparatively much more extended coastlines, is paralleled by the multiplicity of the peoples and languages that have here made history by taking over, each in its turn, the cardinal role in action and creation. The countries and peoples of the West present a unique picture.

Over and above this, it is possible to outline the spiritual character of the West in a series of typical features:

(2) The West knows the idea of *political liberty*. There arose in Greece, although only as a transient phenomenon, a liberty that had come into being nowhere else in the world. A sworn brotherhood of free men prevailed over the universal despotism of a totalitarian organisation that

claimed to be bringing happiness to the nations. With this action the *polis* laid the foundations of all Western libertarian consciousness, of the reality as well as the idea of freedom. In this political sense China and India know nothing of liberty.

From that point a radiance shines out through our Western history—and also a demand. The period from the sixth century on, when the liberty of Greek thought, Greek man and the Greek *polis* came into being and then, in the Persian war, proved itself and reached its highest, though short, florescence, is the great turning-point in the history of the West. It was not a universal priestly culture, not the Orphic mysteries nor the doctrines of Pythagoras, but the formation of the free States that constituted the Greek ethos and presented mankind with a prodigious opportunity and danger. Since that time the possibility of freedom has been abroad in the world.

(3) A *rationality* that pursues its course without stay, holds itself open to the cogency of logically consistent thought and of empirical facts that must carry conviction to all men everywhere. In contrast to the East, Greek rationality contains a strain of consistency that laid the foundations of mathematics and perfected formal logic. Modern rationality became decisively different from anything brought forth by the East with the end of the Middle Ages. At this point scientific research, operating with the critical faculty, entered on an unending path that enables it to reach definitive findings in the particular to the constant accompaniment of incompleteness in the whole. The attempt was made to confer the maximum degree of calculability upon the daily life of society through the legal decisions of the State based on the rule of law. In economic undertakings exact computation determined every step.

By the same token, however, the West experienced the limitations of rationality with a clarity and force unknown to the rest of the world.

(4) The *conscious inwardness of personal selfhood* achieved, in Jewish prophets, Greek philosophers and Roman statesmen, a perennially decisive absoluteness.

This however, since the days of the sophists, also made it possible to break away from the matrix of nature and human community, to step into the void. Western man has experienced in the highest freedom the limits of freedom in nothingness. In the most decisive selfhood he experienced the bestowal upon himself of precisely that which, in a false fixation as a mere ego, he imagined he could leave to its own resources—as though man were beginning and creator.

(5) Western man is continually confronted by the world in its reality as that which he cannot circumvent.

To be sure, the West, like the other great cultures, knows the dichotomy of human nature; on the one hand unrestrained life, on the other unworldly mysticism—on the one hand the monsters, on the other the saints. But the West endeavours to rid itself of this dichotomy by finding the path that leads to the moulding of the world itself; it seeks not only to gaze upon the true in the realm of ideals, but to realise it, to attain through ideas the enhancement of reality itself. The West knows, with unique forcefulness, the postulate that man must shape his world. He feels the meaning of the world's reality, which represents the unending task of accomplishing cognition, contemplation and realisation within and from the world itself. The world cannot be passed over. It is within the world and not outside it that Western man finds his assurance.

This has rendered Western man capable of experiencing the reality of the world in such a way as to know disaster in the profound sense that reaches beyond all interpretation. The tragic spirit becomes simultaneously reality and consciousness. Tragedy is known only to the West.

(6) Like all cultures, the West realises the forms of a universal. But in the West *this universal does not coagulate into a dogmatic fixity of definitive institutions and notions*, neither into life under a caste-system nor into life under a cosmic order. In no sense does the West become stabilised.

In the West it is the 'exceptions', which break through the universal, that generate the motive forces of the limitless Western dynamism: The West gives the exception room to move. From time to time it admits an absolutely new mode of living and creating—which it is then capable of destroying just as radically. Human nature reaches a height that is certainly not shared by all and to which, it may be, hardly anyone ascends. But like lofty beacons these heights afford the West a multi-dimensional orientation. In this is rooted the perpetual disquiet of the West, its continual dissatisfaction, its inability to be content with any sort of fulfilment.

Thus there sprang to life as one extreme, in apparently fortuitous situations, the possibilities that look like impossibilities. In this manner the prophetic religion of the *Jews* came into being while they stood powerless between two warring empires and were delivered over to powers against which all struggle was vain, when politically their world was in ruins. In a similar fashion the Nordic culture and ethos of the *Icelanders* blossomed in resistance to State regimentation on the fringe of the world of political powers.

In contradiction to its liberty and infinite fluidity, the West now developed the opposite extreme in the shape of the *claim to exclusive truth* by the various Biblical religions, including Islam. It was only in the West that the totality of this claim appeared as a principle that ran without interruption through the whole further course of history.

In the sequel, however, it was of essential importance that although the energy of this claim lent added vigour to men, the claim was at the same time held within bounds by the cleavages into the numerous Biblical religions and also by the dissension between State and Church. The claim to a single paramountcy, by impinging upon the same claim in other guises, brought not only fanaticism, but also the irresistible movement of unceasing questioning.

The very fact that there was no one single paramountcy, but that State and Church competed with one another, both claiming the right to total dominance and only relaxing this claim from time to time under the necessity for compromise, may perhaps—through the constant spiritual and political tension that it engendered—have lent the West its high level of spiritual energy, its liberty, its untiring questing and discovery, and the breadth of its experience, in contrast to the uniformity and relative freedom from tension of all Oriental empires, from Byzantium to China.

(7) In a world that is not closed up by any universal, but always directing itself toward a universal, in a world in which exceptions break through and win recognition as truth, and in which the claim to exclusive truth on the part of the historical creeds takes both these manifestations into itself—in such a world, tension of this kind is bound to carry man to the uttermost bournes of the spirit.

Hence the West is typified by a *resoluteness* that takes things to extremes, elucidates them down to the last detail, places them before the either–or, and so brings awareness of the underlying principles and sets up battle-fronts in the inmost recesses of the mind.

This resoluteness is manifested in the concrete historical tensions, into which almost everything at work in the West is forced; such tensions are those, for example, between Christianity and culture, between State and Church, between empire and nations, between the Romance and Teutonic nations, between Catholicism and Protestantism, between theology and philosophy. At no one point does Western man feel absolute, firm ground under his feet. Any claim he may make to doing so is immediately questioned.

(8) This world of tensions is perhaps at one and the same time the precondition and the outcome of the fact that nowhere but in the West have there existed, in such amplitude of character, *autonomous personalities*. These personalities range from the Jewish prophets and the Greek philosophers by way of the great Christians to the outstanding figures of the sixteenth to eighteenth centuries.

And then there is the ultimate and pre-eminent factor in the formation of the West: personal love and the power of boundless self-irradiation in never completed movement. Here a measure of openness, of infinite reflection, of inwardness came into being which first caused the full meaning of communication between men, and the horizon of reason proper, to light up.

The West became cognisant of its own reality. It has not given birth to one dominant human type, but to many opposed types. No man is everything, everyone has his place and is of necessity not only bound up with others, but also separated from them. Hence no one can desire the whole.

7

ORIENT AND OCCIDENT: THE EASTERN AND THE WESTERN WORLD

In placing the three historical movements in China, India and the West side by side, we have disregarded the pre-eminence which Europeans are accustomed to abrogate to themselves. In the foregoing section we gave an interpretive outline of the European self-consciousness, which no European can throw off.

The fact that the European line of development alone led on to the Age of Technology, which today gives the whole world a European countenance, and that, in addition, a rational mode of thought has become omnipresent, seems to confirm this pre-eminence. To be sure, Chinese and Indians have also felt themselves to be the truly human peoples and have asserted the self-evidence of their pre-eminence with no less conviction than the Europeans. But it does not seem to be quite the same thing if every culture considers itself the centre of the world. For Europe alone appears to have confirmed its pre-eminence by practical achievement.

From the outset, that is since the time of the Greeks, the West was built up out of an inner polarity of Orient and Occident. Ever since Herodotus, men have been aware of the antithesis of West and East as an eternal antithesis that is for ever reappearing in fresh shapes. It was only with this awareness that the antithesis became truly real at all, for not until a thing is known does it become a reality in a spiritual sense. The Greeks founded the West, but in such a manner that it only continues to exist as long as it keeps its eyes steadily on the East, faces up to it, comprehends it and withdraws from it, takes over cultural elements from it and works over them till they become its own, and engages in a struggle with it in which now the West and now the East gains the upper hand.

It is not simply the antithesis between Greeks and Barbarians. This situation is pictured in an essentially analogous fashion by the Chinese, Egyptians and Indians vis-à-vis the other peoples. In the divorce of the Occident from the Orient, the Orient remains both politically and spiritually an equal and admired power, a force from which the West can learn and which exercises a seductive attraction over it.

We can interpret the antithesis as a form of the self-division to which every spiritual phenomenon is subject. The spirit only comes to life, is set in motion, becomes fruitful and surges upward, when it becomes cognisant of itself in antithesis and finds itself in conflict. But the antithesis that confronts us here is an historical one; its inner implications cannot be reduced to a universal form nor can its contents be exhaustively defined in finite terms. It is like a profound historical enigma running through the ages. In multifarious modifications the original polarity has kept alive throughout the centuries.

The Greeks and the Persians, the division of the Imperium Romanum into the Western and the Eastern Empires, Western and Eastern Christendom, the Western World and Islam, Europe and Asia, which was in turn split up into the Near, Middle and Far East, are the successive shapes taken by the antithesis, in which cultures and peoples simultaneously attract and repel one another. This antithesis has at all times been an element in the make-up of Europe, whereas the Orient merely took it over from Europe and understood it in a European sense.

Now although objective historical analysis reveals that the West has played a paramount role in shaping the world, it also discloses an incompleteness and deficiency in the West which render it perennially apposite and fruitful to ask of the Orient: What shall we find there that is supplementary to ourselves?

What became real there and what became truth, that we have let slip? What is the cost of our paramountcy?

It is true that the West possesses reliable historical records stretching farthest back into the depths of time. No place on earth has an earlier history than Mesopotamia and Egypt. During the last few centuries the West has given its imprint to the whole world. The West has the richest and most clearly marked articulation in its history and in its creations, the most sublime struggles of the spirit, the greatest plenitude of graphically visible great men.

Looking at things from this point of view, we ask the ubiquitous question: What rudimentary beginnings can we find in the Orient of the various achievements of the West, of science, rational methodology, personal selfhood, the life of the State, or of an economic order bearing the imprint of capitalism, etc.? We then look for that which is identical with the West and ask why it never unfolded fully in the Orient.

We fall under the suggestion that there is really nothing new to be found in Asia. Everything we meet is already known to us with no other differences than those of emphasis. No doubt it is the typical self-sufficiency of the European that leads us to regard this alien world as a mere curiosity. We either take the view that the same conceptions have arisen there as arose in a more lucid form in the West, or we resign ourselves to the opinion that we are only able to understand what the East took over from us and not what had its origins there.

Asia only becomes essential to us, however, when we ask: What is it that, despite all Europe's pre-eminence, has been lost to the West? What we lack and what vitally concerns us is to be found in Asia! Questions come to us from over there that lie deep in our own minds. For what we have produced, accomplished and become we have paid a price. We are by no means on the road to the self-perfection of man. Asia is an indispensable need for our completion. Even though we only understand things from our own vantage point, by recognising what we ourselves are, we may still be able to recognise that which is so deeply buried and concealed within us that it would never have risen into consciousness if we did not see it reflected in this world that is at first so strange to us. We should understand by expanding ourselves within it, while that which lies dormant within us blossoms out. And then the history of Chinese and Indian philosophy is no mere superfluous repetition of our own, nor is it simply a reality in which we can study interesting sociological effects. On the contrary, it is something that directly concerns us because it appraises us of human potentialities that we have not realised and brings us into *rapport* with the authentic origin of another humanity—a humanity that is not ours in actuality and yet is ours potentially, and that represents an irreplaceable historical entity.

The self-evident equation of a closed circle of Western culture with world history as such has been broken through. We can no longer leave the great cultural worlds of Asia on one side as being made up of unhistorical peoples in a state of perpetual spiritual stagnation. The compass of world history is universal. The picture we form of mankind becomes incomplete and distorted if we narrow this compass. But if we turn our eyes upon the magnitude and efficacy of Asia we may easily be deceived into an exaggerated and indeterminate conception of it:

In comparison with infinitesimal Europe, Asia seems huge in space. In time it appears the all-embracing matrix of the whole human race. It is immeasurable, mighty in its extent and in the human masses it contains, everlasting and slow of movement.

Greek culture seems like a peripheral phenomenon of Asia. Europe broke prematurely away from its Asiatic mother. The question arose: Where and when and through what step did this break take place? Is it possible that Europe will once more lose itself in Asia? In Asia's depths and in its levelling-down that is destitute of consciousness?

If the West emerged from the matrix of Asia, its emergence has the appearance of an act of daring in which human potentialities are set free. This act brings with it two dangers: first, that Europe might lose the foundations of its soul, and then, once it has attained consciousness, the continual danger that it might sink back again into Asia.

If this danger of sinking back into Asia were to be realised today, however, it would be under new technological conditions which are transforming and destroying Asia itself; Western liberty, the idea of personality, the amplitude of Western categories and its lucid consciousness would go by the board. In their place would remain the eternal characteristics of Asia: The despotic form of existence, the absence of history and of decision, the stabilisation of the spirit in fatalism. Asia would be the universal, enduring world that outlives Europe and includes it. Whatever fashions itself out of Asia and must sink back into Asia is transitory.

Such contrasting images linked with visions of decline may possess a momentary evidence. But in fact they are untrue and unjust.

The realities of China and India for three thousand years have been just as much attempts to emerge from the indeterminate matrix of Asia. Emergence is a universal historical process, not a peculiarity of Europe's attitude to Asia. It happens within Asia itself. It is the path of mankind and of authentic history.

Asia is turned into a mythical principle, that falls apart when it is analysed objectively as an historical reality. The antithesis Europe–Asia must not be metaphysically hypostasised. Then it becomes a terrifying spectre. As a mythical language at moments of decision it serves as a cryptogram that represents a truth only so long as it operates as an abbreviation for something historically concrete and intellectually lucid, and is not meant as an apperception of the whole. But Europe–Asia is a cryptogram that accompanies the whole of Western history.

8

ONCE MORE: A SCHEMA OF WORLD HISTORY

Before we turn to the present, let us once more cast our eyes on the structure which the sum-total of history has assumed for us. We have found the whole of history to be divided into three successive phases: prehistory, history and world history.

(1) The long *prehistory* embraces the course of man's becoming that ran through the formation of languages and races to the inception of the historical cultures. It leads us into the enigma of humanity, to consciousness of the uniqueness of man amongst the creatures of the earth, it sets us before the problem of our freedom, which must be connected with the origin of all things, and which confronts us nowhere else in the world.

(2) *History* embraces the events of about five thousand years in China, India and the Near Orient together with Europe. It is China and India, not the geographical totality of Asia, that are to be placed alongside Europe.

Here the ancient civilisations first developed: The Sumerian Culture, the Egyptian, Aegean Culture, pre-Aryan India, the culture on the Hwang-ho.

Then further cultural developments were set in motion by conquests. They were determined by the mutual interaction of victors and vanquished and the adoption of the existing aboriginal cultures by the victors—in China, in Aryan India, by the Babylonians, by the Persians and by the Greeks and Romans.

In contrast to all these geographically small areas there stood the isolated processes of the cultures in Mexico and Peru, and the multifarious cultures of the primitive peoples that covered the earth up to the time of the discovery of the world by Europe.

(3) The planetary unity of the world and of mankind, which is becoming a reality today, opens up the factual universal history of the earth, world history. Its preliminary stages lie in the Age of Discovery and it really began in our own century.

The internal structure of each of these three phases is essentially different. The first phase, in so far as it is not a field for hypotheses, is only accessible to us as the contactless co-existence of an endless multiplicity of men that resembles a mass of isolated natural phenomena. There must have been a common fund of spiritual possessions and modes of thought arising out of the common soil of the natural predisposition of man, and not essentially out of history. All the grandiose images of the origin of the human race, of the dispersion of the peoples and their spread over the earth, of the forgetting which produced in the self-deceiving consciousness the idea of a multiple origin, are either ingenious symbols or hypotheses.

The structure of the second phase is centred on the break-through represented by the Axial Period of history.

The third phase belongs, for the most part, to the future. In order to perceive it we must go back to those features of the past which are like an anticipation or preparation of it: to the great unifications that took place in history (the empires), to the great universal human figures of Antiquity and the Modern Age, those men of rich content who do not represent points at which understanding arose out of an empty humanity as such, but who grew from the roots of their own people as figures of absolute humanity and are therefore able to speak to mankind through their existence and their words.

The structures of the three phases have the following additional characteristics:

(1) In the *first phase* everything that happened was akin to the unconscious processes of nature. The prehistoric and unhistoric peoples (the primitives till they died out or became material for technological civilisation) were split up into *de facto* communities of language and spheres of culture. These spread out in silent movements that can only be observed in their outcome. Direct and conscious contact between men was mostly confined to very restricted areas within an overall pattern of scattered units. Factual contact through the diffusion of the acquisitions of civilisation covered very wide areas, in some degree the whole earth, but without the knowledge of men.

Within prehistory the processes of culture already existed. At some points they can be observed in typical forms that seem to anticipate the historical cultures. There remains the difference that they did not come to history, but collapsed at their first contact with the historical peoples; within their own limited range they achieved astonishing things, but they were as though bound to the substratum of natural life, into which they continually threatened to slip back.

Primitive cultures were scattered over the whole earth. Every people has its own peculiar ethos, even the most primitive, such as the Pygmies or the Bushmen, or the peoples of the extreme north, such as the Eskimoes; amongst the Polynesians it is in splendid evidence.

The American peoples in Mexico and Peru justify comparison with Babylon and Egypt.

(2) In the *second phase*, the small number of major cultural developments that began to unfold proceeded side by side, despite occasional contacts. They are separate histories.

The unity of these lines of historical development is no more than an idea. The sum-total of achievement was certainly not known and effective everywhere. On the contrary, the most sublime and important developments were restricted to small areas and short periods. They blossomed, died down and seemed to slip for long ages—perhaps for ever—into oblivion. Transmission of the cultural heritage is not dependable. The sum-total of a sphere of culture seems to enter into a continuity of communication, it spreads and endures; and then of a sudden it ebbs away and vanishes.

And yet, on relatively small areas of the earth's surface, there did arise something amounting, in the sense of its spiritual significance, to a single, universal history, in which everything becomes manifest that was thought by man and that concerns ourselves.

The various developments become articulated to one another. The processes that went to make up a whole in the course of some centuries can be seen in the sequence of styles running from the first blossoming out to the conclusion in the later periods of decline. We see the typical sequences of the generations, which together comprise about a century (diffusion, perfection, disintegration). From time to time we may even see one of Spengler's millennial processes.

But all the time there was continued movement. There were no lasting periods of decline, there was no endless 'fellaheen existence', no final rigidification. Again and again something new and original broke through, even in India and China.

Attempts to comprehend the course of history as a whole have proved vain. Seeing the road that leads from Babylon *via* Greece and Rome to the North, historians said that the course of history runs from east to west and made the prognostication that, pursuing the same direction, the road would lead on to America. In India, however, the road ran from the Indus region (early Vedic period) *via* the central area (period of the Upanishads) to the Ganges (Buddha and his period), that is from west to east. All such schemata are valid only from certain points of view for limited worlds, and even there only with reservations.

The world of Hither Asia and Europe constitutes a relative whole *vis-à-vis* the two others—India and China. The West has existed as an internally coherent world from Babylon and Egypt till the present day. But since the times of the Greeks this Western cultural continent has been inwardly articulated into Orient and Occident. Thus the Old Testament, the Iranian-Persian ethos and Christianity belong to the West—as opposed to India and China— and yet they are the Orient. The territories between India and Egypt have always been subject to an Indian influence as well—this is an intermediate region possessing unique historical fascination—but it is of such a kind as to render simple, clearly discernible analysis in terms of universal history impossible.

(3) In the *third phase*, the unity of the whole—beyond which, with the defin-
     itive closing up of space, it becomes impossible to pass—comes into its
     own. Its presupposition is the possibility of universal communications
     which has now been attained. This phase has not yet reached the level
     of an historical reality; it is still only a future possibility. Hence it is not
     an object of empirical investigation, but a shape that can be adumbrated
     by calling into consciousness the present and our own situation.

This present situation has been created by *Europe*. How did it come about?

The great incisions and leaps that characterise Western history lend it
the appearance of being fragmented and of continually giving birth to itself afresh in a series of radical metamorphoses. By comparison, India and
China, notwithstanding the movement that took place there too, give an
impression of uniformity.

There have been times when the West has sunk so deep into its substratum
as to look almost as though it were finally extinguished. A visitor from some
other planet who had travelled around the earth in about A.D. 700 would
perhaps have found in Tshangan, then the capital of China, the highest seat
of the spiritual life of the earth, and in Constantinople a remarkable residue;
the northern districts of Europe would have appeared to him mere realms of
barbarism. By 1400 the overall life of Europe, India and China had reached
a uniform level of civilisation. The events that occurred after 1500, however,
in which Europe discovered the world and stamped it with its own characteristic imprint, give rise to the question of what caused them, of what new
and peculiar quality Europe possessed that enabled it to carry out this development and what were the steps in which it proceeded. This becomes the
fundamental question of universal history. For a break took place that was
unique in its importance to the West and, in its consequences, to the whole
world; a break whose results make up our own situation and whose ultimate
significance is still open.

The major steps leading up to it were: The prophetic religion of the Jews
set the minds of men free from magic and the transcendence of objects with
a radicality such as had not occurred anywhere else on earth; although it
did so only for an historically limited moment and for a small number of
men, it left its message in the Book for all who came after and who were
capable of hearing it. The Greeks created a clarity of distinctions, a plasticity
of spiritual forms and a consistency in the operations of reason never before

attained anywhere in the world. Christianity realised awareness of the most extreme transcendence—as India and China also succeeded in doing—but with the difference that Christianity fettered this realisation to the world of immanence, and thereby brought about the perpetual unrest involved in the task of giving a Christian conformation to the world.

But the great break really took place after the late Middle Ages. These steps and the memory of them may have been preconditions. The break itself is the fresh great enigma. It is by no means a transparent, rectilinear evolution. Development of the preliminary stages of modern science in late medieval nominalism was accompanied and immediately followed by the orgies of witchcraft. The changes that, in the sequel, occurred in the reality of man's existence, while he was creating science and technology and winning mastery over the whole surface of the globe, are in horrifying contrast to these palpable achievements.

The steps that separate the whole historical past from the still veiled future were only definitively taken during the nineteenth century. Again and again the question arises: What goes to the making of Europe's character as the moulder of the earth, what is the quality that may perhaps be glimpsed from the beginning, that again and again springs into prominence and seems at other times to be gripped by paralysis? What is it that develops after the nominalists as science, spreads across the planet after the fifteenth century, begins to operate on a broad front after the seventeenth century and becomes definitive during the nineteenth century?

Europe's exceptional spiritual achievements from 1500 to 1800, that outshine science and technology—Michelangelo, Raphael, Leonardo, Shakespeare, Rembrandt, Goethe, Spinoza, Kant, Bach, Mozart—challenge comparison with the Axial Period of two and a half millennia earlier. Is a second Axial Period to be discerned in these later centuries?

The difference is considerable. The purity and clarity, the ingenuousness and freshness of the worlds of the first axis are not repeated. Everything stands in the shadow of exacting traditions and follows false roads; it is as if in spite of these false directions that the great figures, the solitary ones, find their way to the most miraculous successes. On the other hand, however, possibilities are open to the second axis that were unknown to the first. Because it was able to take over experiences and appropriate ideas, it possessed from the outset both more variety of meaning and greater inner wealth. Its very fragmentation caused profundities of human nature to become manifest that had not previously been visible. For this reason pre-eminence might be given to the second axis, because, while making an original contribution to the continuity of Western culture and at the same time enjoying a more sweeping view through its position on the shoulders of its predecessor, it achieved the greater breadth and the greater depth. But it must be relegated to second place because it did not live entirely on its own resources and because it suffered and connived at extraordinary distortions and aberrations. It is our own immediate historical matrix. We are alternately at war and on intimate terms with it; we are unable to look at it in the same calm of distance as that in which we see the first axis. Above all, however, it is a purely European phenomenon and for that reason alone has no claim to the title of second axis.

To be sure, these centuries are the most fruitful period for us Europeans; they constitute the indispensable fundament of our culture and the richest source of our intuitions and insights. But they do not represent a universally human, world-embracing axis, and it is improbable that they might become such in the sequel. A quite different axis was established by the activities of the Europeans, with their consequences in science and technology, which first made their appearance when the West, whose spirit and soul were already in decline, impinged upon an India and China whose spirit and soul had reached their nadir.

At the end of the nineteenth century Europe seemed to dominate the world. The situation was thought to be final. Hegel's words seemed to be confirmed: 'The Europeans have sailed round the world and for them it is a sphere. Whatever has not yet fallen under their sway is either not worth the trouble, or it is destined to fall under it.'

What a transformation since then! The world has become European through the adoption of European technology and the European demands of nationalism, and it is successfully turning both against Europe. Europe, as the old Europe, is no longer the dominant factor in the world. It has abdicated, overshadowed by America and Russia, upon whose policies the fate of Europe hangs—if Europe does not gather itself together at the last moment and become strong enough to stay neutral when a new world war plunges the planet into storms of destruction.

It is true that America and Russia are also permeated by the spirit of Europe; but they are not Europe. The Americans (despite their European provenance) may not yet have found a new autonomous consciousness and a new origin in their own soil, but it is certainly their aim to do so. The Russians have an historical matrix of their own in the East and in the mingled European and Asiatic origin of their peoples; spiritually their matrix is Byzantium.

China and India, however, who do not wield any decisive power today, will increase in importance. Their vast populations, possessed of a profound and irreplaceable cultural heritage, are becoming an element of mankind—in common with all other peoples which are seeking their way in the present great metamorphosis of humanity, into which all are being pressed.

PART 2

PRESENT AND FUTURE

9

THE INTRINSICALLY NEW: SCIENCE AND TECHNOLOGY

INTRODUCTION

The purpose of an overall philosophical view of history, such as we are seeking to arrive at, is to illumine our own situation within the totality of history.
It serves to light up the consciousness of the present epoch and shows us
where we stand.

It is only when judged by the standards of world history that the depth
of the dividing-line that has been made in our time, and for which two
centuries have prepared the way, becomes visible. In the wealth of its consequences, this dividing-line is beyond comparison with anything that we
know from the past five thousand years.

The sole specifically new and radically different element, that bears no
resemblance to anything that has come out of Asia, is entirely autonomous,
and foreign even to the Greeks, is modern European science and technology.
In retrospect, the overall picture of history up to the present exhibits a continuity, indeed a uniformity, whose last splendid delineation was contained
in Hegel's conception of history. This changed with the advent of modern
technology. Hence there was a considerable similarity between Europe and

Asia until about A.D. 1500, whereas a very great diversity has arisen during the last few centuries.

It is not easy to see the radically new element in modern science and technology clearly. Since clarity on this point is crucial for the interpretation of our own present—for its spiritual as well as its material opportunities and perils—we must endeavour to set forth the new in its full significance by a comparison with what went before. This requires a somewhat detailed analysis.

I. MODERN SCIENCE

Looking at world history, we see three steps in cognition: First, rationalisation in general, which in some form or other is common to all mankind, made its appearance as soon as man as such appeared, and, in the guise of 'pre-scientific science', rationalised myths and magic; second, science that became logically and methodologically conscious, Greek science, of which there were rudimentary parallels in China and India; third, modern science, which has developed since the end of the Middle Ages, became decisive since the seventeenth century, and reached full unfolding since the nineteenth century. At all events, this science distinguishes Europe from all other cultures since the seventeenth century. Let us visualise the uniqueness of modern science within world history.

In range, amplitude and manifoldness of cognition alone the facts of modern science are without their like in the whole preceding course of history. The history of this modern science presents an inexhaustible picture. The most strikingly new element is probably the natural scientific knowledge gained by the application of mathematical theory since Kepler and Galileo; it has had unprecedented effects through its consequences for technology. But it is only one link in a more comprehensive process of cognition. The expeditions of discovery led to the first voyage round the world and to establishment of the fact that sailing towards the west resulted in the loss of a day. That was only four hundred years ago. Never before had man been cognisant of the earth as a sphere in this real sense (not as a mere surmise). The first geographical globe was produced. Experience of things nearby followed the same lines as of those at a distance. Human anatomy (Vesal) was laid bare through the dissection of corpses with a hitherto unknown passion for research. With the aid of the microscope, the seething activity in a drop of water was disclosed to Leeuwenhoek. In the telescope Galileo saw planets and moons never seen before. From the eighteenth century onward excavations brought to light bygone and forgotten historical realities (Pompeii), enabled whole cultures to be reconstructed, and fulfilled Schliemann's yearning for the reality of the Homeric age. The deciphering of scripts and languages made audible the men who lived thousands of years ago. Prehistory became an indubitable reality through archaeological discoveries. Today we know more about the history of early Greece, of the Near East and of Egypt than the Greeks themselves did. The horizon of history has been pushed thousands of years farther back into the past, the history of the earth is spread out before our eyes, the immeasurable depths of the starry firmament are disclosed to us. The modern world seems at all points to give birth to fresh sciences that are independent of one another, but spring from a common spirit. Natural science grew up in the workshops of painters and architects, geography developed in attendance upon navigation, and economics upon the interests of the State: all of them arose out of the initial impulse to gain practical advantages and were then pursued for their own sakes, independently of utilitarian purposes. In theology historical criticism of the Bible made its appearance. This picture, which can be endlessly extended, leads us to ask: Does modern science, which has attained an unparalleled scope, contain any radically new and singular characteristics?

A. CHARACTERISATION OF MODERN SCIENCE

Science possesses three indispensable traits: It is methodical cognition, cogently certain and universally valid.

I know scientifically only if I am also cognisant of the *method* by which I gained my knowledge, and can therefore explain it and demonstrate its limits.

I know scientifically only if I know with *cogent certainty*. In this way I also know uncertainty, probability or improbability.

I know scientifically only what is *universally valid*. Because the insight can be cogently experienced by every intelligence, scientific knowledge can be spread abroad and yet retain the same meaning. Unanimity is a hallmark of universal validity. Where the unanimity of all thinkers throughout the ages has not been achieved, universal validity is doubtful.

By these criteria, however, science was already present in the Greek sciences, even though the task of working it out to full purity remains uncompleted today. These three factors apart, what is modern science?

(1) In spirit, modern science is *universal*. In the long run nothing can elude it. Whatever takes place in the world is subject to observation, enquiry and investigation, no matter whether it involves the facts of nature, the actions and statements of men, or their creations and destinies. Religion, too, and every kind of authority, is investigated. And not only every reality, but also every intellectual possibility becomes an object of investigation. There are no limits to enquiry and research.

(2) Modern science is in principle *incomplete*. The Greeks did not know the science that advances without limits—not even where, as in mathematics, astronomy and medicine, they themselves did in fact advance for a time. Amongst the Greeks, research itself had the character of an operation carried out within a closed circle. This character of completeness knows neither the desire for universal knowledge nor the explosive force of the will to truth. Since the times of sophistry, the Greeks got no further than reflections of fundamental doubt on the one hand, and on the other, a negligent trifling with the knowledge of particular things, no matter how magnificent the latter may have been in the case of men like Thucydides, Euclid or Archimedes. Modern science is motivated by the ardent desire to reach the limits, to break through all definitive forms of knowledge, ever and again to revise all knowledge from its very foundations. Hence the sudden reversals that take place at every break-through, accompanied by the preservation of factual acquisitions as an element in the new interpretation. There is a constant awareness of the underlying hypotheses, that is of the presuppositions that constitute the point of departure for research at any given time. Everything is there to be overcome (for the presuppositions are explained in terms of more comprehensive presuppositions and so relativised); when it is facts that are involved they are used as a means to further advances in the continuity of increasing and more penetrating knowledge.

This forever incomplete cognition is, by intent, directed toward something that exists and that will be disclosed by cognition. But while cognition presses illimitably forward, it is not capable of apprehending the eternal certitude of Being as a whole. In other words: Through the infinity of the existent it is directed toward Being, which, however, it never reaches—and it knows this through self-criticism.

Because the content of knowledge is unclosed and unclosable (contrary to the Greek cosmos), this science thinks in terms of unlimited advance and in its self-consciousness lies the idea of progress. This begins by lending wings to science, and then causes it to be overcome by a feeling of senselessness: if the goal can never be reached and every piece of work is merely a step for posterity to rise upon, what is the point of it all?

(3) Nothing is indifferent to modern science: it considers everything worth knowing and directs its attention to the smallest and most individual phenomenon, to every fact as such. The manner in which the modern European appears to immerse himself in all sorts of things he would otherwise despise, simply because they are empirically real, is a source of continual amazement. In comparison, Greek science seems to have no love for reality, to choose its point of attack fortuitously, guided by ideals, types, forms, by a pre-existent knowledge that causes it to by-pass the majority of realities. This applies equally to the minutiae of its attitude to the empirical object and to many of the Hippocratic writings.

This self-surrender to every object, to chance, to the misshapen equally with the well-shapen, has its roots in an all-embracing self-consciousness that is both restless and sure of itself. Everything that is must and shall be known. Nothing may be left out of consideration.

The breadth of devotion to everything capable of being experienced, the multi-dimensionality of emotional concern with everything that occurs in the world, is essentially modern.

(4) Modern science, devoted to the most individual phenomenon, looks for its own universal interconnexions. It is not able to apprehend the cosmos of Being, but it is able to apprehend the cosmos of the sciences. The idea of the coherence of all the sciences brings about dissatisfaction with every isolated cognition. Modern science is not only universal but lives for the unity of the sciences, though it never attains it.

Each science is determined by its method and its object. Each science is a vista onto the world, no science comprehends the world, each science lights upon one sector of reality, not reality itself—one facet of all reality perhaps, but not reality in its entirety. There are distinct sciences, not the one science as the science of the real. Thus every science is particular and specialised, but each one belongs to a world that is without confines and yet is held together.

What connects the sciences and in what sense do they form a cosmos?

This is more easily recognised *negatively* than positively. The unity of the sciences does not consist in the unity of the reality of which they give knowledge. The sum-total of the sciences does not give us reality in its entirety. They do not constitute a hierarchy through increasing approximation to reality. They do not constitute a unitary system that becomes master of the whole province of the real.

Repeated vain attempts have been made to formulate a world system incorporating the sum-total of knowledge. To modern science such attempts are nonsensical. They are the outcome of the continued operation of the Greek idea of a cosmos and are disruptive of genuine cognition and the false substitute for a philosophy. In fact, pure philosophy becomes possible for the first time today, on the basis of the sciences but with a different origin and a different goal.

Positively it can be said:

The interconnexion of the sciences consists in the *form of cognition*. They are all of them methodical, they all think in categories, are cogent in their particular cognition, but at the same time restricted by current presuppositions and by the delimitation of the object.

Then there are the interconnexions that arise from the *relation* between the sciences, which render one another mutual assistance through their findings and methods. They become auxiliary sciences to one another. One science becomes the material of another.

They have a common fundament in the subjective impulse to *universal knowledge*.

Through the guiding idea of the particular fields of cognition there speaks an idea of indefinable unity, as a *demand* for the openness of everything real and thinkable. All science is a *path*. The paths cross, separate, combine again, and do not show the destination. But all of them want to be followed.

The sciences are articulated within themselves—into categories and methods—and related to one another. Endless multiplicity in research and the idea of unity set up a tension and drive science from the one to the other.

In modern cognition, the *systematic* character of knowledge, instead of leading to a world system, leads to the problem of the system of the sciences. The system of the sciences is mobile, manifold in its possible classifications, open. But it is characteristic of it that it is also a permanent problem, and that no mode of knowledge and no knowledge is to be left out of consideration.

Objectively, the striving after the interconnexion of all knowledge out of the idea of the unity of the sciences is visible:

Textbooks present the systematologies of individual sciences as fruitful incentives to research (not systems of established facts; when they do this they descend from the modern level to that of the Greeks.)

The organisation of materials, of works of reference, of the publication of texts, of museums and of laboratories is concerned to place all knowledge at the disposal of the seeker.

The universities represent an all-embracing scientific activity in operation.

(5) The *radicality of enquiry* carried to the extreme—but with the proviso that it be accomplished in *concrete cognition*, and does not operate in ultimate universals which it reaches by overpassing intermediate stages—has assumed very great proportions in modern science. Thought that contradicts visible appearances (which began in Antiquity in astronomy), not in order to submerge itself in the void, but precisely for the purpose of comprehending visible appearances in a better and unexpected fashion, dares everything. The manner in which physics deals with that which is beyond imagination, through non-perceptual mathematics, is an example.

The capacity for repeatedly breaking away from the rounding off and totalisation of a form of knowledge makes it possible to experiment with new hypotheses that at first seem highly paradoxical, as in modern physics. An unparalleled freedom of experiment has become possible at certain highpoints. Every question is asked afresh. There is always one more enquiry into the possibility of presuppositions that have been overlooked. And in the play of preparatory cognition, the most audacious presuppositions are tried out.

(6) One might be tempted to regard *certain categories* and their effects as being typical of modern science:

Such as the infinite as the basis of antinomies, as a problem which, susceptible of the finest differentiation, ultimately always presents the breakdown of thought.

Or the causal category, which does not lead, as with Aristotle, to the subsumption of phenomena under the neatly defined *modi* of causality and to a definitive explanation *in toto*, but to the real investigation of questions that are always determinate and particular. In Greek thought the answer to a question always arises from deliberation and plausibility, in modern thought from experiment and progressive observation. In the thought of the ancients an investigation meant simply meditating on the problem, only in modern thought does it come to imply action.

But what is typical of modern science is neither a category nor an object, but *universality in the working out of categories and methods*. Every form is tried out and every object dealt with that appears mathematically, physically, biologically, hermeneutically or speculatively possible. The results are a world of categories capable of limitless expansion and a correspondingly unclosed theory of categories.

The problem becomes that of the suitability of categories and methods and not the superiority of any one of them. Where reality is involved experience itself is reliably defined. Where speculation is appropriate this is carried out as a sovereign act with full knowledge of its meaning. The crucial problem is to avoid confusing the one with the other.

(7) In the modern world a *scientific attitude* has become possible that is able to question, investigate, test and reflect upon everything it encounters from the viewpoint of all-inclusive reason. This attitude is not one of scientific dogmatism, it does not swear by findings and axioms, it stands aloof from all sects and all communities of creed and conviction, in order to keep free in science the realm of the knowable.

The scientific attitude differentiates between that which is compellingly known and that which is not compellingly known; it desires its cognition to be accompanied by knowledge of method, that is by knowledge of the meaning and confines of knowledge; it seeks unrestricted criticism. It has an urge to the clarity of the definite, as opposed to the approximations of everyday speech; it demands concreteness in explanation.

Human veracity is determined by scientificity, once science has become truly scientific. Hence it is an element in the dignity of man, and possesses the enchantment that comes from illumination of the world. Hence, too, however, it knows the anguish caused in spiritual commerce by the unscientificness of blind assertion that is unaware of itself and therefore impassioned and uncritical. It renders the lies of life transparent. *Sapere aude* refers to its courageousness.

Any man who is scientific through his own research-work will be capable of understanding authentic science everywhere. To be sure, specialist routine and *de facto* achievements can exist without a scientific attitude *in toto*. But no one's scientificity can be relied upon who has not himself taken part in science at some point.

B. THE ORIGIN OF MODERN SCIENCE

Light can perhaps be cast upon the problem of the emergence of the new science from various angles, but it cannot be completely understood. Like everything spiritually creative it is an enigma of history.

The statement that it arose out of the aptitudes of the Nordic peoples tells us nothing. These aptitudes are manifest in precisely this effect and by no other signs, so that this argument is a tautology.

Many circumstances combined during the latter centuries to produce the unique concatenation of conditions that made the new science possible.

Sociological conditions can be pointed to: The freedom of States and cities—the leisure of the aristocracy and the middle class—the fragmentation of the numerous European States, freedom of movement and opportunities for emigration, competition between powers and individuals—the wide contacts between Europe and alien cultures after the crusades—the spiritual conflict between Church and State, the need felt by all powers to justify themselves with regard to questions of faith and justice, in general the need to substantiate political claims and interests on the plane of spiritual struggle—the technical tasks arising in the various workshops—the dissemination of ideas made possible by printing and the resulting increase in their exchange and discussion. In this unfolding of the sciences it seemed as though every activity was destined to foster the development of every other activity and to furnish it with opportunities: The tearing open of the earth's surface for technological purposes led fortuitously to archaeological and prehistoric finds. Greed for gain and lust for adventure resulted in the discovery of all areas of the globe, till eventually journeys of disinterested exploration were undertaken. The missionary zeal of the Churches laid bare the souls of strange peoples and cultures and made possible immersion in their spirit, so that it sometimes came about that Christian missionaries turned into missionaries for the Chinese or Indian spirit in Europe. Technological advances often produced devices serving purposes quite different from those originally aimed at, from the printing press to the innumerable apparatuses which, in almost all the sciences, have led to greater refinement of observation, the establishment of facts and the restoration of that which had been lost. Private hobbies and the driving passions of the individual acted as aids to knowledge, particularly through the medium of special collections (e.g. of lichens, etc.), special skills, and sport-like competitiveness. With or without intent, the labour of many men, embracing everything that exists, seemed to work toward a goal of cognition which is at bottom unknown. The manner in which scientists made their appearance under totally diverse conditions in Italy, Germany, England and France is amazing. Scientists emerged from remote corners of the land, seizing upon their tasks and electing their roads in their own right and of their own free will, and laying the foundations of new spiritual possibilities. The question is: Why have there always been in Europe such isolated individuals, who were independent of one another but met each other? Why were they absent from Spain, later on from Italy, and for a long time from Germany?

Sociological investigation will be able to disclose some interconnexions. Let us enquire further into the motives that may have led to modern science.

It has often been said that modern science springs from the will to power. Mastery of nature, ability, utility, 'knowledge is power', this has been the watchword since Bacon. He and Descartes sketched the outlines of a technological future. To be sure, it is not crude force that avails against nature, but knowledge of her laws. Natura parendo vincitur. An authentic cognition is one that gives birth to its object and so confirms the cognition: 'I know only that which I can make.' The creative consciousness of ability lends wings to this type of cognition.

Two things must be differentiated in such an interpretation of modern knowledge. Firstly: The power consciousness that it expressed in the technological will, in the coercion of things, and whose goal is ability. Secondly: The will to knowledge that desires to penetrate the processes of nature. The scientist is the man who examines the witnesses (Kant). A pure will to knowledge exists, even without the aims of technology.

The opinion has been put forward that both these impulses contain aggression. For this kind of cognition, that has not yet been focused on technological power, is not the contemplation, self-surrender and fitting in with nature of authentic, loving cognition, but is already a struggle with and coercion of the existent, from which exploitation duly follows.

This must be entirely contradicted; we have only to look at the psychic attitude of the great scientists to see how false it is. They are characterised by a feeling for necessity. Readiness to fit in with nature has always been part of the ethos of the natural scientist. But he wants to know what nature does and what happens in nature. For this will to knowledge, this freedom of the knower, who suffers, endures and lives, not blindly but with his eyes open, is something quite different from aggressivity and will to power. It is a will to power not as dominion, but as inner independence. This liberty of consciousness of the knower is able precisely to grasp pure factuality as a genuine hieroglyph of Being. It is not aggressivity that is contained in the ethos of cogent, universally valid knowledge—in contrast to the plausible, approximate, fluid, and ultimately capricious—but will to clarity and trustworthiness.

In particular, research by experiment is taken to be aggressive. In contrast to simple contemplation the purpose of the alternation of theoretical speculation with verification by experiment is to afford an insight which is not only trustworthy, but penetrates ever deeper into the laws governing unconscious processes. The motive is not aggression, but the questioning of nature.

On the other hand, of course, what modern science does may be misunderstood and misused. Hence the will to power and the will to destruction, which are themselves unhistorical and for ever on the point of disappearing from the scene, have also taken possession of science for purposes of aggressivity in speech, action and practical application; but always in such a fashion that science gets lost in the process.

The most horrifying example of this was experiments on humans. That no experiments may be carried out on a human being without his insight and consent—so that dangerous experiments should only be carried out by the experimenter on himself—does not, it is true, follow from the spirit of science, but from the basic principles of humanity and the rights of man.

Two thousand years ago an Indian prince carried out experiments on criminals, something like this: 'Put the man alive in a tub, close this with its lid, cover it with a thick coating of lime, place it in a baker's oven and light the fire. This was done.—When we knew that the man must be dead, the tub was pulled out, the lid removed and we looked cautiously inside to see whether we could perceive the vital spirit escaping: but we observed no vital spirit escaping.' This is analogous to the experiments on humans perpetrated by the national socialists. They have nothing to do with modern science as such, but come under the heading of misuse, which can be practised on science as on everything else brought forth by man.

The position with regard to historically determined motives is different from that which obtains for the unhistorical will to power. The birth of modern science is perhaps unthinkable without the state of mind and the impulses that have their historical roots in Biblical religion. Three motives that impel research forward to the limit seem to have their origin here:

(1) The *ethos* of Biblical religion demands *veracity* at all costs. Through it veracity was pursued at the highest pitch and in all its problematic nature. The demand for truth put forward by God does not permit cognition to be pursued as a game, not as a noble pastime for the idle hour, but requires that cognition shall be regarded with all the seriousness of a vocation in which everything is at stake.

(2) The world is *God's creation*. The Greeks know the cosmos as the perfect and orderly, as the rational and law-abiding, as the eternally enduring. But if the world is God's creation, then everything that is, as the creation of God, is worthy of being known; there is nothing that it is not necessary to apprehend and know. Cognition is like a re-thinking of the thoughts of God. And God—in the words of Luther—is present as creator even in the intestine of a louse. The Greek is bogged down in closed world systems, in the beauty of his thought cosmos, in the logical transparency of the thought whole; he either causes himself to group everything in schemata of grades and classifications, or he causes that which has been thought to be deduced in interconnexions by means of syllogisms, or he comprehends an eternal process obeying set laws. Not only Aristotle and Democritus, but also St. Thomas and also Descartes[1] obey this Greek impulse to the closed form, which paralyses science.

Entirely dissimilar is the new impulse that desires to hold itself open to all creation without limits. Out of this impulse cognition strives toward precisely that piece of reality which does not accord with the classifications and laws so far discovered. Within the *logos* itself there develops the urge to bring about its own downfall—not in order to deliver itself up, but in order to win itself back in a new, more ample, more fully realised shape, and to continue this process *ad infinitum*, since it can never reach any final conclusion. This science springs from the *logos* that does not enclose itself within itself, but, open to the *alogon*, penetrates the latter by subordinating itself to it.

The continual and incessant interaction between the formulation of a theoretical construction and experimental experience is a simple and great example and symbol of this universal process that is kindled by the impact
between *logos* and *alogon*.

For the new urge to cognition, the world is also no longer intrinsically
beautiful. This cognition is directed upon the beautiful and upon the ugly,
upon the good and upon the evil. Granted that in the last resort *omne ens est*
bonum, namely as having been created by God. But this goodness is no longer
the visible, self-sufficient beauty of the Greeks; it is present only in the love
felt toward every existent as having been created by God, and consequently
also in the confidence that is felt in the meaning of research. The knowledge
that every worldly thing is a creature of God gives peace of mind before the
chasms of reality in the disquiet of boundless questioning and the attendant
forward-thrusting research.

But known and knowable worldly being, as createdness, is only second-
grade being. Hence the world in itself is without foundations, for it has
its matrix in another, in the Creator; in itself it is not closed and therefore
cannot be closed by cognition either. Worldly Being can nowhere be apprehended as final, absolute reality; it always points to something else.

The idea of creation makes the created thing worthy of love as the work
of God, and thereby makes possible a hitherto unknown closeness to reality.
At the same time, however, it engenders the greatest remoteness from Being,
which is after all only created Being, not Being itself, not God.

(3)   The reality of the world is full of horror and dread for man. His will to
truth has to note 'it is thus'. If *God* is the creator of the world, however,
He is *so to speak made answerable* for His creation. The question of the vindication of God becomes in Job a struggle round the Godhead in the
knowledge of worldly reality. It is a struggle against God for God. The
existence of God is not in doubt. The very fact that it is not in doubt
intensifies the struggle. It would cease if belief were extinguished.

This God, with His demand for absolute truthfulness, does not want to be
grasped through illusions. He spurns the theologians, who seek to console
and exhort Job with intellectual sophistries. This God demands knowledge,
the content of which seems again and again to impeach Him himself. Hence
the audacity of cognition, the demand for unconditional cognition—and at

the same time the aversion to it. There is a polarity, as if man heard at one and the same time: The will of God is unlimited research; research is the service of God—it is an impugnment of God; not everything is to be disclosed.

This conflict goes hand in hand with the investigator's conflict with his own, with that which is dearest and most desirable to him, with his ideals and principles: they must all be put to the test and substantiated or transformed. Just as God is not truly believed if He does not submit to the questions that grow out of the facts of reality, and just as the quest for God is a process of making things difficult for oneself by depriving oneself of illusions, so the genuine will to research is the struggle with one's own desires and expectations.

This combat finds its ultimate confirmation in the combat of the scientist with his own theses. It has become the decisive hallmark of the scientific man that in his researches he seeks his antagonists, and that he seeks most ardently for those who call everything in question with concrete and clearly defined ideas. Here something apparently self-destructive becomes productive. And it is the hallmark of loss of science when discussion is avoided, even declined, when thought is confined to like-minded circles and destructive aggressivity turned outward in vague generalities.

C. ABERRATIONS AND TASKS OF MODERN SCIENCE

Science, at first slowly and in a series of leaps, then rapidly and continuously unfolded in the collaboration of scientists from all parts of the world, has, in the course of the last three centuries become an inexorable destiny and opportunity.

Science is today universally disseminated and recognised; everyone believes himself to have a share in it. But at the same time, pure science and the lucidity of the scientific attitude are exceedingly rare. There is the mass of scientific findings, which are simply accepted; there is the plenitude of specialist ability without participation in universal scientificity; there is the broad stream that is made up of an intermingling of science with unscientific elements. In our world, however, authentic scientificity, the attitude of universal knowledge, trustworthy methodological criticism, enquiring cognition, is no more than a thin thread in the maze of aberrations.

Science cannot be acquired without effort. The vast majority of men still have little or no idea what science is. That is the flaw in the consciousness of our epoch. Science comes naturally to very few. It is one of the cardinal features of the age and yet, with its true nature, it is still spiritually powerless, because the mass of men do not enter into it when they take possession of technological findings or appropriate dogmatically facts that can be learnt by question and answer.

Science has enjoyed an immense prestige in our era. Everything was expected of it; penetrating knowledge of all Being and help in every kind of need. This fallacious expectation is superstitious belief in science, the ensuing disillusionment leads to contempt for science. Mystical trust in something that one thinks one knows all about is superstition, the experience of its failure leads to contempt for knowledge. Neither has anything to do with science itself. Thus science is indeed the hallmark of our era, but in a shape in which it ceases to be science.

The path of this error is the following: In research we make a presupposition of the knowability of the world. For without this presupposition all research would be senseless. But this presupposition is susceptible of two interpretations: Firstly, that of the knowability of the objects in the world; secondly, that of the knowability of the world as a whole. The first supposition alone is correct, and it is impossible to know how much further cognition in the world can be carried. The second presupposition, on the contrary, is incorrect. That it is fallacious is demonstrated by the radical difficulties which, while placing no restrictions on research into contents, show the limit of knowledge; this limit is represented by the fact that not only does the world as a whole, as a single closed entity, evade cognition, but also that the world in the sense of something that can be thought and experienced without contradiction does not exist for us at all. These limits become clearly visible when we see the fallacious presupposition of the knowability of the world-as-a-whole come to grief on the facts of research. Insight into the error is by no means easy. The error entered into modern science through the supposition that it is a philosophy; it dates from Descartes. Hence the great and pressing task of our epoch is the pure apprehension of the meaning and limits of modern science.

One misleading consequence of the fallacious scientific conception that the world is knowable in its entirety and in principle, has been to regard it as fundamentally beautiful. The view became current that from now on it was only a matter of good will, on the basis of knowledge, to organise the world in such a manner as to create for mankind a permanent state of well-being and happiness. This introduced a new phenomenon into history during the last few centuries: The will not merely to help oneself in a meaningful manner through knowledge, in the world and within the incalculable totality of human conditions, but through knowledge of this totality (which the deified scientist was supposed to possess) to put the world as a whole in order by means of intelligence alone.

This typically modern superstition expects something that science is not capable of achieving. It takes supposed scientific total-interpretations of things to represent definitive knowledge. It uncritically accepts results without knowing the methodological road along which they were obtained, and without knowing the limits within which the scientific results are valid at any given moment. It conceives of all truth and all reality as being employable by our intelligence. It has absolute confidence in science and obeys without question the authority wielded by official bodies of experts.

When this superstitious belief in science was disappointed, however, the reaction produced repudiation of science and the invocation of feeling, instinct, impulse. Every calamity was then ascribed to the evolution of modern science. Such disillusionment is the inevitable consequence of superstitious expectation of the impossible. Reorganisation of the world fails to materialise, the finest plans come to naught, catastrophes take place in the condition of man, and their extent is rendered all the more unbearable by the previous expectation of final progress. Symbolic of what lies within the potential scope of science is the fact that the physician, despite the unparalleled increase in his ability that has taken place in our day, remains unable either to cure all diseases or to prevent death. Again and again man comes up against his limits.

In this situation the task is to gain for ourselves that genuine science which is as clearly aware of what can be known as it is decisively conscious of its limits. Only in this way can the dual errors of superstitious belief in science and hatred of science be eluded. The crucial factor in deciding the ultimate fate of man will be whether, with the passage of time, science can be safeguarded, deepened and brought to reality in an increasingly large number of men.

This is no easy matter. For authentic, all-embracing science is bound to the historically determined structure of a profound soul. It rests on very fragile foundations that cannot be confidently guaranteed to persist through generations. This science springs from a complexity of motives so involved that when one of them is lacking science itself becomes paralysed or empty; the consequence is that throughout the centuries of the modern world, science as the reality of the total scientific attitude has always been rare and has perhaps become rarer. The prevailing sound and fury of findings relating to the conformation of the material world and to the twists and turns of the 'enlightened' view of the world, so much talked about all over the globe, cannot blind us to the fact that science, which appears to be so widely current, is in fact the most deeply concealed rarity. For the most part, modern man as such does not know at all what science is; he has never really experienced what drives a man toward it. Scientists themselves, who continue to make discoveries in their own special fields—unconsciously carrying on a little while longer a movement that was set going by other forces—often do not know what science is; they betray this in their comportment outside that narrow field in which they are still masters. Modern philosophers discuss science as though they knew it, and then permit it to degenerate into an historically passing ideological error. Even philosophers of the stature of Hegel know little or nothing about this science.

II. MODERN TECHNOLOGY

Today we are all conscious of standing at a turning-point of history; a hundred years ago this turning-point was likened to the decline of the ancient world. Since then, however, it has been more and more deeply felt to be the great moment of destiny not only for Europe or the West, but for the whole world. It is the Age of Technology, which seems to leave nothing standing of what man has acquired in the course of millennia in the way of methods of work, forms of life, modes of thought and symbols.

The German idealism of Fichte, Hegel and Schelling interpreted its own period as the most profound turning-point of history. It did so on the basis of the conception of the Christian axis, which was supposed to have just reached its climax or consummation. This was the overweening boldness of spiritual self-deception. By contrast, we are now in a position to say with certainty: the present is no second Axial Period. In the most pronounced contrast to the latter, it is a period of catastrophic descent to poverty of spirit, of humanity, love and creative energy; one thing alone is still great enough to stand comparison with all that went before: the production of science and technology.

But what sort of greatness is this? We understand the joy of the discoverer and inventor; at the same time we see them as functional components in the chain of a fundamentally anonymous creative process, in which every link fits into another and the participants do not operate as human beings, in the greatness of an all-embracing soul. Despite a high level of creative inspiration, of patient and persevering labour, and audacity in tentative hypotheses, the overall picture leaves us with the impression that the spirit itself has been sucked into the technological process, which even subordinates the sciences to itself—and this with an intensity that grows from generation to generation. This explains the astonishing stupidity of so many scientists outside their own special field; it explains the intellectual helplessness of so many technicians outside the tasks which, though they are for them the ultimate ones, are in themselves not so at all; it explains the secret lack of happiness in this world that is becoming ever more inhuman.

If we seek an analogy for our epoch, we find it not in the Axial Period, but rather in another technological age, of which we have no transmitted knowledge: the age of the invention of tools and the use of fire. When man, with a single jump involving the whole world, found entirely new preconditions for his potentialities. The long ages of mere repetition and expansion that followed, during which everything remained fundamentally the same, have been left behind. Hence the past century was enthusiastically aware, as we still are today, of the fact that immense and unprecedented possibilities are open to humanity in every phase of existence. Hence, too, recorded history furnishes us with nothing comparable to the events of our era. For this reason we today, misunderstanding ourselves, see ourselves in our technological ability as creators of salvation on earth without parallel—or we see ourselves as equally without parallel in our spiritual perplexity. There is nothing in history by which we can measure ourselves.

If there is to be a new Axial Period it can only lie in the future, just as the first Axial Period followed, after a long interval, the period of foundation-laying discoveries which finally differentiated human life from the animal kingdom: the Promethean Age. This new Axial Period, which perhaps stands before us and which would constitute a single, world-embracing reality, is beyond our powers of imagination. To anticipate it in phantasy would mean to create it. No one can know what it will bring.

Technology is the procedure by which scientific man masters nature for the purpose of moulding his existence, delivering himself from want, and giving his environment the form that appeals to him. The appearance given to nature by human technology and how his technological procedure reacts upon man, that is, the manner in which his mode of work, work organisation, and shaping of the environment modify him himself, constitutes one of the ground-lines of history.

But it took modern technology to make this palpable as the fate of man. In contrast to the relative stability of technological conditions for thousands of years, there has taken place since the end of the eighteenth century a revolution in technology, and thereby in human existence as a whole, whose velocity has continually increased up to our own day. Karl Marx was the first to recognise this in grand style.

Man's attachment to nature is made manifest in a new fashion by modern technology. Nature threatens to overpower man himself, in a manner previously unforeseen, through his tremendously increased mastery of her. Through the nature of the man engaged in technological work, nature really does become the tyrant of humanity. The danger threatens that man will stifle in the second nature, to which he gives birth technologically as his own product, whereas he may appear relatively free *vis-à-vis* unsubdued nature in his perpetual struggle for existence.

Technology has wrought a radical transformation in the day-by-day existence of man in his environment; it has forced his mode of work and his society into entirely new channels: the channels of mass-production, the metamorphosis of his whole existence into a technically perfect piece of machinery and of the planet into a single great factory. In the process man has been and is being deprived of all roots. He is becoming a dweller on the earth with no home. He is losing the continuity of tradition. The spirit is being reduced to the learning of facts and training for utilitarian functions.

In its first effects this age of metamorphosis is disastrous. We are living today in the impossibility of finding a legitimate form of life. Little that is true and trustworthy and that could sustain the individual in his self-consciousness comes to us out of the contemporary world.

Hence the individual is either overcome by a profound dissatisfaction with himself, or he delivers himself up in self-oblivion to become a functional component of the machine, to abandon himself unthinking to his vital existence, which has become impersonal, to lose the horizon of past and future and shrink into a narrow present, untrue to himself, barterable and available for any purpose asked of him, under the evil spell of unquestioned, untested, static, undialectic and easily interchangeable pseudo-certainties.

But whoever retains in himself the troubled mind that comes from dissatisfaction becomes perpetually false to himself. He is compelled to live in masks and to change the masks according to the situation and the people with whom he is dealing. He speaks entirely in terms of the 'as if' and does not gain himself, because in the end, thanks to all the masks, he does not know who he really is.

If no ground is firm enough to stand on—if there is no echo for authentic selfhood—if there is no more respect because masks and wrappings do not command respect, but only make possible fetishistic deification—if men do not bring me to an upsurge through the hidden demand of their selfhood speaking out of their existence—then the troubled mind grows into the despair that was prophetically lived through by Kierkegaard and Nietzsche and that attained its most lucid expression in their interpretations of the epoch.

Along with all this there has taken place a breaking-off of history, a destruction or submersion of the past to an extent from which all the millennia of history afford no analogies or parallels. The first inception of the kindling of fire and the development of the first tools are alone comparable with the events of our time; the discovery of atomic energy does indeed seem analogous to the discovery of fire: a prodigious opportunity and a prodigious danger. But we know nothing of those ages of beginning. As then, mankind is starting from scratch—or else it is about to lay itself in the grave of unconsciousness to the accompaniment of stupendous destruction.

On account of the magnitude of the question of what it may make of man, technology is perhaps the cardinal theme for the comprehension of our present situation. The importance of the irruption of modern technology and its consequences for absolutely all the problems of life cannot be overestimated. As a general rule, historical thought blindly clings to the fallacious idea that modern technology is a direct continuation of the past and draws wrongheaded comparisons between our existence and that which preceded us. Whenever historical parallels to our epoch are adduced, it behoves us to ask whether sufficient account has been taken of the radical difference which results from our technology. If this is done, comparison will focus attention all the more sharply on what continually recurs in man and what are the permanent basic human conditions. The question is, what remains unaffected by the transformation wrought by technology or re-establishes itself in its primary form in spite of it.

We must therefore proceed to a more detailed and precise analysis of what has so far been characterised and asserted in general terms only. We shall begin by discussing technology and work as they form part of man's life at any time, in order, by means of comparison, to present a graphic picture of the depth of the dividing-line established by modern technology and work.

A. THE NATURE OF TECHNOLOGY

1. Definition of technology

Technology as means: Technology comes into being through the interposition of means to the attainment of an end. Immediate activities, such as breathing, movement, or ingestion, do not involve technique. Only when their functioning is faulty and measures are intentionally taken to perform them correctly, do we speak of breathing-technique, etc. The following are the essential characteristics of technology:

Understanding: Technology rests on the work of the understanding, on calculation in conjunction with anticipatory feeling and the estimation of possibilities. It thinks in terms of mechanisms and transforms everything into quantities and relations. It is a part of rationalisation in general.

Power: Technology is an ability whose procedure in relation to the aim is external. This ability is one of fabrication and utilisation not of creating and causing to grow.

By setting natural force against natural force, technology masters nature indirectly through nature itself. This mastery rests on knowledge. It is in this sense that we say: Knowledge is power.

The meaning of technology: Power over nature has meaning only in terms of human purposes: The easing of existence, the lessening of the daily struggle for the physical prerequisites of existence, a gain in leisure and comfort. 'The meaning of technology is freedom in relation to nature.' Its purpose is to liberate man from his animal imprisonment in nature, with its want, its menace, and its bondage. Hence the principle of technology is purposive activity carried out on substances and forces in the service of man's determination of his own life. Technological man does not simply take things as he finds them. He sees them in their utility for human purposes and seeks the approximation of their forms as utility forms to the particularity of these purposes (Dessauer).

There is more than this to the meaning of technology, however. Its role as a means, expressed in the making of tools, is subservient to the idea of a unity, namely the unity of man's moulding of his environment—a process which, within its own closed circle, is continually expanding. The animal finds its environment ready-made and is unconsciously bound to it. Despite being likewise bound, man brings forth his environment in boundless overpassing of his ties. Life in an environment that he has created himself, simultaneously with life in the natural environment, is the hallmark of humanity. He finds himself in his own creation, not only through release from want, but also in the appeal that the beauty, appropriateness and form of his creation has for him. He augments his reality with the breadth of his environment.

Kinds of technology: A distinction is made between the technology that produces power and the technology that produces goods. Man obtains operational power for himself by such means as the training of animals, wind- and water-mills, etc.; the technology that produces goods is made possible by various special techniques, such as spinning, weaving, pottery, building and medical treatment.

Dessauer expounds the view that, furthermore, technology not only produces means to the attainment of a goal that is set in advance, but also produces constructs whose further utilisation cannot be foreseen at the time of their invention—as was the case with musical instruments, the printing press, etc. Here technological creations become, so to speak, keys with which to open rooms for the activity of man, so that he can expand his being and make fresh discoveries.

In general, technology is defined as operation with the substances and forces of nature for the purpose of producing useful objects and effects. It is only in analogy to this that we speak of technique in relation to all other planned procedures in so far as they lead to regulation and mechanical repetition; thus we use the term in reference to the organisation of human relationships, to the carrying on of institutions, to the self-treatment of body and mind.

Invention and repetitive labour: Technological rules are those that can be learnt, handed on and applied in identical form. Technology as theory states the methods appropriate to the attainment of ends, i.e. methods which are, firstly, objectively correct, and secondly, avoid superfluous activities and involve the economical application of only such activity as is essential. Technology consists in procedures and constructs invented by men and capable of subsequent realisation in *ad libitum* repetition and quantity.

Hence there is an essential diversity between the creative activity that leads to technological inventions, and the performance of work that merely applies the invention repetitively in order to produce greater quantities.

Deviations: If the meaning of technology lies in the unity of the moulding of the environment for the purposes of human existence, then a deviation is involved wherever tools and activities make themselves independent of their mediate function, wherever the end-purpose is forgotten and the means themselves become the end, become absolute.

Wherever in day-to-day work the meaning of the whole, as motive and field of vision, is lost sight of, technology degenerates into an endlessly multifarious mode of action and becomes, for the worker, senseless and a plundering of life.

Where that element of technological activity which consists of performances that can be learnt by practice becomes self-enjoying routine, it ceases to be an enrichment of life (through ensuring its rudiments and services) and becomes instead an impoverishment of life. Work, without the spiritual effort which is an indispensable means of enhancing consciousness, becomes instead sufficient to itself. Man sinks down into unconsciousness or loss of consciousness.

2. The great historical dividing-line within technology

Technology, in the sense of the utilisation of implements, has existed as long as men have existed. It existed as far back as our historical memory reaches, on the basis of the natural physics of the primitives, in handicrafts and the use of weapons, in the employment of the wheel, the spade, the plough, the boat, of the work-power of animals, of the sail and fire. In the civilisation of Antiquity, particularly in the West, a highly evolved science of mechanics became the means of moving immense weights, erecting buildings, building roads and ships, and constructing machines of siege and defence.

Yet all this technology remained within a comparatively measurable framework that was not too large for men to see as a whole. Everything that was done was accomplished by human power supplemented by animal power, tensile force, fire, wind and water power, but here too within the province of the natural human world. The position became completely different after the end of the eighteenth century. It is erroneous to suppose that no decisive leap ever took place in technological evolution. It occurred at this date, and it occurred in the technological life-form as a whole.

After the passage of centuries, during which rudimentary beginnings had been attempted while a technological, technocratic ideology was adumbrated in imaginative constructions and its initial scientific prerequisites slowly and fragmentarily created, a realisation took place in the nineteenth century that exceeded all imagination. We shall enquire what this new manifestation was. It cannot be reduced to a single principle.

The most tangible fact is: Machines were invented that produced consumer goods automatically. What had previously been done by man as a handicraftsman was now done by machine. The machine spun, wove, sawed, planed, pressed, cast; it fabricated complete objects. Whereas a hundred workmen had to blow laboriously to manufacture a few thousand bottles a day, one bottle-machine made 20,000 bottles daily and required only a few workmen to serve it.

Further machines had to be contrived to supply the power with which to drive the production machines. The steam engine was the turning-point (1776), then the electric motor (dynamo, 1867) became the universal power machine. Energy was transformed out of coal or water-power and conveyed to wherever it was needed. The mechanical science of the ancients, which had reigned supreme for thousands of years, was now confronted by the modern science of energy. The old mechanical science had at its disposal only limited power in the shape of the muscular performance of man and beast, and of wind and water for mills. The new factor was the thousandfold greater power, which at first seemed capable of multiplication *ad infinitum*, that was now at man's disposal.

This development was only possible on the basis of the modern exact sciences. These afforded knowledge and possibilities which were entirely unknown to the earlier science of mechanics. Above all, the development of the theory of electricity and of chemistry became an indispensable prerequisite for the new technological realities. That which was initially invisible and only disclosed to the eye of research, furnished man with those almost boundless energies which are today employed all over the planet.

One further prerequisite was needed, however, to lift the various inventions from the level of a spare-time hobby or a refined luxury-activity and bring them to economic realisation, which alone made them a factor in human existence. Modern social liberty—in which slaves were unknown and free competition permitted at the individual's own risk—afforded bold entrepreneurs the opportunity of trying out the improbable and that which seemed to the majority impossible. This was facilitated firstly by the credit system, which placed funds at the disposal of the efficient in a sum which formerly not even the wealthiest man would have possessed, and secondly by an organisation of labour with free labour forces which could be engaged for any desired work-operation and, since they were paid at a fixed daily rate, represented a predictable element in the calculation of the entrepreneur's costs. And attendant upon both of them was a calculable legal system, which enforced observance of contracts.

Thus there arose in the West the technological-scientific battle of the entrepreneurs of the nineteenth century, in which the old handicrafts went under with the exception of a few indispensable remnants and everyone engaged in technologically useless activity was ruthlessly destroyed. To be sure, even the best ideas might come to naught. On the other hand, however, miraculous successes were achieved. A process of natural selection by the touchstone of success took place. Whoever failed to accomplish what the undertaking demanded went bankrupt or was dismissed from his post. For a time at least—at the commencement of these creative enterprises—a selection of the most competent occurred.

The genesis of the modern technological world therefore contains the following inseparable elements: Natural science, the spirit of invention, the organisation of labour. Common to each of these three factors is rationality. Even those scientific discoveries which are *per se* technologically utilisable, are by no means susceptible of immediate application. They require the flash of technological inspiration before they can be put to use. It took Morse to make telegraphy. There is no predictable relationship between science and technology.

(2)   The *spirit of invention* is able to perform amazing feats even without specifically modern science. The achievements of primitive peoples—e.g. the boomerang—are astonishing, and numerous inventions were made in China (e.g. porcelain, lacquer, silk, paper, printing, the compass, and gunpowder). Equally astonishing, however, is the contemporaneous ossification in laborious traditional methods of work, where the simplest, and for us, most obvious mechanical inventions could be of assistance. It is as if a normal absence of ideas held man fast to inappropriate methods. In contrast to this attachment to tradition, during the last century and a half a multitude of inventions have been made in all fields, which

fall within the framework of that which has long been possible without any need of modern science: e.g. heating-stoves, the slow-burning fire, central heating, kitchen utensils, and many domestic appliances, and medical equipment such as the ophthalmoscope. For other things modern knowledge was a prerequisite of discovery, though the old means would have sufficed for their execution: this is true of a great part of the control of epidemics and to the use of anaesthetics and antiseptics in operations. The traditional apathy in living, together with the patient endurance of discomfort and inappropriate ways of doing things, seems to have been overcome in our epoch by the spirit of invention.

To this we must add the specifically modern element represented by the systematisation of invention. No longer are fortuitous inventions made here and there by individuals; the process of technological invention has become a movement in which numberless men participate. From time to time inventions that are new in principle lend fresh impetus to this movement. For the most part it consists in the development of existing inventions, in continual improvements and further exploitation. Everything becomes anonymous. The achievement of the individual disappears in the achievement of the totality. In this way perfected forms, e.g. of the bicycle or the automobile, came into being in a relatively short space of time.

The technologically utilisable must also be economically utilisable. The spirit of invention as such, however, holds itself free from this compulsion. In its major impulses it proceeds, as it were, toward the creation of a second world. Nevertheless, that which it creates is only given technological realisation to the extent of the space made available to it by economic utility in free competition or by the will that disposes of despotic power.

(3) The *organisation of labour* becomes a social and political problem. The machine leads to the production not only of luxury goods, but also of the mass-goods of everyday need to all; this results in the majority of men being drawn into the production process, into this method of work by machine, as component parts in the machinery. If almost everyone becomes a link in the technological work process, the organisation of labour becomes a question addressed to humanity. Because the ultimate consideration for man is man and not technology, and because technology is meant to serve man and not man technology, a sociological-political process has been set in motion on the basis of

modern technology which strives passionately for a reversal of the initial circumstances that permitted an *ad libitum* subordination of man, as a unit of labour, to technological and economic purposes.

To understand the meaning of such demands it is necessary to form a clear picture of the nature of work, first of all in a general sense, and then in the metamorphosis wrought in it by the incisive effects of technology.

B. THE NATURE OF WORK

Everything realised by technology has at all times demanded work. And wherever man works he applies some form of technology. The nature of the technology determines the mode of work. Modifications in technology modify work. A radical transformation of technology is inevitably accompanied by a radical transformation of work.

Not until the metamorphosis that took place in the nineteenth century did both technology and work become a problem. At no time prior to this were either of them discussed from so many angles or in such detail as since this date.

Let us next call to mind what work as such is, and what it has been since the beginning. Only with the aid of this yardstick can the specific characteristics of work in the new technological world be recognised.

1. *Definition of work*

The definition of work is threefold:

Work is physical labour.

Work is planned activity.

Work is the basic feature of man's nature in contradistinction to the animal: it is what gives rise to his world.

Firstly: Work is *physical labour*. It is effort, e.g. the work of the muscles, and leads to fatigue and exhaustion. In this sense the animal works just as much as the human.

Secondly: *Work is planned activity*. It is activity undertaken with purpose and aim. The effort is willed in order to gain the means of satisfying needs. This work already distinguishes man from the animal.

The animal satisfies its needs directly through nature. It finds what it requires for its needs ready-made. Man can only satisfy his needs through the conscious and planned interposition of means. This interposition is made through the medium of work. Although he finds the material for his work in nature, this material is suited to the satisfaction of his needs only when he has worked it up.

The animal's instinct consumes and causes to disappear—work constructs tools and creates that which endures in the shape of goods and products. The tool serves to remove man from direct connexion with nature. It prevents destruction of the object by transforming it.

Natural skill is not sufficient for work. The individual only acquires skill through learning the universal rules of work.

Work is both physical and mental. Mental work is the more difficult. Forms of work that can be learnt by practice and then carried out almost unconsciously are infinitely easier. We are always ready to flee from creative work into that which is automatic, from mental to physical. On days when the savant makes no progress in his researches, he is still able to give an expert opinion.

Thirdly: *Work is a basic form of human behaviour.* It transmutes the existing world of nature into a human world. The shape of the total environment of man at any given moment is the world intentionally and unintentionally created by communal work. The world of man, the overall condition in which he lives, grows out of communal work. Hence it always calls for division and organisation of labour.

Division of labour: It is not possible for everyone to do everything. Special skills are required. The man who is skilled in a specialty can produce more and better goods of this particular kind than the man who is unskilled. Furthermore, not everyone possesses the means and materials for every kind of work. Work in the community therefore leads straight to the division of labour, because work is necessarily of many kinds.

Workers are differentiated in classes according to the type of work they do. They are differentiated according to the nature of their human culture, their mores, their mental outlook, and their standing: husbandmen, artisans, merchants, etc. A process that binds a man to his work takes place.

Organisation of labour: Where there is division of labour, collaboration is necessary. The performance of my special work has meaning only if I am a co-worker in a society where all performances are mutually valuable. Work gains its meaning from its position in an organisation of work.

The latter develops in part without a plan and of itself through the market, and in part according to a plan through the distribution of work. A society derives its essential character from whether it is organised, as a whole, on the basis of planning or of the operation of the free market.

Where there is division of labour, products are changed from direct consumer goods into merchandise, and must therefore be exchanged, put on the market, or distributed. This renders the standard provided by an abstract value imperative. This standard of value is called money. The value of merchandise in terms of money either develops freely through the processes of the market, or to order through planned price-fixing.

Today it is perfectly obvious that the social structure and human existence are determined, in all their ramifications, by the nature of work and its distribution. Hegel already saw this; Marx and Engels disseminated the knowledge in epoch-making interpretations.

The question of the extent of this connexion and to what extent other causes—religious and political factors for instance—operate to curtail its importance, is a matter for special historico-sociological investigation.

Over-emphasis of this connexion, resulting in a monocausal conception of human history, is certainly fallacious. That this conception has been essayed since Marx and Engels, rests upon the fact that in our epoch the connexion between work and social structure has acquired very great importance and has therefore become more perceptible than ever before.

Division of labour and organisation of labour are certainly responsible for essential structures of our existence in our society. But the crucial factor for the consciousness of all who are working is what work is being done, to what end, with what meaning, and how this presents itself to the consciousness of the worker. Discussion of these questions is all too naturally based on the presupposition that it is the system of human needs—food, clothing, housing, etc.—that determines work. This is true, but it is by no means the whole truth.

Pleasure in work, in so far as it is not simply functional pleasure in the use of the muscles or the exercise of skill, is the consciousness of participating in the creation of our environment. The worker becomes conscious of himself in the mirror of that which he has produced. His serenity springs from sharing in the life of the existential forms which he has helped to create, from the construction of something that exists.

Much more than this may lie in work, however. Hegel speaks of 'religious labour that brings forth works of devotion which are not intended for any finite purpose. ... Such labour is itself an act of worship. ... Work as pure creation and as perennial labour is its own purpose and hence is for ever unfinished.' This work runs 'from the merely bodily movement of the dance to the stupendous and gigantic works of architecture ... all these works fall into the category of sacrifice ... the very activity is an offering; no longer of a purely external thing, but of the inner subjectivity ... in this producing the sacrifice is spiritual activity and the effort which, as a negation of the particular self-consciousness, holds fast to the purpose that lives within and in imagination, and brings it forth to outward view' (15, 248 ff.).

Thus Hegel points out potentialities of the meaning of work which today have been almost forgotten. It is a superficial view that divides the content of work into the satisfaction of vital needs and of the demands of luxury. The meaning of work reaches a great deal further. It is precisely what is called luxury from this viewpoint—all forms and goods that are not indispensable to vital satisfaction—which conceals the essential factor: how and as what man creates his world, in which he becomes aware of himself and of being itself, of transcendence, and of his own specific nature.

This briefly summarises work in general. We shall now turn to a consideration of the incision made by modern technology.

2. Work after the dividing-line of modern technology

(1) *Technology saves labour, but at the same time increases labour.* Technology aims at saving labour. Work is to be carried out by machines, instead of by human muscles, by the automatism of apparatuses, instead of by repeated efforts of thought. The unique achievement of an inventor spares the exertion of muscles and intelligence. The limit to the realisation of this technology is the fact that there remains one form of work which has to be carried out by men again and again and for which there is no technological substitute, and that fresh tasks become necessary which did not exist before. The machines themselves have to be built again and again. Even if machines become almost independent beings, human labour is still required to serve, mind and repair them; furthermore, it

is needed to obtain the raw materials for the machines to work on. All that happens is that labour is shifted to different points. It is altered, not abolished. Somewhere or other there remains the immemorial toil that no technology can do away with.

Thus technology does indeed make work easier. But it also gives rise to new possibilities of production and engenders new needs through its achievements. Through the increase of needs, new, augmented work arises. And above all technology produces, in the shape of weapons of war, new means of destruction which intensify the demands on labour to the utmost, first through the obligation to manufacture the maximum quantity of armaments, and then through the obligation to start all over again amidst the chaos and the ruins.

On the whole it is doubtful whether, in respect of our contemporary reality, technology does in fact ease and diminish work; it looks much more as though technology places a strain on man's forces such as they have never before been called upon to bear. At all events, modern technology has brought about an immense initial increase in the labour of those who are actively engaged in it. Nonetheless, technological potentialities do contain the principle of a reduction of physically ruinous labour, and modern technology has established the lasting idea of a growing release of man from the burden of physical labour in the interests of leisure for the unfolding of his free potentialities.

(2) *Technology changes work.* In contrast to the magnificence of inventive creation there stands the dependence of uncreative application. Invention springs from leisure, inspiration, and perseverance; application demands repetitive labour, order and reliability.

In executive technological work the observation and service of the machine is reckoned as positive; a disciplined, deliberate, reflective attitude of mind is developed; joy in meaningful activity and ability, indeed a love for the machines, becomes possible. Against this the automatisation of labour, for the many whose work consists of continuous repetitive motions at the conveyor belt, becomes negative; the aridity of this empty labour that brings nothing but fatigue becomes an intolerable burden to all but those of a fundamentally apathetic disposition.

Hegel already saw the consequences for work arising out of the leap from the tool to the machine. Initially the prodigious advance. The tool is no more than an inert thing with which I am only formally active and make myself into a thing; for it is man who supplies the power. The machine, on the other hand, is an independent implement; by means of it nature is tricked by man, in that he causes her to work for him.

The trickery comes home to rest on the trickster, however: 'By causing nature to work through the medium of the machine, he does not do away with the necessity for his own work … he removes it from nature and does not direct it toward her as a living object … the work that is left to him becomes itself more mechanical; the more mechanical work becomes, the less value it possesses and the more he has to work in this fashion.' 'Work becomes more lifeless … the skill of the individual infinitely more restricted, and the consciousness of the factory-hand reaches the lowest possible level of apathy; the connexion of the individual type of work to the whole infinite mass of needs is completely lost sight of and replaced by a blind obedience, so that an operation carried out far away often puts a sudden brake on the work of a whole class of men, who have been satisfying their needs by it, and renders it superfluous and useless.'

(3) *Technology compels the adoption of a certain magnitude of organisation.* The technological goal can be completely and economically realised only in factories of considerable compass. How large this organisation must be is a question that must be answered separately for each factory. There remains, however, the further question of how far any number of large-scale organisations can advantageously develop without monopoly in the free market, of how far, outside the framework of legal rights, the planned establishment of an all-embracing world-factory is to be held in view, in which all forms of production are to be geared to each other, so that neither too much nor too little is produced in the various individual fields.

In either case the individual is dependent upon the large-scale organisations and the place he occupies in them. Just as machine manufacture leaves no room for joy in the individual product, so it also puts an end to personal freedom in the possession of the tools of a craft and in production to personal order. The vast majority of men are no longer in a position to visualise the purpose and meaning of their own work. Human standards have been overpassed.

The dual dependence of work upon the machine and upon the organisation of labour, which in turn is a kind of machine, results in man himself coming to resemble a machine-component. Creative inventors and organisers of new units of work become rare exceptions: they continue to build onto the machine. By contrast, more and more men are forced to become parts of the machine.

Technicisation, however, spreads out from the working up of nature to the whole fabric of human life, to the bureaucratic conduct of everything, to politics, even to pastimes and pleasures, which now constitute a continuation of the accustomed forms of life and have ceased to spring from creative pleasure. Man no longer knows what to do with his free time if it is not in turn filled with technologically organised activity—in so far as he does not give himself over to a state of twilight trance in order to recover from his exertions.

Man's life as a component of the machine may be characterised by comparison with the life he used to live: Man is uprooted, he loses his soil and his homeland and in return he is given a place at the machine; the house and land that are apportioned to him are themselves of the type of the machine, transient, interchangeable, not landscape and not unique home. The surface of the earth takes on the appearance of a machine-landscape. The horizons of man's life become extraordinarily restricted in respect of the past and the future; he loses his cultural heritage and his quest for the final goal; he lives in the present alone. But this present becomes increasingly empty, the less it is sustained by the substance of memory and the less it bears the already germinating seeds of future possibilities. Work becomes mere effort in exertion and haste, expenditure of energy is followed by fatigue, both of them devoid of reflection. In fatigue nothing is left but the instincts, the need for pleasure and sensation. Man lives on the cinema and the newspaper, in listening to the news and looking at pictures, everywhere within the range of the mechanically conventional. The multiplication of technologically produced consumer goods enables this mass of men to increase to an apparently limitless extent; at any rate our epoch has, in a short space of time, brought about a multiplication of the total population of the earth.

The transformation of man into parts of the vast machinery is revealed by the conception of man arrived at through so-called tests. Individually variant attributes are tested and people are classified by numbers and quantities, on the basis of which they are arranged in groups, types, and grades. Man as an individual resists being transformed into a material which can be interchanged, he resists being arranged by label. But the course of events throughout the world compels the adoption of this technique of selection. At the same time the selectors themselves are human. Who selects the selectors? The selector himself becomes a part of the machinery. The apparatuses and measurements are operated by him mechanically.

Consciousness of being thus dragged into a machinery that is alien to man was expressed by a twenty-one-year-old Lieutenant in the American Air Force at an interview after he had received the highest decorations for outstanding performances in bombing planes: 'I am a cog in the inferno of a vast machine. The more I think about it, the more it seems to me as though I had been a cog in one thing after another since the day I was born. Whenever I started to do something I wanted to do, a thing much larger than I came along and pushed me into a place that was waiting for me. It's not exactly pleasant, but that's how it is.'

C. APPRAISAL OF WORK AND TECHNOLOGY

Appraisal of work

Contradictory opinions concerning work have been expressed since early times: The Greeks despised all physical labour as appropriate only to a low mentality. The complete man, they thought, is an aristocrat, does not work, is possessed of leisure, practises politics, lives in competition, goes to war, gives birth to works of the spirit. Jews and Christians saw in work a punishment for sins. Man has been driven forth from Paradise, he bears the consequences of the fall, he is destined to eat his bread in the sweat of his brow. Pascal intensified this conception: Work is not only a burden, but a distraction from the authentic task of man; work reveals the emptiness of mundane pursuits, the sham of industriousness; it entices to diversions and veils that which is essential. Protestants, however, see in work the great blessing. Milton portrayed the salvation of man in the expulsion from Paradise; Adam and Eve soon dry their tears:

The world was all before them, where to choose
Thir place of rest, and Providence thir Guide. ...

The angel Michael says to Adam:

    ... onely add

    Deeds to thy knowledge answerable ...

    ... then wilt thou not be loath

    To leave this Paradise, but shall possess

    A Paradise within thee, happier farr.

Calvinism deemed success in work a sign of having been chosen by God. The concept of the worldly profession as a duty, which was the outcome of religious conceptions, lived on independently of religion. Pleasure in work and work as a blessing, the honour of work, and achievement as a touchstone of human value grew on this soil. It is the foundation both of the postulate: 'He who does not work shall not eat', and also of the inner benediction: 'Work and despair not.'

In the modern world the affirmation of work is universal. As soon, however, as work became the dignity of man, the distinguishing feature of his nature as a human being, a dual aspect of work was disclosed: on the one hand in the ideal of the working human being, and on the other in the picture of the real average working conditions, in which man is estranged from himself through the mode of work and work-organisation.

From this duality springs the impulse to change the world of man, so that man shall find his way to the proper mode of work in the creation of the totality of his world. The false, compulsive mode of work, that estranges him from himself, must be done away with. The criterion is contained in Hegel's words: 'This is the infinite right of the subject, that he find his own satisfaction in activity and work' (11, 50).

The problem of work in its connexion with the dignity, the rights and the duties of humanity, is fallaciously simplified if we see work as one single whole. In truth work is extremely diverse in the multiplicity of types of work, by virtue of the esteem accorded to the particular type of work, by virtue of the extent of participation in the enjoyment of the goods produced, by virtue of the way the work is organised, the manner in which authority is exercised, and the degree of *esprit de corps* and solidarity felt by the workers.

The tasks of changing the structure of work to the advantage of the dignity of man cannot, therefore, be resolved by the application of a single principle, nor can they be reduced to a single denominator. The following have been recognised as tasks of this order: Changes in the concrete material conditions

under which work is performed, in order to render them more humane—
changes in the organisation of work in order to render the position of the
individual worker, and the methods of establishing authority and subordination, compatible with liberty—changes in society, in order to render the
distribution of goods more equitable and to safeguard the status of every
man, whether in terms of his achievement, or simply as a human being.

These problems have only taken shape through the metamorphosis of
work and forms of life wrought by technology. Appraisal of modern work is
inseparable from the appraisal of modern technology. Through modern technology the burden of work acquires new weight, but perhaps to the accompaniment of opportunities for new fulfilments.

Appraisal of modern technology

For a hundred years technology has been glorified, or condemned, or looked
at with horror.

In the nineteenth century there was the creative urge of the inventor, and
there were the. workers who revolted and smashed the machines.

The initial enthusiasm contains a meaning that has been held fast until
today and has been most recently interpreted by Dessauer. The idea of the
moulding of man's environment accomplished by the inventiveness of man,
who, as the image and likeness of the deity, discovers eternal creative ideas
and creates fresh realities that are like a second nature. The 'spirit of technology' then implies something more than merely a means: it implies an
all-embracing realisation of the allegedly true and legitimate environment
of man. An autonomous world comes into being. Technology is not simply
outward existence, it is an inwardly fulfilled realm of spiritual life. From this
enthusiastic standpoint it appears improbable 'that a world-transforming
force should be nothing more than a system of means with borrowed goals'.

If Dessauer is right, an environment radically different from that created
by man is now in the process of coming into being out of the spirit of technology itself. In the current crises arising out of the melting down of the old,
the new environment has not yet found its shape. It appears in rudimentary
beginnings, while the overall picture seems, in this creative transition, to be
one of anarchy and ruin. The idea of a new environment for man may be
contained in technology of a modern character. Perhaps technological evolution is not proceeding *ad infinitum*, but is following a direction to a conclusion

that would be a new kind of perfection in the material substratum of human existence.

In opposition to this conception there stands the other: The way of technology is not liberation from nature through the mastery of nature, but rather the destruction of nature and of man himself. An unhalting course of the murder of the living will lead ultimately to total destruction. The horror which, from the beginning, gripped great men at the sight of technology was a vision of the truth.

Vis-à-vis these two radical positions there is a third. It asserts the neutrality of technology. Technology is per se neither good nor evil, but it can be used for either good or evil. In itself it contains no idea, neither an idea of perfection nor a diabolical idea of destruction. Both of them spring from other origins, in man, from which alone technology is lent meaning.

It seems characteristic that in Europe today the Promethean enthusiasm for technology has almost vanished, without the inventive spirit being paralysed. The dangerous infantile joy in technology is gone or has been passed on to more primitive peoples, who are just becoming acquainted with technology, which they are in the process of making their own.

Along the route of the Age of Technology, however, whose goal and end are neither clear nor certain, there is certainly taking place at the moment that process of melting down and equivocal refashioning, which we shall discuss with reference to some individual facets:

1. REMOTENESS FROM NATURE AND NEW NEARNESS TO NATURE

Man is torn out of his given, merely 'natural' environment. The first step in the process of becoming human was the domestication which man carried out on himself. But up till a hundred years ago this remained easily surveyable, a real environment, a whole.

At present a new environment is being created; somehow or other a 'natural environment'—now as dependent and relative—must re-establish itself within this new environment, with a fundamentally different consciousness.

In technological activity fabrication is the essential operation. The purpose, and with it the technological apparatus, occupies the foreground of consciousness; the naturally given, on the contrary, recedes into obscurity. The nature which technological activity has in view is nature in its mechanical aspect and the invisible forces known through research (such as electricity), with which I can operate indirectly within the permanent framework of the mechanical environment.

Anyone who does not acquire this knowledge, but confines himself to its utilisation—in pressing the switch, in travelling by electric railway—merely exercises a primitive sleight of hand without having the least idea of what is really going on. Thus men can make use of uncomprehended technology without any relationship to nature—at any rate in many fields—whereas the natural mechanical science of the past demanded practice and the ability expressed in physical skill.

In many realms, however, the nature given to technology demands that we come close to it in respect of the functions peculiar to these realms. Many technological apparatuses call for a specific physical skill, from the type-writer to the automobile, and more intensely so with the aeroplane. But it is almost always a one-sided, particular and extreme skill and a capacity for physical endurance, not a thoroughgoing cultivation of the life of the body as a whole (this can be seen in the difference between the skill of the cyclist and that of the walker). Furthermore, the use of technological apparatus requires knowledge. The practical essential is then skill in the exploitation of technological knowledge, in order on every occasion to find the right starting-point from which to attain the purpose, and, when confronted by a breakdown of the apparatus, to proceed from tentative experimentation to methodological penetration and effective repair.

Thus technology can affect us who live within it in either of two ways: It can remove us from nature entirely and leave us in the position of unthinking utilisation of mechanical appliances, or it can bring us close to nature in the shape of the known but invisible findings of research.

Technology does not only bring us close to the nature that is investigated in the categories of physics, however. Through technology a new world comes into being for us and man is presented with new possibilities of existence in the world, which bring with them a new closeness to nature.

(a) First of all the *beauty of technological constructs*: Consummate technological forms are attained in vehicles, in machines, in technologically manufactured objects of daily use. In technological fabrication the growth and creation of a second nature does, in fact, take place. The question is, in what does this beauty of the technologically successful product consist. It is not mere fitness for purpose, but rather functionally perfect integration into the human world. Still less does it consist in superfluous ornamentation and embellishment, which, on the contrary, impress us as ugly, but in something which causes a natural necessity to be felt in the totally functional construct; this natural necessity is first manifest in a pure form in the work of man, and is then recognised afresh in the unconscious productions of life (in the structures of the bodies of animals and plants, for instance). There are solutions inherent in the thing itself, which are found, as it were, through the striving after eternal, predetermined forms.

(b) Further, technology makes possible an enormous *extension of real apprehension*. Through it great and small things become visible that are closed to natural perception. The microscope and the telescope are unnatural, but they open up a new world of nature. Technology, through the medium of the various means of transport, enables man to be almost omnipresent; he can move about everywhere—when his passage is not barred by the State, war, and politics—so as to immerse himself on the spot in that which can be experienced, seen, and heard in a particular locality. Visual image and sound make present to him in his own home what was previously offered to his senses only in a scanty or fantastic form through inadequate and erroneous notions, or did not enter the field of knowledge at all; gramophone and film keep past events present to memory. Possibilities of observation have been unprecedentedly refined and enriched in all directions.

(c) Finally, there develops a *new consciousness of the world*. Since the inception of the modern system of communications and news-distribution, the feeling that we have of the spaces of the earth has come to take in the whole planet. We visualise the globe and it is filled with the daily news that comes to us from all parts of it. The real imbrication of forces and interests all over the globe renders it a closed whole.

Thus the technological world contains humanity's new possibilities, the specific pleasures of technology, the achievement of technology in extending experience of the world, in rendering the whole planet and all the elements of existence present to concrete experience; the foundations are laid for a playful mastery of matter that will lead to pure experiences of the sublime. At the present time, however, all this is still a rare exception.

Apart from skill, this new nearness to nature and to all things postulates the sovereignty of man, who, penetrating with his power of apprehension into the realm of that which is alien to nature, creates presentness out of the whole, which is not immediately existent. The spirit is decisive.

Much easier is silting up in thoughtlessness, empty and mechanical functioning, alienation in automatism, losing oneself in diversions, growing unconsciousness, the residue of nervous excitation.

2. MISJUDGEMENT OF THE LIMITS OF TECHNOLOGY

The appraisal of technology depends upon what is expected of it. A clear appraisal presupposes clarity concerning the limits of technology.

Fallacious limits have frequently been placed upon technology on the basis of a dogmatic knowledge of nature; thus, for example, about half a century ago flight, and even the airship, were from time to time declared to be impossible. The fact is that the extent of the mastery over nature which man may be able to achieve is unpredictable. Phantasy is free to formulate the most extraordinary pictures, unrestrained by any absolute impossibility. Such pictures include the technological utilisation of atomic energy, which might provide a substitute after the supplies of coal and oil have been exhausted, the intentional explosion of the globe, or the spaceship. Although *perpetuum mobile* has rightly been recognised as impossible, the discovery of a practically inexhaustible source of energy nonetheless remains possible. But the wide range of technological potentialities must not deceive us as to the limits of technology. The limits of technology lie in those presuppositions of all technological realisations which can never be overcome.

(1) *Technology is a means and requires direction:* There would be no technology in Paradise. Technology serves the purpose of ridding man of the burden of want; this first compels him to maintain his physical existence by work and then enables him, without the compulsion of want, to extend his existence into the incalculable structure of an environment which he himself has shaped.

Technologically creative invention is in the service of a need, is guided by it and hence is valued according to its utility. It is true that another process is also present in invention: Pleasure in the creation of previously non-existent constructs which perform certain tasks. The inventor is capable of building his contrivances without any regard for utility. In this manner the automata and playthings of the Baroque Period came into being. Nonetheless, the selection and therefore the ultimately decisive direction of invention proceed from usefulness. The technological inventor does not create any fundamentally

new needs, even though, by satisfying existing needs, he expands and multiplies them. The goal must be given; as a rule it is self-evident: the easing of
work, the manufacture of consumer goods, mass-production. Such utilitarian considerations constitute technology's *raison d'être*.

The limitation of technology consists in the fact that it cannot exist out of
itself for itself, but is always a means. This renders it equivocal. Because it
does not set itself any goals, it is beyond or before all good and evil. It can
serve the purposes of salvation or calamity. In itself it is neutral toward both
of them. This is precisely why it requires direction.

Is it possible for this direction to spring from the existential appropriateness of the natural environment as a whole? from discovery itself and
from extended needs? Such questions are aimed at the unknown, and yet
perhaps meaningful, element in the course of things, as if this course were
the realisation of a plan—or as if a devil were taking possession of it. We
have little reason to pin our faith to any such unconscious course of things.
The direction of technology cannot be looked for in technology itself, but must
be sought in a conscious ethos. Man himself must find his way back to the
guiding reins. He must achieve clarity concerning his needs, he must put
them to the test and determine their hierarchy.

(2) *Technology is restricted to the mechanism, to the lifeless, to the universal:* Technology
     never has more than the mechanically intelligible in its grasp. It trans-
     forms its objects into a mechanism, and thereby into an apparatus and
     a machine. In the face of the unexpectedly magnificent successes of
     these mechanical potentialities, everything may appear technologically
     possible. Then there develops a basic attitude of illusory expectation
     of being able to do everything. However, such absolutisations of the
     technological misjudge reality, which always demands more than tech-
     nology; notwithstanding the fact that all activity contains technique as
     a presupposition, mechanism only furnishes the skeleton, so to speak.
     The steps to be taken with regard to nature in cultivation and breeding,
     with regard to man in education and communication, the creation of
     the works of the spirit, indeed invention itself, cannot be performed
     according to the rules of technique. It is erroneously hoped to fabricate
     by technique that which can be created only out of the living spirit.
     Painting, poetry, and science make use of technique as a means, but
     they are empty things if they are the products of technique alone.

One limitation of technology is its restriction to the lifeless. The understanding that dominates the fabrication of technology is adapted only to the lifeless, to the mechanical in the widest sense. Therefore technology can only deal with the living organism by treating it as it would something without life, e.g. in agricultural chemistry, in modern breeding methods and treatments with hormones and vitamins for such purposes as maximum milk production, etc. There is also a notable difference between technological cultivation (modern ways of growing flowers, for instance), which aims at sensational, extreme effects from the viewpoint of breaking records, and the historical methods of cultivation as practised in China for thousands of years; it is the same difference as that between the manufactured article and the living work of art.

The product of technology has a universal, not an individual character. To be sure, technology can be employed to produce a unique construct in an historical process of creation. But technology as such aims at types and at mass-production. The limitation of technology by its attachment to the universal renders it accessible to all peoples in its unrestricted transferability. It is not bound to cultural presuppositions. Hence, in itself, it is something inexpressive, impersonal, inhuman. Its character as a construct of the understanding confines it to the understanding that is the same everywhere, although something more than mere technology always makes itself felt in the 'spirit' of discoveries and in particular constructions.

(3) *At any given moment technology is bound to substances and forces which are limited:* Technology needs substances and forces with which it operates. In so far as these are available to man in limited quantities only, e.g. coal, petroleum, ores—it uses up what it cannot replace. The day will come when they are at an end, unless new sources of energy are discovered. We think of atomic energy, but we do not know how far the ores will go from which it is obtained.

In addition to the sources of energy available from the surface of the earth, which are for the most part limited and not to be recovered once they have been used up, the possibility of using solar energy may be considered. It is already accessible to us indirectly through water-power, which is itself limited but perpetually renewed. Whether it will ever be possible to utilise solar energy directly is an open question for future technology. Beyond this, deeper and more extensive boring into the earth's surface is conceivable.

In practice we have not yet reached the end, the cellar of mankind is still full. But where calculations can be made—as for coal and petroleum—the end is imminent within an historically comparatively short time.

If, however, the energies necessary to technology had been used up, this would indeed mean the end of the Age of Technology, but human existence would not, on that account, have ceased. The human population of the earth would decrease greatly in numbers and would live under the presuppositions with which all previous historical epochs managed, without coal and petroleum, without modern technology.

(4) *Technology is bound to human beings, through whose labour it is realised:* Human beings must desire, and must be prepared for, service. What man's humanity leads him to demand will decide, when the limit has been reached, whether he no longer wishes to live or whether he will revolt at the risk of his life. Then either the running of the machinery of technology will be upset or brought to a halt, or it will be reshaped under conditions laid down by humanity as such.

(5) *The course of technological invention is perhaps confined to a possible goal and predetermined by an end:* From time to time great new discoveries have come to pass, which, after a relative consummation of our cognition appeared to have been reached, have resulted in further groups of discoveries, of which we had no presentiment and for which they were the prerequisites. The diesel engine and the radio were new beginnings of this sort; now it seems as though atomic energy will be another. The limit to such new thrusts will have been reached when everything accessible to man has been made use of. Up to now, the technological process as a whole has proceeded at increasing, break-neck speed over a period of rather more than a century and a half. It may look as though the end has been fundamentally reached. If the end were already here in essentials, there would still remain the gigantic qualitative intensification to be brought about by the transformation of the whole of the earth's surface into a single field of utilisation.

No proof can be given of a potential consummation or end of technological inventions. But there are indications and probabilities: Comparison of the number of new inventions prior to 1939 in the USA, England, Germany, France and Russia reveals such immense disparities that the situation can only be described as one of paralysis in certain regions, and eruption in others. The conditions and opportunities and the common 'spirit' within a population play such an important role, that the ease with which this spirit can be destroyed places the whole activity of invention on an insecure footing. Perhaps technology itself has an unfavourable retroaction on men: The constrained life occasioned by technology causes the extinction of the prerequisite for scientific-technological evolution, a crucial factor in which is freedom of spirit. A prodigious dissimilarity is already manifest between the great inventors and entrepreneurs of the nineteenth century and the organised and increasingly anonymous forward drive of today. The new tendency to withhold publicity from research work and invention of military importance might be a symptom of the end, especially in view of the unpredictable compass of the sphere of research involved.

3. PERCEPTION OF THE DEMONISM OF TECHNOLOGY

The word 'demonism' is not intended to imply that demons are at work. There are no demons. The word refers rather to something created by man and yet unwilled; something coercive, which has consequences for the whole of existence; the resistant that remains impenetrable; that which takes place at the backdoor, so to speak; the unmanifest.

At an early stage, men of vision were seized with horror of the technological world, without really understanding it. Goethe's attacks upon Newton are only intelligible in terms of the upheaval produced in him by the exact sciences through his unconscious knowledge of the catastrophe which was even then beginning to threaten the world of man. J. Burckhardt had an intense dislike of railways and tunnels and yet made use of them. Men deprived of their handicraft and their livelihood by machines, destroyed machines.

In opposition to this view, there stood the creed of progress, which foresaw nothing but good fortune from the new knowledge of nature and from technology. This creed was blind. For it saw only misuse within technology, which seemed to be penetrable and capable of correction. It did not see the more profound perils hidden in technology. The creed of progress failed to recognise that progress was limited to knowledge and technology and that this could not possibly lead to progress in the sum-total of humanity. Today what has been called the demonism of technology is clearly revealed. Let us summarise these unexpected inversions, which turn upon man out of technology, in a few propositions that have already been stated:

A growing proportion of work leads to the mechanisation and automatisation of the people doing it. It is not the easing of the stubborn labour of working up nature that determines work, but the transformation of man into a component of the machine.

Mechanisation of the instruments of work, with the accompanying complication, enlargement and necessity for collaboration, results in an organisation which not only surpasses all earlier forms in its compass, but is radically different, because the whole of human existence—and not merely a sector for particular purposes—is slowly drawn into this organisation.

Technological thinking spreads to all spheres of human action. The revolution goes as far as the sciences; it is manifest in the technicisation of medicine, in the industrialisation of research into nature, in organisational arrangements, which lead, in a number of sciences, to research being carried out in factory-like organisms. Circumstances demand it, if the desired success is to be achieved.

In consequence of the fact that the fashioning of life has become the work of machines, the whole of society is transformed into one great machine, into a single organisation embracing the whole of life. The bureaucracies of Egypt, or the Roman Empire, were only precursors of the modern civil service State. From now on, everything that wishes to be effective has to be fashioned after the pattern of the machine, that is, it has to take on an exact, constrained character and be bound by outward rules. The greatest power emanates from the greatest and most perfectly evolved machine.

The consequences of this mechanisation are the outcome of the absolute paramountcy of mechanical constraint, of calculability and dependability. Everything belonging to the realm of the soul or of faith, on the other hand, is admissible only on condition that it is of utility to the purposes of the machine. Man himself becomes one of the raw materials to be purposefully worked over. Hence that which was previously the substance and meaning of the whole—man—becomes a means. A veil of humaneness is permitted, indeed fostered and, in speech, put forward as the cardinal concern; but humaneness is radically violated where the purpose demands it. The greatest power is attendant upon the greatest ruthlessness. Therefore the cultural heritage, in so far as it contains absolute demands, is destroyed; men are turned into a heap of sand, which is all the more easily made use of the more destitute of origins it is. The feeling for life divorces life in the service of the machine from private life. But this private life itself becomes empty, free time is also mechanised, enjoyment becomes another type of work.

The technological mechanism is able to coerce men in masses as never before. For example, the original liberation of the spirit through the omnipresence of news is turned into the dominance of all through controlled news. The will of the State, through the communications system, can make itself effective at any moment over wide areas, right into every home.

Technology renders everyone dependent in his vital existence upon the functioning of the apparatus that has been built up. When this apparatus breaks down the life of comfort is immediately reduced to one of utter destitution, such was unknown in the past. Man is then more at the mercy of circumstances than the peasant in his natural existence. There are no further reserves.[2]

One thing is certain: Technology is in the process of transforming man himself, along with his whole working existence. Man can no longer extricate himself from the technology to which he himself gave birth. It is certain too that technology brings not only incalculable opportunities, but also incalculable perils. Technology has become an independent, impetuous force. Man has fallen into its clutches without noticing the fact or how it happened. And who today dare say that he can penetrate the obscurity of these events! Yet the demonism of technology is only to be vanquished by following the road that leads to our penetration of it. Whatever mischief it gives rise to may perhaps be within our power to master. Organisation of the market, for example, can afford deliverance from temporary want and then enable a free market to be re-established, instead of ending in annihilation, in which there is nothing more to distribute. But again every plan conceals the possibility of that 'demonism', of the unforeseen. Technological mastery of the mischief wrought by technology may add to this mischief. Absolute technocracy is, for its part, an impossibility.

To look upon the task of vanquishing technology by means of technology itself as one that can be achieved in toto will open up a fresh road to calamity. The fanaticism of narrow judgement abandons the technologically possible in favour of an alleged technology. But the question remains as to how man is to impose himself upon technology, which has become his master. The fate of man depends upon the fashion in which he masters the consequences of technology for his life (from the arrangement of its whole structure, as it presents itself at any particular time, to personal conduct at every hour of the day).

All the elements of technology combine with connexions whose origins lie elsewhere to confer upon man the consciousness, in the lucidity of contemporary understanding, of being at the mercy of an uncanny process that is the inexorable and compelling outcome of man's own actions.

Taking it all in all, the event of technology, because its obscurity has not been penetrated, is not only a fatality but also a task. The projects of phantasy are at the same time like invitations to humanity to become their master. Are all the potentialities of man as an individual to cease, is meditation to vanish from the earth? Does not man possess an origin which renders everything technological ultimately conditional upon him, instead of man becoming the slave of technology?

The reality of technology gave rise to the monstrous break in the history of mankind—whose ultimate consequences no phantasy can anticipate, although we ourselves are in the midst of it—that consists in the mechanisation and technicisation of human life.

This much is in any case obvious: Technology is only a means, in itself it is neither good nor evil. Everything depends upon what man makes of it, for what purpose it serves him, under what conditions he places it. The question is, what kind of man will take possession of it, what sort of creature will man prove himself to be through the use he makes of it. Technology is independent of what can be done with it; as an autonomous entity it is an empty power, in the last resort a paralysing triumph of the means over the end. Is it possible for technology, released from human meaning, to become a frenzy in the hands of monsters—or for the earth, together with its human population, to be reduced to the level of material for a single, gigantic factory, for the whole world to become an ant-heap that has transformed everything into a part of itself and lives on only as a cycle of production and consumption in the idle running of a contentless process? The understanding may construe it as possible; the consciousness of our humanity will always say: in its entirety this is impossible.

Thought alone will never master technology. The world historical decision as to the shape in which man's possibilities are afforded him under the radically new conditions of his life, will be reached now and in the coming centuries. All previous attempts at the realisation of man are faced with the question of what they still mean to us, how they can be repeated, and what account they give of themselves.

Philosophy must look this reality in the eye. It is true that it engenders only ideas, an inner attitude, judgements of value, and possibilities for the individual; but the individual may, incalculably, become a salient factor in the march of events.

NOTES

1   (Page 104): My book *Descartes und die Philosophie,* Berlin 1937; French translation, *Descartes et la Philosophie,* Paris 1938.

2   (Page 138): To elucidate such tendencies means to demonstrate possibilities, the compass of whose realisation remains uncertain. It is a different matter to treat the technological world as a whole as something that has been seen through, whether as the manifestation of a new heroic figure of humanity, or as the work of the devil. The demonism of technology is then substantiated into something really demonic; with this interpretation, the meaning of labour is either heightened, or denied altogether, technology's world of work is either glorified or repudiated. Both arise out of the possibilities inherent in technological labour. But these opposed possibilities are both fallacious in their absolutisation. This is the manner in which they are presented by the brothers Jünger in writings that make a strong impression on the reader.

Ernst Jünger—in his book *Der Arbeiter, 3. Auflage,* Hamburg 1932—sketched a visionary picture of the technological world: labour as total mobilisation, culminating in the battle of equipment—the figure of the worker hard as bronze—the sense of the nihilistic, aimless, intrinsically destructive. Jünger adumbrates the 'figure of the worker' as the future lord of the earth. The latter is beyond humanity and barbarism, beyond individual and mass. Work is his life-form, he knows himself responsible in the total fabric of work. Technology objectifies everything as a means to power. Through it, man becomes master of himself and of the earth. Man, as this new man, as the figure of the worker, acquires a countenance bearing the stamp of rigidity. He no longer asks: why and to what purpose? He wills and believes, irrespective of the contents which this volition and faith give themselves.

Friedrich Georg Jünger (*Über die Perfektion der Technik,* Frankfurt 1944), on the other hand, presents a desolate, hopeless picture of technology: The elemental, coerced by technology, spreads precisely within technology. Rational thinking, itself so poor in elemental forces, here sets huge elemental forces in motion, but through coercion, by hostile forcible means. 'The industrial landscape has something volcanic about it', all the phenomena of a volcanic eruption recur in it: 'Lava, ashes, fumes, smoke, night-clouds lit up by fire, and widespread devastation.'

F. G. Jünger impugns the thesis that technology diminishes man's labour and increases his leisure. He rightly points out that there is no question today of a decrease in the labour-quantum. But on the whole it is certainly incorrect to say, as he does, that every seeming reduction of work is bought at the expense of an increase at another point. When he contests the thesis that technology increases wealth, he does so with a leap into a different signification of 'wealth', according to which wealth is a being, not a having. It is also no stricture on technology, when Jünger erroneously imputes to rationalisation the want (entirely due to military destruction) which it is intended to combat. His topical depiction of this organisation of want hits the nail on the head: It does not create wealth, but is a procedure for the distribution of what little there is in times of shortage. The organisation of distribution in an economy operating at a loss remains inviolable amidst the ruins; it grows all the more powerful the greater the poverty becomes. Its collapse comes about only when there is nothing left to distribute. Such statements obviously relate not to technology, but to a terrible phenomenon resulting from the war, which we happen to be living through today, and which has been fallaciously construed as the necessary outcome of technology.

The two formulations of the brothers Jünger are contrary in character in respect of the general tone of their evaluation of technology—but they are similar to one another in their mode of thought. This is analogous to mythological thinking: not cognition, but an image—not analysis, but the adumbration of a vision—but through the medium of modern categories of thought, so that the reader may be of the opinion that he is dealing with rational cognition.

Hence the one-sidedness and fervour. There is no sifting of the evidence, no contrary instances are adduced save those selected in such a manner that, by their demolition, the speaker increases the height of his own platform.

There is no sobriety of cognition, but an emotionalism which is not overcome either in the comportment of exactly formulating sobriety, nor in the cold climate of dictatorial observations and valuations. It is above all an aesthetic attitude that draws its sustenance from delight in the spiritual product, and which has indeed, in the case of Ernst Jünger, led to works of the highest literary merit.

Seriously speaking, there is no element of truth in thinking of this kind. But it is seductive on that inordinately modern plane, on which reflection has been lost, methodical cognition abandoned, basic knowledge, or the life-long search for it, cast aside. Hence the tone of decisive authority lacks any authentic nexus perceptible to the reader. It is an easy matter to vary the content, indeed the whole approach and atmosphere: the way of thinking remains; subject, opinion and aim alter.

10

THE PRESENT SITUATION OF THE WORLD

INTRODUCTION

Of the past we have but an incomplete recollection, the future is obscure. Of the present alone we might expect to form a lucid picture. After all, we are in the midst of it. But it is precisely the present as such that is opaque to us, for it would grow clear only through complete knowledge of the past, by which it is borne, and of the future, which it conceals within it. We should like to achieve awareness of the situation of our epoch. But this situation contains hidden possibilities, which will only become visible once they have been realised.

What is historically new and, for the first time in history, decisive about our situation is the real unity of mankind on the earth. The planet has become for man a single whole dominated by the technology of communications; it is 'smaller' than the Roman Empire was formerly.

The course of development since the Age of Discovery, four hundred years ago, led up to this moment. Until the end of the nineteenth century, however, history remained for us essentially European history. To the European consciousness of that time, the rest of the world was colonial territory, of secondary importance, destined as a source of booty for Europe. It was only unintentionally that the foundations of the world history which is at present unfolding were already laid at that time by the powers that were seeking to win the great spaces of the earth for themselves. In the First World War these spaces were already brought into play. It was still a European war, however. America withdrew again. It was only in the Second World War that all of them, the whole globe, were committed to the full. The war in Eastern Asia was as grave a matter as the war in Europe. In fact it was the first real World War. World history, as one single history of the whole world, had begun. From our vantage point, the interlude of previous history has the appearance of an area scattered with mutually independent endeavours, as the multiple origin of the potentialities of man. Now the whole world has become the problem and task. With this a total metamorphosis of history has taken place.

The essential fact is: There is no longer anything outside. The world is closed. The unity of the earth has arrived. New perils and new opportunities are revealed. All the crucial problems have become world problems, the situation a situation of mankind.

A. CHARACTERISATION OF THE PRESENT SITUATION

1. *The masses have become a decisive factor in the historical process*

All previous history occurred under conditions that were relatively stable in comparison with those of today. The peasantry represented the mass of the population and remained fairly constant in its mode of life, despite catastrophic political events. It constituted the unhistorical substance of the population. The agrarian crises that occurred again and again in historical times brought upheavals, but no radical changes. The mutations of social conditions proceeded slowly and only affected individual classes and groups, within an overall condition that was felt to be permanent. As far as their consciousness was concerned, men remained comparatively secure in immutable orders, even if they had to starve. They endured and submitted, and lived in a pervading religious faith.

Today things are different. Social conditions are in ceaseless flux. This flux has become conscious. The whole population of the earth has been torn out of its immemorial traditional orders and forms of consciousness. Consciousness of security is constantly diminishing. Human masses are becoming more integral. Everyone is learning to read and write. If they did not they could not come to knowledge, could not acquire a language in which to express their will, nor make their influence felt.

The masses are becoming a decisive factor. To be sure, the individual is more powerless than ever, but the individual as a member of the mass, the 'we', seems to be gaining possession of a will.

This will cannot grow originally in an anonymous mass, however. It is aroused and guided by propaganda. The masses need ideas and slogans. They have to be told what they want. But the soil for that which is told them must be ready within them. The statesman, the thinker, the artist, the poet must appeal to forces in the masses, if he wishes to have any effect. What forces these will be cannot be stated in advance. Leaders are characterised by the impulses, value judgements, and passions to which they appeal. But what they stimulate in the masses has a retroactive effect on the leaders. The masses determine what the leaders themselves must be and what they must become in reaction. They are exponents of the will of the masses, unless they become dictators over masses of directed slaves.

Mass[1] is a concept capable of several interpretations, however. The mass means either the bulk of the population (and as such is present at all times), or the momentary expression and comportment of people under the influence of suggestion (and as such appears as suddenly as it vanishes again), or it is the inferiority of the many, of the average, whose existence determines everything by the mass pressure which it exercises (and as such is the manifestation of an historical situation under certain conditions and by no means definitively inferior).

A distinction must be made between mass and people:

The people is subdivided into orders, is conscious of itself in ways of life, modes of thought, and cultural heritage. A people is something substantial and qualitative, it possesses a communal atmosphere; the individual from the people has a personal character that is partly derived from the strength of the people by which he is borne.

The mass, on the other hand, is not subdivided, is unconscious of itself, uniform and quantitative, devoid of specific character and cultural heritage, without foundations and empty. It is the object of propaganda, destitute of responsibility, and lives at the lowest level of consciousness.

Masses arise where men come to be without an authentic world, without provenance or roots, disposable and exchangeable. In consequence of technology this state of affairs is growing more and more widespread: the narrowed horizon, life that does not look ahead and is devoid of effective recollection, the compulsion of meaningless labour, amusement in the dissipation of leisure, excitation of the nerves masquerading as life, deception in the illusion of love, fidelity and trust, betrayal, especially in youth, resulting in cynicism: no one who has been involved in this sort of thing can still respect himself. *Via* despair in the garb of liveliness and obstinacy the road leads into oblivion and indifference, into the condition in which corporate human life is a sandheap that can be made use of, set to work, or deported, and that is treated in the light of qualities which can be given a number and counted by means of tests.

The individual is both people and mass at the same time. He feels quite differently, however, where he is people and where he is mass. The situation forces him into the mass, man holds fast to the people. Illustrated by some comparative examples: As mass I thrust into the universal, into the current fashion, into the cinema, into the mere today; as people I want corporeal, irreplaceable reality, the living theatre, the historically present—as mass I applaud the star on the conductor's dais; as people I experience in my intimate self the music that soars above life—as mass I think in numbers, accumulate, level; as people I think in hierarchies of value and in structure.

A distinction is to be made between mass and public.

Public is the first step along the path of the transformation of people into mass. It is the echo of poetry, art, literature. When the people no longer lives comprehensively out of its community, there develops a multiplicity of separate publics, amorphous like the mass, but a forum for spiritual things in free competition. For whom does the writer write when he is free? Today he no longer writes for the people, and not yet for the mass. He woos and wins his public, if he is lucky. The people possesses enduring books that accompany its life; the public changes, is without character. But where there is public there is still a lively open forum.

The transformation of the people into public and mass can no longer be brought to a stop. The situation compels the progress of events through the medium of the masses. But mass is not something definitive. It is the mode of existence during the dissolution of humanity. Every individual in it remains a human being. The question is, to what extent is the individual and his intimate world—under the epithet 'private world' today so often the object of overweening contempt—giving birth to the new beginnings which may ultimately lead to the recovery of humanity out of the mass.

We can see the past by its pinnacles. Then it is as if, on the broad substratum of mass-existence, of which little historical information has come down to us, lofty spiritual creation made proper history. It is the life and activities of individuals, who, in the continuity that runs through the ages, call to each other as friends and foes. Every individual has his community, however, the human beings who belong to him and from whom he hears, to whom he is important, he has his circle of friends, his people in the shape of language and spiritual heritage, his public.

Now today this community is inevitably the world that is determined by the masses. That alone will remain which is assimilated by the masses. The path of history today runs inexorably via the masses, or seems to do so. Popular education may put the multitude on the road to spiritual nobility—a de facto process of natural selection, which is going on all the time, may engender a new factual aristocracy without hereditary privileges—the abolition of social repression and political terror may cause the disappearance of the rebellious and negativist way of thinking, by which the masses have, for the moment, been seized.

The school, natural selection operating in free competition, and continual improvement of the still unjust human conditions in the direction of greater social justice, may, to the accompaniment of constant tensions, blaze the trail to growing freedom.

Their failure may open the door to inconceivable horrors of abysmal mass existence. Everyone who wants to be of some account desires to go with the masses. Many thinkers presuppose that the masses are making for some particular point, and that the truth is to know this and act accordingly. Human masses as such, however, are not a person, they do not know or want anything; they are without content and a tool for anyone who flatters their universal psychological impulses and passions. Human masses are easily able to lose the power of deliberation, rush into the intoxication of change for the sake of change, and follow the Pied Piper, who leads them into the inferno. It is easy for the conditions of interaction between unreasoning masses and directing tyrants to develop. But it is also possible that the rationally striving labour of the real spirit may develop in the masses themselves, this labour that takes place in gradual changes of conditions, which no one observes in their entirety, but in which so much reason prevails that an ordered existence, free work and free creation become possible in an incalculable degree.

The world would ascend to a pinnacle of history wherever that which was formerly confined to the aristocracy became real in the masses themselves: education, disciplined moulding of the life and thought of the individual, capacity to learn and to win a part in the spirit, to reflect and deliberate and to find the rational solution historically in the most powerful tensions of men who confront one another at once critically and in solidarity.

Today, however, the monstrous peril is this: Whereas the events of all former history had little effect on the substance of humanity, this substance itself seems now to be in flux, to be threatened at its core. The instability in everything sets the problem of what man, on the basis of knowledge and technology, and out of the origin of his nature, will make of his existence. In this the situation forces us to follow the unavoidable path of the masses.

2. The dissolution of traditional values

Formerly, religions were bound up with the totality of social conditions. Religion was borne by these conditions, which, in turn, it justified. The conduct of everyday life was embedded in religion. The latter was taken for granted as the omnipresent breath of life. Today religion is a matter of choice. It is retained in a world which is no longer permeated by it. Not only do the various religions and confessions stand side by side and, by the mere fact of doing so, cast doubt upon one another; in addition, religion itself has become a special domain, unconnected with the rest of life. The traditional religions are becoming untenable to an increasingly large number of people: almost all dogmas and revelation in its exclusive claim to absolute truth are disbelieved. The *de facto* unchristian lives of the majority of Christians is a criticism to which it is impossible to close one's ears. A Christian life in its manifestness and unquestionable truth may perhaps still be real today as a compelling model for imitation, but it no longer exists for the masses.

In all ages in which men have thought and written since the Axial Period, there has been doubt. But now the dissolution is no longer an affair of isolated individuals and small circles. It has become a ferment in the whole population. Although men have at all times been ready to lose their faith, this apostasy never involved more than a narrow sector. Under the conditions of work and life in ages past, the population remained secure in its religious bonds. The conditions of the Age of Technology, however, have proved conducive to an outbreak of nihilistic possibilities in the whole of the population, that has degenerated into a mass.

The ever-present readiness to loss of faith is today fostered by spiritual movement as such, by misunderstood science—by misunderstanding on the part of the masses. Bacon's words have been proved right: Half knowledge leads to unbelief, whole knowledge to belief.

Our era's growing lack of faith has brought nihilism. Nietzsche is its prophet. He was the first to see it in its calamitous magnitude, to disclose it in all its manifestations, to suffer it himself as the victim of his time, to seek with a mighty effort to overcome it—in vain.

Nihilism, which was previously powerless in its sporadic beginnings, has become a dominant mode of thought. Today it seems possible that the whole of the cultural heritage since the Axial Period will be lost, that history from Homer to Goethe will sink into oblivion. This looks like a threat of the downfall of humanity; in any case, it is impossible to foresee or imagine what will happen to man under these conditions.

Today there is passing through the world the evil spell of a philosophy that finds truth in nihilism, that summons man to a strangely heroic existence without consolation and without hope, in affirmation of all harshness and mercilessness, in what is alleged to be a purely worldly humanism. This is mere repetition of the ideas of Nietzsche without his poignant tension in the will to overcome it.

Man cannot endure the fundamental attitude of nihilism, however. In the situation of universal lack of faith man succumbs rather to a blind faith. Such a faith is an immense substitute, is fragile, and suddenly discarded again; it may embrace the most singular contents; it may be, as it were, an empty faith of mere motion. It interprets itself as a feeling of oneness with nature, with world history. It takes concrete shape in programmes of salvation. It encloses itself in pseudo-scientific total conceptions, in Marxism, in psychoanalysis, in the theory of race (whose scientific elements, which seldom emerge with clarity, are at the same time beyond doubt).[2]

The following are some typical manifestations of this dissolution of faith:

Thinking in ideologies.—An ideology is a complex of ideas or notions which represents itself to the thinker as an absolute truth for the interpretation of the world and his situation within it; it leads the thinker to accomplish an act of self-deception for the purpose of justification, obfuscation, evasion, in some sense or other to his own advantage. Hence the apprehension of a way of thinking as ideology means the unveiling of error and the unmasking of evil. Bestowal of the epithet ideology upon a way of thinking is to reproach it with untruth and untruthfulness and therefore constitutes the most violent attack.

Our era has both given birth to ideologies and seen through them. But the profound insights that have been achieved in this direction, from Hegel to

Marx and Nietzsche, have become a brutal weapon in the war of words leading to the breaking off of communication. The method of this attack is directed against the opponent as such, against all views other than one's own.
However, those very people who spurn everything that is believed, thought,
and imagined as being ideology, are frequently themselves possessed by the
most stubborn ideology consisting in this mode of interpretation.

The high daring of self-reflection, that precondition of all truthfulness,
has degenerated along the path of ideological theory. Certainly an infinite
number of perversions, repressions and obfuscations have taken place; they
have won sociological significance as the type-view of a whole social class:
for example, untruthfulness with regard to matters of sex in the bourgeois
era, the self-justification of economic success, the legitimation of the *status
quo* on the part of the privileged. But it is absolutely necessary to unveil the
method of unveiling itself. From the heights reached by Kierkegaard and
Nietzsche our age has carried the thought that unveils to the very limit of
this intellectual process of unmasking; but now it has ceased to be an unveiling and has become a malicious attack; it is not critical investigation, but
suggestion, not empirical exposition, but mere assertion with some degree
of plausibility. Thus the method of penetrating cognition of truth has ended
up as the abasements of psychoanalysis and vulgar Marxism. When the
thinking that unveils becomes itself dogmatic, it completely loses the truth.
Everything is ideology and this thesis itself is an ideology. Nothing is left.

But perhaps the formation of ideologies really is particularly great in its
compass today. For in hopelessness there arises the need for illusion, in the
aridity of personal existence the need for sensation, in powerlessness the
need to violate those who are even more powerless.

The manner in which malice salves its conscience in this process is exemplified in the following arguments:

If the State commits blatant crimes, the argument runs: The State is sinful
from its origin, I too am a sinner, I obey the commandments of the State,
even when they are sinful, because I am no better and because national duty
demands it. But this is all to the advantage of the man who speaks in these
terms; he joins in the deed and enjoys its fruits, he exhibits his anguish in
the contorted features that are not true anguish, but merely play-acting. He
avails himself of sinfulness as a relief.

One takes part in frightful deeds and says: Life is harsh. The lofty goals
of the nation, of the faith, of the finally free and just world that is coming

demand harshness. One is harsh toward oneself with a safe, partial harshness which is enjoyed and which furnishes sham proof of the genuineness of one's demand for harshness, while in reality it covers up one's own unconditional will to existence and power.

One is conscious of one's own mendacity in the enjoyment of chance situations of advantage while these terrible things are happening. Now one wants to see that which one is not prepared to do oneself, does not wish to experience or suffer, is not capable of being oneself. One craves martyrs. One waxes enthusiastic about the possibility of martyrdom, as though this almost made one a martyr. One attacks others for not being martyrs. One intoxicates oneself with the destiny of men who appear to conform to the image of one's craving, but one has no desire ever to be like that oneself. This distortion of the facts goes so far that later on one sets oneself up as a pattern and becomes a fervent advocate against one's environment of that which, as a contemporary, one paid almost no attention to and, above all, did not do oneself.

We will not continue. There is no end to such illuminating instances. The dissolution of traditional contents is revealed in the mere fact that this type of intellectual unmasking is making itself universal. The age invents the theory to fit its actions. But the theory itself straightway becomes a means of intensifying the evil it is combating.

Simplification.—Simplicity is the shape of that which is true. Simplification is the violence that takes the place of lost simplicity. Simplicity is infinite in its capacity for interpretation, a world *in parvo.* replete and mobile. Simplification is finite in nature, the string by which one is guided like a puppet, incapable of development, empty and rigid.

Ours is the age of simplifications. Slogans, universal theories that explain everything, gross antitheses, meet with success. Whereas simplicity crystallised into mythical symbols, simplification adheres to pseudo-scientific absolutes.

Life out of negation.—Where faith is no longer the basis of the content of life, nothing is left but the vacuum of negation. When one is dissatisfied with oneself, the fault must be someone else's. If one is nothing, one is at least anti-. All ills are heaped onto a phantom that takes its name either from historical formations as they once presented themselves to theoretical cognition: everything is the fault of capitalism, liberalism, Marxism, Christianity, etc.—or else those unable to defend themselves are picked on in individual shapes and serve as scapegoats: everything is the fault of the Jews, the Germans, etc.

All the indissolubly intricate ramifications of causality or responsibility to which blame attaches are uncritically reduced to the blame of one single alien entity that is not oneself. All that matters is to possess the means of giving expression to its no and of attacking it in general. In this process intellectual concepts become banners and badges. Words are used like counterfeit coins, with their meaning reversed but with the emotions formerly attached to them preserved (liberty, fatherland, State, nation, empire, etc.). In the language that has been ruined by the sophistries of propaganda it is finally impossible to tell what words really do mean. Speech deteriorates into a welter of vague phrases, destined only to give expression to a perpetual no, to an anti-, that does not follow from any real pro.

B. WHAT GAVE RISE TO THE PRESENT SITUATION?

The origin of the crisis cannot be apprehended in a single cause. In the infinite web of the material and spiritual interconnexions of historical change we can only bring to mind individual threads. Every total and monocausal interpretation proves fallacious.

We cannot even visualise the fact of an age as a whole, but only more or less essential particular phenomena within this age. The more we get to know, the greater for our consciousness becomes the enigma of the whole.

Now the dividing-line that starts off the Age of Technology cuts unusually deep. It leaves no aspect of human existence undisturbed. Everything of which it is not actually the cause is modified by it. But we must avoid tracing the intricate course of human affairs back to this one solitary factor. Long before technology had these effects, movements were afoot from which the present spiritual situation springs. The fact that technology became operative and was universally adopted was due to this spiritual world, this way of thought and of life, which it found waiting for it.

The Age of Technology certainly brought about the tremendous crisis. Marx and Engels were able to gain an intrinsically illuminating piece of knowledge because they saw this new factor. This new factor was by no means a spiritually new humanity, however. That was the great mistake.

People talked about a new human consciousness, about new man, about spiritual creation, about truth and salvation, they looked into a luminous future—yet this kind of talk was nothing more than the accomplishment of the *tabula rasa*, a symptom of growing loss of consciousness. That which was devoid of any informing idea was noisily propagated as idea. Then, after great men had taken the wrong path, the world became a theatre for petty place-seekers and obedient intriguers, who knew no difference between true and false or good and evil, but were merely tools submissive to the function of power.

Or else people talked about lack of faith as being the consequence of technology. The latter was supposed to have deprived men of their roots, to have torn them out of all security, placed them, as it were, in an empty space, dispossessed them of air and with it of breath and of their souls, and to have left nothing of them over save that which can be made use of in the operation of machines.

The events of the Age of Technology, however, though they were furthered by the consequences of technology, had quite different presuppositions. The spiritual movements that led up to ourselves began long before the world was altered by technology. The great change that introduced the Enlightenment at the end of the seventeenth century, the French Revolution, the equivocal consciousness of crisis and consummation that informed German philosophical idealism, these are steps in our direction, independent of technology.

The Enlightenment. Lack of faith is deemed to be a consequence of the Enlightenment. Because men know too much, are acquainted with the dangerous books and are daily surrounded by the aura of their language in the press, they no longer believe. The discovery of the world of alien cultures and religious convictions has brought scepticism toward one's own faith through comparison. But this road need not have led to loss of faith. Only half and misconstrued enlightenment leads into nothingness, whereas total and unrestricted enlightenment renders the enigma of the origin really audible for the first time.

Carried further, this thesis propounded the view that a dialectic of spiritual evolution, impelled by Christian motives, led from Christianity to such a radical illumination of truth that this religion brought about the reversal against itself, out of its own forces. But again this road need not have led to loss of faith. To be sure, dogmatic positions were lost in this transition process of painful and perilous melting down and recasting, but the transformation of Biblical religion remained a possibility.

The French Revolution. This event, which either gave expression to the modern crisis or set it in motion, is today still an object of contradictory interpretation:

Kant, deeply moved by the attempt of reason to stand on its own feet, never reversed his high appraisal of the outset: 'That will never be forgotten.' Burke, on the other hand, was from the very first moment a critic as perspicacious as he was hostile. One saw in this event the consummation of the wonderful developments and aspirations of the eighteenth century, the other the ruin and corruption of these same tendencies which, in the French Revolution, had run off the rails—a fatality by which the eighteenth century was being not consummated, but overwhelmed.

The French Revolution grew on the soil of feudalism and absolute monarchy; as an essential phenomenon, therefore, it is not a universally European process, but confined to regions of this particular type. The soul of England or of Switzerland remained unaffected by it.

Even on the soil of feudalism, however, it was an ambiguous manifestation, because, although it desired liberty and reason, it made room for despotism and violence. It determines our thinking in both directions: In the justice of the struggle against the evil of repression and exploitation, in the name of the rights of man and the liberty of every individual—and in the error of the opinion that the world as a whole can be founded on reason, instead of transforming by the use of reason historical bonds, authority and the order of values, without recourse to violence.

Founded with fanaticism in boundless belief in reason, it is not the fountainhead of modern freedom, whose roots lie rather in the continuity of genuine freedom in England, America, Holland and Switzerland. To this extent, notwithstanding the heroic upsurge of its beginning, it is the expression and origin of modern unbelief.

Philosophical idealism. The philosophy of German idealism—especially of Fichte and Hegel—brought about an enhancement of philosophical self-confidence, an alleged total knowledge that knows what God is and desires, and loses all capacity for astonishment because it fancies itself in possession of absolute truth. This kind of sham faith was bound to swing over to lack of faith. It is true that this philosophy unfolded in the particular, conceptions that can never be lost; it was one of the manifestations of human thought that possessed genius, and its speculative grandeur cannot be doubted. But the distrust of its world, which has erroneously spread to all German philosophy, is justified. Here the *hubris* and waywardness of genius became an unparalleled seduction. Whoever drunk of this potion became intoxicated, a promoter of ruin, through the fact that a spiritual firework of a high order caused loss of faith, which presupposes sobriety.

Even these facts, however—the Enlightenment, the French Revolution, and German philosophic idealism—are not sufficient to explain our spiritual situation. They themselves often seem less like the cause than the initial manifestation of the crisis. There remains the burning and inadequately answered question as to how lack of faith came about. The question contains the hope of mastering lack of faith through the right answer.

This urge would be deprived of all prospect of success if certain metaphysical interpretations of the course of history, and thereby of the provenance of our situation, were correct. An age of consummate perplexity is supposed to be the outcome of a loss of substance. A ceaseless total process is conceived of, that was finally put into words by Klages in the statement that during the nineteenth century the earth-essence deserted the planet.

Such an imprecise notion of a loss of substance seems, however, unacceptable. It is not an insight, but a metaphor for the radically pessimistic outlook. This sort of notion is more of an obfuscation than an illumination. Yet the idea of some unrecognised total process forces itself upon us again and again. Only it is neither a natural happening analogous to biological processes, nor in any other sense an objective, tangible happening; it is the Comprehensive, in which we are but which we do not recognise. It is the enigma of world history, which we deepen but do not dissolve, and in the excogitation of which we must not submit to any construct of thought as being supposedly necessary in its entirety; if we do we shall surrender both the openness of our possibilities of knowledge and the freedom of our inner being, of our choice and of our decision to a subordinate conception.

Preferable to any form of alleged total knowledge is the simple notion (which does not provide us with the key either): There is immutable evil in man, which has always led to the recurrence of senseless wars, but which has today brought about a quantitative increase both of their diffusion over the earth and of the measure of destruction they cause, the results of which give rise to the phenomena of both civilisational and spiritual disintegration.

No adequate answer is possible to the question of the provenance of crises and lack of faith, no matter whether it is sought along the path of empirical causality, intellectual understanding, or metaphysical interpretation.

C. SUMMARY

The importance of the fact that the whole of mankind, that all the old cultures, have been drawn into this one common stream of destruction or renewal has only become conscious during the last few decades. The older ones amongst us were, as children, still living entirely within the European consciousness. India and China were alien, untouched worlds of their own that one did not learn about in history. Anyone who felt dissatisfied, or for whom things were going badly, emigrated. The world was open.

In 1918 the following sentences of de Groot's in his book on China (Universism) still affected me deeply as something absolutely new:

> The universist system represents the highest point to which the spiritual culture of China has been able to evolve. The only power capable of undermining it and bringing about its downfall is sound science. If ever the time should come when science is seriously cultivated in China, there can be no doubt that a complete revolution will take place in the whole of its spiritual life, which will either put China utterly out of joint or cause it to undergo a rebirth after which China will no longer be China and the Chinese no longer the Chinese. China herself possesses no second system with which to replace the old; consequently breakdown of the old would inevitably result in dissolution and anarchy, in short in the most complete fulfilment of their own sacred doctrine, according to which catastrophe and downfall are certain if mankind loses Tao. ... If it should be ordained in the order of the world that the horrible work of demolition is to take its course, so that the days of China's ancient universist culture are numbered—then at least let her last day not be also the day of the corruption of a people of millions, that has been cast into misfortune by foreign influences.

It is a remarkable world phenomenon that contemporaneously with and already prior to the emergence of the Age of Technology, a spiritual and psychical retrogression took place all over the world which has today become a European movement, as well. It is true that Europe continued to blossom spiritually for a short time when, after the seventeenth century, China and India were already going downhill. At the moment when these peoples were overpowered by the European technique of warfare, they were already lying at the nadir of their spiritual culture. Europe came up against a China and India that were not florescent, but very nearly oblivious of themselves.

Today, for the first time, there is a real unity of mankind which consists in the fact that nothing essential can happen anywhere that does not concern all. In this situation the technological revolution effected by the Europeans through science and discoveries is merely the material basis and precipitating cause of the spiritual catastrophe. To the success of the process of melting down and recasting that is now beginning, de Groot's remarks concerning China—once it is complete China will no longer be China, the Chinese no longer Chinese—may apply for the whole of mankind. Europe too will no longer be Europe, the Europeans will no longer be Europeans in the sense in which they felt themselves to be in de Groot's day. There will be new Chinese, new Europeans, however, whose image we cannot yet see.

Out of this experience of our historical situation as the turning-point of the ages, our gaze returns again and again. To the question: have such radical metamorphoses taken place before? our answer was: we know nothing of the events of the Promethean Age, when man first came into possession of his world through tools, fire and speech. But within history the greatest turning-point was the Axial Period, which we have discussed. If we have now entered into a new radical metamorphosis of humanity, this is no repetition of the Axial Period, but a happening that is different to its very roots.

First of all *outwardly*. Our Age of Technology is not merely relatively universal, like the events in those three mutually independent worlds of the Axial Period, but absolutely universal, because it is planetary. It is not a process that is mutually related in meaning, yet separate in fact; it is a single whole in continual mutual intercourse. Today it is taking place with consciousness of universality. It is bound to bring a different decision concerning humanity from the one that was reached then. For whereas all previous periods of crucial change were local and susceptible of being supplemented by other happenings, in other places, in other worlds, so that even if they failed the possibility of the salvation of man by other movements was left open, what is happening now is absolutely decisive. There is no longer anything outside it.

Inwardly, however, something manifestly quite different from the Axial Period is involved. Then the plenitude, now the emptiness. If we become aware of the turning-point, we know that we are only in the preparatory stage. The present age is one of real technological and political remoulding, not yet of eternal spiritual creations. We may more readily liken ourselves, with our grandiose scientific discoveries and technological inventions, to the epoch of the invention of tools and weapons, of the first use of domestic animals and horses, than with the age of Confucius, Buddha and Socrates. The fact that we are tackling the high task of reconstructing humanity from its origin, that we sense the fateful question as to how we can, in faith, become specifically human beings, is, however, evinced in the current tendency, which is becoming increasingly strong, to look back toward our origin. The deep matrix from which we sprang, the specific reality which was concealed by the veil of secondary cultural constructions, turns of phrase, conventions and institutions, is to become articulate once more. In this process of self-understanding through the knowledge of whence we come the mirror of the great Axial Period of humanity will perhaps, once more, prove one of the essential assurances.

NOTES

1 (Page 145): Concerning the 'mass': Le Bon, *La psychologie des foules,* Paris 1895. Ortega y Gasset, *La rebelión de las masas,* 1930.
2 (Page 149): See note 4, Chapter 11.

11

THE FUTURE

A conception of history intended to cover the totality of human affairs must take in the future. This was the case with the Christian view of world history as running from the Creation to the Last Judgement.

This contains a truth that holds good even if the Christian view of history is disbelieved. For to renounce the future is to render the historical picture of the past final and complete and hence to falsify it. No philosophical consciousness of history is possible without consciousness of the future.

The future is not accessible to research however. Research can be carried out only on that which has reality, in other words, on that which has already happened. Yet the future lies concealed in the past and the present; we see it and think it out in real possibilities. In fact we are at all times sustained by a consciousness of the future.

We ought not to allow this consciousness of the future to run wild in arbitrary phantasies of our desires or terrors, but to give it solid foundations, first by research into the past and then by the pure apprehension of the present. What matters is to discern, in and through the struggles of the day, the more profound struggles that are being waged round humanity itself.

Under these circumstances, the objectivity of a history that deals merely with that which is past, and remains withdrawn from the struggle of the day, is no longer appropriate; instead the present itself becomes the origin and goal of historical consciousness as well.

But it is as crucially necessary to look at the present from the viewpoint of the future as from that of the past. The ideas we have of the future guide the manner in which we look into the past and the present.

Prognostic historical thinking determines our actions. The soul shaken by concern and hope renders us clairvoyant. Or else we suppress the emergent images of possibilities and let things take their course.

Let us call to mind a few examples of earlier prognoses, the truth content of which is today already open to examination and which, in some cases, strike us as uncanny prophecies. Ever since the eighteenth century the future has been the object of conscious meditation and empirically founded vision. From then until our own time prognostication concerning the future has been a major literary theme.

During the eighteenth century, in the process of liberation from authorities that had lost their souls and been misused, at the time of the initial, unprecedented achievements of science and technology, of the increase of wealth, in the jubilation of this success, many men lived as though progress were assured, as though everything would continually improve. They lived free from concern about the future.

This changed after the French Revolution. Increasing pessimism regarding the future traversed the nineteenth century.

In 1825 Goethe already looked into the impending century of the machine. It will be the century of efficient intelligences, of practical people with a quick grasp of facts, who, equipped with greater mental agility, will feel themselves superior to the multitude, even though their gifts do not reach the highest level. Then, however, he had a vision of something worse: I see the time coming in which God will find no more joy in mankind and will have to obliterate it, in order to begin Creation afresh.

Tocqueville wrote in 1835 (*Democracy in America*, translated by Henry Reeve 1835; Oxford University Press edition, pp. 285 ff.):

The time will therefore come when one hundred and fifty millions of men will be living in North America, equal in condition, the progeny of one race, owing their origin to the same cause, and preserving the same civilisation, the same language, the same religion, the same habits, the same manners, and imbued with the same opinions, propagated under the same forms. The rest is uncertain, but this is certain; and it is a fact new to the world—a fact fraught with such portentous consequences as to baffle the efforts even of the imagination.

There are, at the present time, two great nations in the world which seem to tend toward the same end, although they started from different points: I allude to the Russians and the Americans. Both of them have grown up unnoticed; and while the attention of mankind was directed elsewhere, they have suddenly assumed the most prominent place among the nations; and the world learned their existence and their greatness at almost the same time.

All other nations seem to have nearly reached their natural limits, and only to be charged with the maintenance of their power; but these are still in the act of growth; all the others are stopped, or continue to advance with extreme difficulty; these are proceeding with ease and celerity along a path to which the human eye can assign no term. The American struggles against the natural obstacles which oppose him; the adversaries of the Russian are men; the former combats the wilderness and savage life; the latter, civilisation with all its weapons and its arts: the conquests of the one are therefore gained by the ploughshare; those of the other by the sword. The Anglo-American relies upon personal interest to accomplish his ends, and gives free scope to the unguided exertions and common sense of the citizens; the Russian centres all the authority of society in a single arm: the principal instrument of the former is freedom; of the latter servitude. Their starting-point is different, and their courses are not the same; yet each of them seems to be marked out by the will of Heaven to sway the destinies of half the globe.

Burckhardt wrote of the future for his *Weltgeschichtliche Betrachtungen* in the year 1870 (first printed in Werner Kaegi's edition, Bern 1941, p. 218):

Resignation will prevail instead of reasoning, the single whole instead of individuals and the many.

In place of culture, mere existence will once more occupy the stage. ...

The State will again exercise dominion over culture and even give the latter a manifold new orientation on the lines of its own taste. Perhaps culture will, of its own accord, turn to the State for instructions.

At the outset, the most severe and repeated reminders will be given that the business of earning a living and social intercourse are not the cardinal factors in human life.

A considerable proportion of the luxury pursuits of scientific research and communication, and also of the arts, is likely to die out; that which survives will have to double its exertions.

Harsh utilitarianism will be the dominant pattern of life.

Future wars will do everything else needed firmly to establish this state of affairs. The State itself will take on a physiognomy such that, for a long time, the representatives of other political viewpoints will be unable to gain possession of it.

Some sort of reaction on the part of free idealism will take place, but only at the cost of superhuman effort.

In 1872 he wrote in a letter: 'The ways of the army must now become the pattern for all existence ... in the machinery of the State and of government ... in school and cultural life. The most remarkable things will happen to the workers; I have a presentiment which sounds at the moment utterly crazy, but of which I cannot rid myself. The military State will have to become a large-scale manufacturer. The masses accumulated in the big workshops must not be left for ever to their want and their greed; a definite and supervised measure of misery, accompanied by promotion, and begun and concluded daily in uniform and to the roll of drums—that is what must logically come.'

Nietzsche adumbrated a picture of the age and of the future: The machine in its effect upon life and as a model for the whole of existence; the rise of the masses and their reduction of everything to the same level; the theatrical nature of this existence, in which everything is falsified and nothing is really valid any more; intoxication in place of reflection as an element of life—'God is dead'. Nihilism is raising its head: 'The whole of our European culture has for a long time been moving, with a torment of tension that is increasing from one decade to another, in the direction of catastrophe; like a river that wants to reach its end, that no longer reflects, that is afraid to reflect.'

Nietzsche drew a grotesque picture of the man of the last stages of the epoch to come:

The earth hath then become small, and on it there hoppeth the last man who maketh everything small. His species is ineradicable like that of the ground-flea; the last man liveth longest.

"We have discovered happiness", say the last men, and blink thereby ...

A little poison now and then: that maketh pleasant dreams. And much poison at last for a pleasant death.

One still worketh, for work is a pastime. But one is careful lest the pastime should hurt one.

No shepherd, and one herd! Every one wanteth the same; every one is equal: he who hath other sentiments goeth voluntarily into the madhouse.

"Formerly all the world was insane", say the subtlest of them and blink thereby.

They are clever and know all that hath happened: so there is no end to their raillery.

"We have found happiness", say the last men, and blink thereby.

(Thus Spake Zarathustra, English translation by Thomas Common, T. N. Foulis, Edinburgh, 1914.)

Since then many writers have pictured the ant-life of the future, a life in which men derive their happiness from hygienic measures, hour by hour instructions, and the ladling out of all things in doses, through the agency of total planning.

These pessimistic visions are still today opposed by popular images, originating in the eighteenth-century idea of progress, of coming splendour, of a world in which man will live in peace, liberty and justice, a world order of the living equipoise of continually ascending forces—vague images of salvation to come, to which anyone is referred who is discontented.

The idea of progress has its roots in science and technology, and here alone lies its real meaning. But it too leads to questions of concern: Are there, in principle, limits to the future revelations of scientific research, as well as to technological ability? The question is whether science, which is today in full flower and bearing fruit, is approaching a conclusion that will, for the time being, bring its advance to a stop. Whether it will later make a fresh start, or whether, by and large, it will only preserve its results for a time and then lose part of them, until it is reduced to automatic operation with technological constructs and conventional thought-patterns, in such a manner as merely to satisfy the basic demands of existence. Here all prevision is vain. One can do no more than devise interesting and internally consistent Utopias, as has been repeatedly done for half a century.

Another question: Will man one day come to feel cramped on the globe? Will the situation arise in which he will have no further way out, in which no further distance will be open to him, in which, as far as space and matter are concerned, he will only be able to turn round in a circle?

The prognosis is in doubt even as regards the mere provision of necessities to the human masses. If a world order came about there would, it is true, be no threat from barbarian peoples without—the threat would come from nature. The limited potentialities of nature will shortly bring history into new situations. At the present rate of consumption, supplies of coal will be exhausted in a thousand years, of petroleum in less time than that, and of iron already in two hundred years; supplies of phosphorus, which is indispensable to agricultural production, will come to an end even more rapidly than that. It is not yet possible to calculate how soon the uranium ores, which will continue to furnish us with atomic energy for a long time, will be used up. No exact computation is possible in any particular case. But the carefree prodigality with which our limited resources are being used, makes it safe to predict as possible, or even probable, that they will be exhausted within a foreseeable period.

It is impossible to predict whether the human population of the earth will sink to the numbers of five hundred years ago, or whether new expedients will be found. What historical phenomena and upheavals in the human soul will accompany these catastrophic breakdowns cannot be foreseen. One thing alone is certain: as before, there will be no stable conditions.

In our own time, numerous prognoses have been made on *biological* grounds. Observations of a particular kind, alleged total processes of life, have been carried over onto man; on the basis of these processes man's decline has been predicted unless it is prevented by biological planning and breeding. The point of departure was a total conception that was becoming the vogue in current biological thought.

Thus *miscegenation* was supposed to be disastrous, and racial purity a precondition to high value. History, if this sort of thing were susceptible of proof at all (biological proof does not apply to races, but is in fact confined to hereditary interrelationships of individual characteristics, which are by no means easily grasped), would tend to demonstrate the contrary.

Thus, on the basis of alleged observations of psychopathic families, mankind was supposed to be subject to a general process of *decay*. All attempts at a closer and more detailed definition of this theory have long ago been refuted.

Thus, by analogy with the consequences of *domestication* in animals, man was supposed to lose vigour and discipline in the process of domestication, because organised society relieves him of all those difficulties in the overcoming of which he previously became truly human. Whereas amongst wild geese 'marriage' is contracted on the presupposition of certain qualities in the partners and after resistances have been overcome, but then for life and to the accompaniment of the upbringing and protection of the offspring, domestic geese pair at will but are able to leave care of the offspring to the breeder, and have no other task than 'indiscriminate and immoderate feeding and procreation'. Domesticated man is supposed to degenerate in a similar manner. The comparison is fallacious however (*vide* p. 43).

All such fears for the future determined by 'race', 'heredity', 'decadence', or 'domestication' are groundless, if they are directed toward the totality of the process of mankind. They have a very restricted significance. These theories are immeasurably more dangerous (on account of the outlook engendered by their untruth) than that which they themselves envisage as a danger. It is as though real concern for the future sought a way of escape for itself by obscuring the situation with palpable fears of objective natural processes, against whose dubious effects no practical measures could be taken.

Concern for the future of man of quite a different kind has made its appearance in the world, however, a concern that has never been felt before. This is *concern for humanity itself*, which found expression in the works of Burckhardt and Nietzsche: Man might lose himself, mankind might slip, partly unnoticed and partly as the result of stupendous disasters, into a levelling down and mechanisation, into a life without liberty and without fulfilment, into a sombre malignancy destitute of humanity.

What man may come to has today, almost in a flash, become manifest through a monstrous reality that stands before our eyes like a symbol of everything unspeakably horrible: The national-socialist concentration camps[1] with their tortures, at the end of which stood the gas-chambers and incinerators for millions of people—realities that correspond to reports of similar processes in other totalitarian régimes, although none but the national socialists have perpetrated outright mass murder by the gas-chamber. A chasm has opened up. We have seen what man can do—not according to a plan drawn up in *toto* at the outset, but in a circle along which he moves at ever increasing speed once he has set foot upon it. It is a circle into which the participants are dragged without the majority of them knowing or desiring what they will suffer or do as they advance unceasingly around it.

It appears possible to destroy man whilst he is physically still alive. Comparison with the psychoses forces itself upon us. It is a horrifying fact, and one that cannot without dishonesty be fitted into a conception of the world as for ever harmonious, that man can become insane. Our natural fundament is such that, while the body is still alive, we can see communication between us sundered and our fellow man slip down into madness. But we are not to blame for this extreme phenomenon, and there is no danger of mental illnesses becoming epidemics. The dehumanisation perpetrated in the concentration camps, however, was not the work of nature but of man himself, and it can become universal. What does this mean?

Man is capable—under the conditions of political terror—of becoming something of which no one had any inkling. What happened there we only see from outside, unless we are amongst those who either perished in it or survived it. What was possible to the individual, how he suffered, what he did, and how he met his death, remains his secret. Seen from without the impression we gain from the phenomena is that men ceased to be human: almost without a doubt in the case of the active elements, more questionably as regards the tortured victims, who suffered different and greater agonies than those which every man undergoes in the torments of disease and which reduce us to wretched creatures.

The fact that this can happen presupposes in the active elements (who to a great extent were drawn from the internees themselves) a readiness, which was already present prior to this realisation, not only in the existence of the social outcast, but also in the apparent harmlessness of the trusty bureaucrat or the tranquil life of the bourgeois. It is this readiness that inspires our horror, when subsequent events reveal it as having been there all the time. It is the implementation of unconscious lack of faith, the disappearance of faith without conscious nihilism, life without roots or the life of apparently secure puppets on the strings of decorous convention, which can be exchanged without more ado for the strings of life in the concentration camp.

That man, in the passivity of torment in a life in which every minute is under compulsion, turns into this mechanism of reflexes is the outcome of a technico-operative procedure which our era alone has been capable of evolving, in the intensification of tortures that were known to earlier periods also.

This reality of the concentration camps, this interaction in the circular process between torturer and tortured, the manner of this dehumanisation, is an intimation of future possibilities, before which everything threatens to vanish.

After dealing with reports of the concentration camps, one hardly dare continue to speak. This peril goes deeper than the atom bomb, because here it menaces the soul of man. We may easily fall prey to the consciousness of utter despair. This is not the last word, if we believe in man. Then alone does the crushing prognosis, to which these realities give rise, cease to appear absolutely inescapable.

Those individuals who, in all the frightfulness of suffering, although they could not save themselves from being miserable creatures in bodily anguish, yet refused to participate in their souls and who, although they could not avoid injury, yet remained intact as human souls, encourage us to hold fast to the ancient faith in man.

In the face of all the perspectives of the future, we dare to state the proposition: Man cannot get lost entirely, because he is created in the 'image of the Deity'; he is not God, but he is bound to Him with oft-forgotten and always imperceptible, but fundamentally unsunderable, ties. Man cannot altogether cease to be man. Sleep is possible, absence and forgetfulness of himself. But man as a whole can neither become, in the course of history, an ape or an ant, nor, in the present, a reflex machine, save in the horrifying circumstances that brought him to this brink, from which he returns to himself, if he does not die as an individual. These are menacing spectres. That they menace and at times weigh down upon us like an incubus is itself a demonstration of our humanity, that wants to rid itself of evil dreams.

The future of humanity does not come of itself, however, like a natural happening. What men do today and at every moment, what they think and expect, at once becomes an origin of the future, which is in their hands. The only hope is for horror to become conscious. Nothing but the most lucid consciousness can help us. Dread of such a future may perhaps prevent it. The terrible forgetting must not be allowed to take place. The fact that these things have happened causes anxiety: They may be repeated, they may spread, they may conquer the globe. We must keep our anxiety, which is transmuted into active concern.

Anxiety in the face of the horrible facts is repressed in consciousness of powerlessness. Mankind seeks to veil these frightful things from itself. People become indifferent, but in the background of anxiety at the destination toward which mankind is heading. If we think about it, it seems inevitable; we see everything, including ourselves, going under. That which makes humanity human and life worth living will cease to be. We have not yet reached that point. As long as disaster is not upon us we will not think about it.

Consciousness of powerlessness may regard the course of history as being similar to a natural happening. We set ourselves free from responsibility, by seeking to extinguish ourselves as free men. But there is a radical diversity between the historical process and the process of a mental illness. A mental illness is a natural process which it may one day be possible to combat with natural means, but against which we have till then no defence. This path of humanity, however, rests with man himself. To be sure, the individual is defenceless, the peril can only be vanquished in community. But every individual perceives that his free will is involved. Hence the recoil from anxiety to more intense anxiety: It depends upon man, each individual man, upon the decision. It must not be, it shall not be—it is not inevitable. That which has happened is a warning. To forget it is guilt. It must be continually remembered. It was possible for this to happen, and it remains possible for it to happen again at any minute. Only in knowledge can it be prevented.

Here lies the danger. Unwillingness to know, forgetfulness and even disbelief (there are still people who deny the reality of what took place in the concentration camps); then the evil of docile readiness to accept mechanisation—and finally indifference that seeks peace of mind in the nearby and the present, and the passivity of impotence leading to resignation in the face of the supposedly necessary.

Man can only counter the menaces of the future, however, by combating the evil potentialities in the world itself. Man alone can master the danger that is approaching from within himself—in the hope that assistance will come to him if he is of good will. He can do it only in a constitution of liberty, in which power can be relied upon to proceed against everything which threatens man's freedom, that is to say, along the road of a legal order that will become a world order.

No prognosis is harmless. Whether it is true or untrue, it ceases to be a contemplative vision and becomes a call to action. What man deems possible moves his inner attitude and his deeds. To see the dangers with just concern is a precondition for his self-assertion, whereas illusionary notions and obfuscations drag him into ruin. Hope and anxiety move him. In view of the lethargy of the average man, it is right to disturb all false peace of mind. It is not the mental distress that springs from the feeling of being personally threatened, but the great distress concerning humanity—perhaps nourished by the former—that may be of assistance. Let us visualise the significance of anxiety.

An anxiety without parallel seems today to be spreading through mankind. It is equivocal and by no means of one single type; it may be superficial and easily forgotten again, or deep and burning, unadmitted or overt—it may be at a vital or at an existential level—and it seems to be all of this at the same time.

In the democratic countries anxiety is caused by the indefiniteness of the danger, by uncertainty, by excess of liberty—in the totalitarian countries anxiety springs from political terror, which leaves the individual no chance save in obedience and collaboration.

When anxiety ceases in nihilism, in so far as that is possible (for as long as we continue to believe in man, a hidden seed of humanity remains undestroyed), man seems like an extinguished being, unconsciously consuming himself in vital passions. As long as there is still anxiety, there is a chance for man in the method by which he overcomes it.

Where it is possible for man to act on his own initiative in the perpetual mutation of conditions and situations, he can overcome anxiety only in the transcendentally founded self-awareness of freedom. Where he is forced to obey and acquires his relatively safe function in blind obedience, anxiety can diminish to a continuously operative motor for the enforcement of obedience.

But an anxiety that is perhaps common to all pervades mankind. Terrible experiences (such as those of the concentration camps), even if they are quickly forgotten, leave behind them a hidden horror.

Anxiety is to be approved. It is a reason for hope.

The arguments so far put forward show the *meaning of prognoses in human affairs*, the course of which depends upon man himself. For precisely this course of human affairs the comportment in prognostic thinking is decisive.

When one's own intentions are expressed in the form of a prognosis (Hitler: 'If there is a war, it will be the end of the Jewish race in Europe'), that is not a prognosis, but a mere declaration of will.

There is no statement concerning the future, however, in so far as the human will is involved in its realisation, that is not, or could not become, a contributory factor. The statement has the effect of impelling us toward something, or of frightening us away from it. In particular, alleged knowledge of the prospective future is a factor that contributes toward bringing it about.

Anyone who regards an impending war as certain is helping on its occurrence, precisely through his certainty. Anyone who regards peace as certain grows carefree and unintentionally impels us into war. Only he who sees the peril and does not for one instant forget it, is able to behave in a rational fashion and to do what is possible to exorcise it.

It is of crucial significance for the course of events whether the individual can endure to remain in suspense, or whether he flees into certainties. The dignity of man in his thinking about the future consists both in the projection of the possible and in a nescience that is founded on knowledge; our principle must be that we do not know what may happen. The most compelling element in our lives is the fact that we do not know the future, but contribute toward its realisation and see it loom before us incalculable in its entirety. To know the future would be the death of our souls.

When we are erroneously convinced that a particular course of events is going to take place, this paralyses us if it is unwanted—or, if it is wanted, it aids our actions in situations of failure, through the certainty of ultimate success; but here too at the price of an untruth, of a narrowness of heart, of a treacherous arrogance, which deprives any such success—in so far as it does, for a while, occur—of all nobility.

All this by no means implies a repudiation of prognoses. Only prognoses must not lose their meaning. They open the area of the possible, they provide points of attack for plan and action, they bring us into the broadest horizons, they enhance our freedom with the consciousness of the possible.

All our activity depends upon what we expect from the future, upon the picture we form of chances and certainties. The goals of our activity are set within the area of that which we deem possible.

But the present alone is real. Absolute certainty of a future may pillage the present. Prognostications of salvation to come may distract us from the present, which is all we have. Only by accepting responsibility for the present can we become responsible for the future.

In the following discussions we do not wish to project images of the future, but to call to mind tendencies of the present, which only represent questions put to the future. We wish to find the decisive phenomena in the indissoluble web of happening. What appears to be essential, seen in the perspectives of universal history?

Three tendencies are today making their way through the world. They may be summed up by the words socialism, world order, and faith.

Firstly: The human masses are striving toward order. Socialism shows the demands of just mass organisation.

Secondly: The unity of the surface of the earth is pressing toward the implementation of this unity in peaceful intercourse. The alternative is shown to be world empire or world order.

Thirdly: Loss of the traditional footholds in the substance of a common faith is pressing toward the authentic origin of faith in man with the question of whence and whither we are living. The alternative is shown to be nihilism or love.

These three great basic tendencies of contemporary human happening and volition converge in the goal of accomplished human liberty. We shall preface these three cardinal themes by a discussion of liberty.

I. THE GOAL: LIBERTY

Amidst all the antitheses of our volition, only one thing seems today to be agreed. With complete unanimity, all peoples, individuals and political régimes demand liberty. But as to what liberty is and what is required to achieve it there is at once a wide divergence of views. Perhaps the deepest human antitheses are determined by the modes of men's consciousness of liberty. What is to the one the road to freedom, seems to the other the reverse. In the name of liberty almost everything is desired by men. In the name of liberty the road into serfdom is trod. To renounce liberty in a free decision counts for many as the highest freedom. Liberty arouses enthusiasm, but liberty also arouses anxiety. It may look as though men do not want liberty at all, indeed as though they would like to avoid the possibility of liberty.

Since the consciousness of the great Western crisis—since the French Revolution of 1789—concern for human freedom has been abroad in Europe. Spirits of the highest calibre have seen the possibility: freedom can be lost. Whereas Hegel still tranquilly saw world history as the history of the consciousness and reality of liberty, more deeply shaken spirits were invaded by dread of the possibility that the liberty of all men might be lost. The question was then put directly to politics and society: the great spirits, Burke, Benjamin Constant, Tocqueville and Max Weber, were concerned for liberty. Our contemporaries, individual thinkers in all parts of the world, adjure mankind in their concern for freedom—men like W. Lippmann, Ferrero, Hayek, Röpke. They are economists, historians, writers, attached to no party, addressing themselves to all, in order to save the one single common possession, without which man would cease to be man.

A. THE PHILOSOPHICAL CONCEPT OF FREEDOM

We speak of political freedom, social freedom, personal freedom, economic freedom—religious freedom, freedom of conscience—freedom of thought, freedom of the press, freedom of assembly, etc. Political freedom occupies the foreground of discussion. Even here the question as to its nature has not received a unanimous answer.

If we take it to be a condition in which every citizen plays a part in the decisions of will of the whole, in which every citizen shares in knowledge and participates in action, history shows us. Political freedom has only been tried in the West. But most of the realisations have come to naught. They teach us what caused the collapse of freedom in Athens, in Rome. The question that is today exciting Europe and mankind is whether the road leads on to liberty, or whether it passes first into the annihilation of liberty for an unpredictable period.

What will happen is, in any case, dependent upon men. Here nothing must be thought of as following a fixed path. All our human, and particularly our spiritual, activity consists in finding our way in open possibilities. What will come to pass depends upon us—upon each individual, although no individual decides the course of history.

The political concept of liberty becomes external and inverted if it does not retain its foundations in the meaning of liberty, which must be considered the authentic being and doing of man. Let us essay a philosophical exposition of the nature of freedom.

(1) Freedom is the *overcoming of the external* and which coerces me. It comes into being where the other ceases to be alien to me, where rather I recognise myself in the other, or where the externally necessary becomes an element of my own existence, and is known and fashioned as such.

But freedom is also the overcoming of *one's own arbitrariness*. Freedom coincides with the inwardly present necessity of the true.

If I am free, I do not desire because I so desire, but because I am convinced of what is right. The demand upon liberty is, therefore, to act neither from caprice nor from blind obedience, but from judgement. Hence the demand to base our desire upon our own origin by casting anchor in the origin of all things.

I may easily deceive myself, however. Arbitrariness re-establishes itself as the claim to the right to hold my own opinion, with the pre-assumption that every opinion is justified by the fact that someone advocates it. Mere opinion is not judgement, however. Freedom demands the conquest of mere opinions.

This conquest takes place through the attachment which we, as individuals, impose upon ourselves in interrelationship with others. Liberty is realised in community. I can be free only to the extent that others are free.

Mere opinion melts away in favour of well-founded judgement in the loving struggle with one's neighbours.

It is transmuted into consciousness of objective truth in the common socio-political condition, in acceptance of opinions through publication of the conflict of opinions, but only in the movement of dialectical discussion.

Freedom demands both: the depth of human communication between individuals in their selfhood, and conscious work on the freedom of public conditions through the forms of judgement and will-formation.

But absolute truth, and with it final freedom, is never attained. Truth, together with freedom, is on the way. We are not living in the eternity of the perfect concord of souls, but in the time of the ever uncompleted imperative of change.

(2) Freedom demands that nothing be omitted. Everything that has being and meaning must be given its due. Extreme latitude is a condition of freedom. Hence the content of freedom is manifested through life in *polarities and antitheses.*

To every position there develops a counter-position. Potentially freedom is everything. It is not only prepared to take what comes from without as an antithesis, but also to incorporate it into itself. Freedom is reason in boundless openness and ability to hear, and it is through freedom in this truly open area of the widest consciousness that the decisions of history are reached. Hence freedom seeks the fruitful polarities in which one side would perish without the other.

Liberty is lost where polarities are surrendered to restriction—either in an order that forgets its own limits—or in extremes that deny order on party grounds—or in the one pole that makes itself the whole. On the other hand, liberty is present where we preserve our possibilities with open minds and in the tension of antitheses, decide historically out of the origin in the mutation of situations and unpredictably discern being in fresh implications.

(3) But if liberty coincides with the necessity of the true, then our liberty remains at all times fragile. For we are never certain of the truth *in toto*

and finally. Our liberty remains dependent upon something else, it is not *causa sui*. If it were so, man would be God. Authentic freedom is aware of its own limits.

In *subjectivity*, man as an individual is familiar with the experience of the origin: that I am not free through myself, but that precisely where I know myself to be authentically free I, at the same time, know myself to be bestowed upon myself out of a transcendental matrix. I can be lacking to myself—this is the mysterious boundary to which the possible experience of being-bestowed-upon-oneself corresponds. Existence, which we are able to be, is therefore only together with transcendence, through which we are. Where existence becomes sure of itself and freedom lucid they will, at the same instant, become certain of transcendence.

In the *objectivity* of free human community, however, it is the case that freedom depends upon the freedom of everyone else. Hence political freedom can never succeed in being the final and secure permanence of a condition. Here too freedom remains on the way.

(4) Freedom seems impossible: In polarities there arise alternatives: within time I must decide in concrete terms for what and to what end I am living, I cannot be everything, I must adopt a bias, I must fight against that which, at the same time, I recognise as inevitable.

In fact, freedom is man's road in time. He makes toward freedom out of the demand for freedom. Hence freedom is in movement and in dialectic.

This movement seems to be possible in thinking by reason. We designate *reason* the all-perceiving openness, which, in every step taken by the understanding, is more than understanding. Reason becomes the representation of the true, which makes use of the forms of thought given by the understanding. It seeks with their unfolding the systematic unity of everything thinkable. But then again, it seeks precisely that which is contradictory. Thus it is the incentive to bring the understanding to those limits upon which it founders. It surrenders itself to antitheses, but at the same time, surpassing the understanding, it is the power to bind them to one another once more. It does not want to allow anything to fall apart finally. It wants to overcome the alternatives of the understanding. Thus it binds together that which, at the same time, it drives into the ultimate antitheticalities: world and transcendence, science and faith, moulding of the world and meditation on eternal being. Hence reason is intensified dialectic; through consciousness, it pursues the factual dialectic to its ultimate consequences.

The overcoming of antitheses, however, gets stranded on the concrete alternatives of the real situation. This happens wherever thinking cannot stop at itself, but is called upon to achieve a realisation in space and time. Here he alone is free who can decide. Whoever decides, takes upon himself an unfreedom that he lays hold of by his decision. With the surrender of possibilities he realises in freedom, but restricts himself. Through realisation freedom acquires a content, but on the path to unfreedom.

Liberty can never be a possession. There is no isolated liberty. Hence the individual sacrifices the rigour of his empty liberty in favour of a liberty that can be won only in being together.

This kind of freedom develops only with the *transformation of man.* It cannot be fabricated by compulsory dispositions for men who do not change, but is bound to the mode of communication between men prepared for mutation. Hence freedom as such cannot be planned, but men become free in the right planning of concrete tasks together.

To bring men to liberty means to bring them to converse with one another. This remains bound up with illusion, however, if there are mental reservations which are not put into words—reserves upon which, inwardly breaking off communication, one draws back—if converse amounts, in fact, to a concealment, a mere gesture of giving, and the exercise of cunning. Genuine converse between men is without restraint and holds nothing back. Only in the complete openness of both parties does truth develop in community.

Contrary to truth in their effects, and thereby contrary to liberty, are both the bourgeois lulling of the mind by conventions and the conditions of dictatorship, in which everyone has to accept one universal ideology, in whose phrases alone it is permissible to speak, and which then dominates communication, even in private letters; equally contrary to truth and to liberty is the fanatical truth-pathos that claims possession of truth in aggressive and offensive terms, but employs it only for the purpose of suppressing others; this fanatical accentuation of truth exhibits its lack of truth precisely through its lack of willingness to enter into converse.

In fact, however, no one is in possession of truth as final and absolute. To seek for truth always means to be ready for communication and to expect communication from others in return. With the man who desires real truth, and therefore also communication, one can, *ipso facto*, speak openly on every subject; he can do the same himself, and in such a manner as neither to injure nor spare him who really wants to hear. The struggle for truth in liberty is a loving struggle.

Has this disquisition taught us what freedom is? No. But that is in the nature of freedom. In reply to the reproach that from all these propositions we have not learnt what freedom is, it is necessary to call into consciousness the fact that freedom is not an object. It has no existence which, through its occurrence in the world, is susceptible of investigation. To scientific-objective cognition of the world there is no such thing as freedom. Hence freedom cannot be visualised in a defined concept. However, that which I cannot know objectively, I can nevertheless become familiar with by thinking, can bring to conceptual actuality in the movement of thought—and then I can speak of freedom as though it existed. But it is inevitable that it will contain a maze of misconceptions.

B. POWER AND POLITICAL FREEDOM

In theoretical reflection on that which is desirable and reasonable we too easily forget the fundamental reality of force, although it is present to us daily, even though covertly. Force is inescapable. But if there is no human existence without the reality of force, whether the individual is aware of the fact or not, and if force is *per se* evil (Burckhardt), the question is: How is force to be set in its right place, how is force itself to become a factor in the attainment of order, till the point is reached at which it need hardly manifest itself at all? Or how is force to be divested of its evil character?

The answer is furnished by the primordial struggle of history: between the rule of law and the rule of force. Justice is to become real through law on the basis of a guiding ideal law, natural law. This ideal law takes shape, however, only in the historical law of the society that gives itself laws by which it abides. The liberty of man begins with the validity of the written law of the State in which he lives.

This liberty is called *political liberty*. The State in which freedom through law prevails is called a *constitutional State*. A constitutional State is one in which laws come into being and are altered exclusively along a legal path. In democracies this path leads *via* the people, *via* its collaboration and participation, whether direct or indirect, through its representatives, who are periodically renewed in unimpeachable free elections.

A State is called free when it possesses sovereignty in relation to other States. When we speak of *political freedom*, however, we mean the freedom of a people in the sense of the *internal freedom* of its political condition.

The external freedom of a State may be associated internally with despotism and unfreedom. The external unfreedom of a State usually results in loss of sovereignty, but not always in internal unfreedom. For if the subjugating State-power desires political freedom, it can permit this to develop in the dependent State to the point at which individuals from the subject people become autonomous members of the all-embracing State order.

The power of internal political liberty springs originally from the political self-education of a people, which therein constitutes itself a political nation. From this point it can arouse and liberate other peoples. But those who have been liberated remain pupils politically speaking. They must, in humility, forgo the pride of a creation of their own.

All this sounds simple, as though, if men were only clear-sighted and of good will, they could live in ideal liberty through natural law and the legal system that emanates from it. In the first place, however, law is always concrete for the particular historical circumstances—hence laws change with changed circumstances—and in the second, it is necessary to subdue force, which is ready at any moment to break the law—hence legally guided force directed against crime.

Where there is force, we are beset by fear—where law prevails, we live in tranquillity. Force is incalculable, arbitrary; the individual is its defenceless victim. Law is calculable, a source of order; it furnishes the individual with the protection of his existence. The rule of law produces a climate of fearlessness, unconstraint, liberty and peace of mind. Where force rules there is fear, silence and concealment, coercion and unrest. In the constitutional State trust prevails, in the State based on force there is universal mistrust.

Trust requires a fixed pole, an inviolable fundament, something that is respected by all, in such a manner that anyone who violates it can, without difficulty, be cast out as a criminal. This inviolable fundament is called legitimacy.

Max Weber distinguishes three types of legitimate sovereignty: *traditional* (belief in the sanctity of traditions effective since the remote past), *rational* (belief in the legality of orders laid down by law, and in those called to sovereignty through these orders), and *charismatic* (belief in the sanctity or the heroic power or the exemplariness of a person). In these three cases the rulers are respectively: *superiors* determined by law, the lord called by tradition (such as that of hereditary right), and the *leader* qualified by his *charisma*.

Ferrero has formulated the alternative, which is perhaps schematic, but illuminating for our epoch, between liberty through legitimacy, or despotism and fear through illegitimacy (in which the charismatic leader is a type of illegitimacy). Ferrero sees legitimacy in, for example, hereditary monarchy or in the expression of the will of the majority through popular suffrage. A legitimate government is able to rule without fear, confident of the consent of the people. An illegitimate government is afraid of the people, its own force arouses force in others; out of fear it has to safeguard itself by means of continually growing political terror, through which, in turn, fear becomes the fundamental state of mind of all. Legitimacy is like a magic spell that creates indispensable order through trust; illegality is violence that engenders violence everywhere, through distrust and fear.

The basis of legitimacy always appears dubious when submitted to a critique, e.g. hereditary right is irrational, because it also legitimises fools and men without character; election by the majority is questionable, because it is partly determined by error and chance, by the momentary effects of mass-suggestion. This is why legitimacy is always in such danger. The understanding can all too easily cast doubts upon it. Since, however, the sole choice is between legitimacy and despotism, legitimacy is the only way along which man can live without fear—especially since the mistakes made along this way can be rectified. Doubts such as these explain the intellectual aversion to the fountainhead of legitimacy. Our age sees it in elections and votes.

In legitimate conditions there is an infinite amount that is inadequate, unjust and inappropriate. Those who are elected may be foolish people, laws may be wrong and injurious, a source of revolt through their effects. Legitimacy does not afford absolute protection to those elected or to the laws however. Fresh elections may remove the former and fresh, legitimate, decisions change the latter. The fact that both operations are carried out through legitimate channels renders rectification without force possible. The consciousness of legitimacy accepts great evils as part of the bargain in order to avoid the absolute evil of terrorism and fear under despotism. Political liberty is not the outcome of pure understanding, but is bound to legitimacy.

In order that force shall not irrupt into universal sovereignty, legitimacy is needed. Only where there is legitimacy is there liberty, because legitimacy puts force in fetters. Where legitimacy disappears liberty too is annihilated.

In the West, certain fundamental determinants of the idea of political freedom have been evolved (originally, above all, in England and America, from
whence they were taken over by France and other States after the French
Revolution; they were elaborated philosophically during the period of the
Enlightenment, for instance by Kant). I shall try briefly to set out the cardinal
points. Political freedom, in the sense of internal political freedom, possesses
the following characteristics:

(1) The liberty of the individual, if every individual is to be free, is only
    possible to the extent that it is compatible with the *simultaneous liberty of*
    everyone else.

Legally, scope is left to the individual for the play of his arbitrary will (negative liberty), through which also he can shut himself off from others.
Ethically, however, liberty consists precisely in the openness of life in being
together that can unfold without compulsion, out of love and reason (positive liberty).

Only when positive liberty has been realised on the basis of the legal
safeguarding of negative liberty, does the proposition apply: Man is free in
the measure in which he sees freedom around him, that is, in the measure
in which all men are free.

(2) The individual has a dual claim: That he shall be protected against
    force, and that his judgement and his will shall have the opportunity
    to make themselves felt. Protection is guaranteed by the constitutional
    State, expression of his judgement and his will is made possible by
    democracy.
(3) Only when force has been overcome by law can freedom be realised.
    Freedom fights for the power that serves the law. It attains its goal in the
    constitutional State.

The laws operate in the same fashion for everyone. An alteration in the laws
can be made only through legal channels.

The operation of the law guides the use of force where this is necessary.
Hence the police do not exercise force outside the framework of those measures against lawbreakers which are safeguarded against arbitrary action by
legal forms. Hence there are no special political police.

The freedom of the individual is ensured as freedom of the person, of property, and of domicile. Its curtailment takes place only under conditions laid down by law and applying to all. Even the intervention of authority must respect certain fundamental rights; for example, no one can be arrested without the reason being stated, and without trial after the elapse of a certain short period of time, or without being afforded the legal means of protest and defence in public court.

(4) To the inviolability of the rights of the individual personality is added its right to participate in the life of the whole. Free conditions are therefore possible only through democracy, that is, where it is possible for everyone to play a part in forming the collective will. Each individual has the chance of making his influence felt to the degree of his political self-education and the extent to which his views carry conviction.

Everyone enjoys the same right to make his influence felt through his vote at elections. The secret ballot is guaranteed. There is no limit to the number of popular groups that can put up candidates. Government comes into being through elections held at fixed intervals.

Hence, in democracy, government can be, and in fact is, changed, brought down, or reconstructed by constitutional means, without recourse to violence. Under free democratic conditions, it is impossible for the same men to remain permanently and uninterruptedly in the exercise of government.

To the protection of the individual against force, corresponds the safeguarding of all against the power of one individual. Even the greatest service to the State does not confer inviolability upon the power of any individual. Man remains man, and even the best is a danger if he is not subject to restraint. Hence there prevails deep-seated distrust of perpetual power, and hence even the most powerful man has, at least for a while, to stand down in the alternation of electoral popularity. There is no deification of man, but there is gratitude and respect for him who, when the time is ripe, gives up his power without opposition.

(5) Formation of the collective will takes place through decision reached on the basis of converse.

Hence freedom demands public, unrestricted *discussion*. So that this may take place within the widest horizons on the basis of the most complete knowledge possible, freedom demands that what is knowable shall be known, including news and the vindication of opinions—and that it shall be known to the whole people. For this reason there must be freedom of the press, freedom of assembly and freedom of speech. To persuade and carry on propaganda are permissible, but only in free competition. Curtailment of this liberty is possible solely in time of war, but even then it can apply only to the public communication of news, not to the communication of opinions. A further curtailment arises out of penal law (protection against libel, slander, etc.).

Everyone reaches his decisions on the basis of converse. The political opponent is not an enemy. Liberty stands firm only when it lives in readiness to work together even with the opponent. In principle, there are no limits to negotiation—except in relation to the criminal; people seek to co-operate in agreement and compromise.

(6) Political freedom is democracy, but through forms and in degrees that have come about historically. They exclude the sovereignty of the masses (ochlocracy), which is always in alliance with tyranny. This is the reason for the paramountcy of an aristocratic stratum, which is continually supplemented from the ranks of the whole people according to achievement, merit and success, and in which the people recognises itself. It is not a class, nor an estate, but a political élite. The creation of this élite through education, through preservation and selection, is the precondition of a free democracy. Democracy postulates that no élite shall be fixed and thereby become a dictatorial minority. It must be kept under perpetual control through free elections, in which it has to justify itself, so that the persons exercising the functions of government come and go, reappear or finally withdraw from the scene.

(7) The conduct of elections and the training of an élite are in the hands of parties. In a free condition there are necessarily several parties—two at the least. In its concept and in its literal sense party means a part. In conditions of freedom it is out of the question for a party to claim the right to be the only one. A single party with a claim to totality is a contradiction of liberty. Its victory spells the end of liberty. Hence free parties desire the existence of other parties. They do not desire to exterminate them. Those parties which are, for the moment, in a minority form the opposition, but they are at all times sustained by their share in

responsibility for the whole. They think in terms of the instant when, following changed electoral results, it will be their turn to take over government. The existence of an effective opposition is the indispensable sign of free conditions.

(8) Democratic technique is bound up with the *democratic way of life*. One without the other would immediately come to grief. A free political condition can only be maintained if the consciousness of freedom in the mass of the population is concerned for the preservation of freedom and is in a state of constant alert against all realities that threaten it. We know at what cost liberty was won, both in the historical process and in the self-education of the whole people.

Democracy is not possible without liberality. It must be consciously bound to liberty. Otherwise it falls prey to ochlocracy and tyranny.

(9) Political freedom is intended to make all other human freedoms possible. Politics are directed toward the *ordering of existence as the basis, not as the final aim, of human life.* Hence political freedom embraces both the passion for liberty and cool-headedness concerning immediate objectives. So that it shall afford man the maximum degree of liberty, the legal order must be confined to necessities of existence. The politics of freedom become impure when they are mingled with other motives. And the impurity of politics becomes a source of unfreedom.

(10) One mark of the condition of political freedom is the *severance of politics from the world view.* To the extent that liberty increases, religious (confessional) conflicts and conflicts relating to the world view are divorced from politics.

Politics are concerned with that which is common to all men, with the interests of existence that are independent of the content of any faith, in which all men can understand one another so as to make room for each other mutually through order, justice and contract.

The question is, at what point does that begin which is not common to all men: world view, historically determined faith, all the particular tendencies that must have room to move. The only thing they have in common is their need for room to move.

Man has an urge to consider his own life-form the only true one, to feel every existence that does not resemble his own to be a reproach, and to hate it.

From this arises the disposition to enforce one's own way of life upon everyone else, as far as possible to model the whole world upon it.

Politics that draw their sustenance from such impulses tend to violence, multiply violence. They do not hear, do not negotiate—save in appearance—but subjugate.

Politics that spring from man's will to liberty, however, effect a self-conquest that leads to moderation. Their aim is confined to the interests of existence, in which they seek to give scope to all human potentialities that are not inimical to that which is indispensably common to all. They are tolerant toward all who do not strive after force through intolerance. They follow the path of a continual diminution of force.

This kind of politics is founded in a faith that desires liberty. Faith is capable of an infinite variety of contents, but common to all men of faith is the earnestness of their unconditional demand for justice and legality in the conditions and processes of human society. Pious men alone are capable of the grandeur of restraint and of trustworthiness in ethico-political activity.

Politics relate, so to speak, to a lower plane of humanity, to existence; therefore, although everything else depends upon them—hence the responsibility and the fervour of their intervention—they have no direct contact with the high goods of inner liberty, of faith and of the spirit. For these they only create the preconditions.

An example: Christianity is a matter of faith. The Christian as such can vote for any party and belong to any party, inasmuch as terrestrial affairs alone are involved; he may vote communist or capitalist, republican or monarchist. For the manner in which terrestrial matters are to be ordered does not follow from the Biblical faith itself, but from ecclesiastically determined particularities of its manifestations. Evil alone the Christian cannot desire. Christianity that has become political as such, has become questionable as a faith.

On the other hand, however, since fervour is possible to politics that soberly restrict themselves to their true meaning only as the outcome of faith, it is the pious Christians who have brought the modern world of liberty into being. Faith does not form the content, but the general outlook of politics.

Another example: Marxism, in the shape of scientific Marxism, was an exceptionally fruitful method of cognition; as an absolutised historico-philosophical and sociological total conception it has become a scientifically demonstrable fallacy and a fanaticising ideology. The socialisation of the means of production in large-scale undertakings, to abolish the private appropriation of surplus value, is a goal that one can deem just and strive after without being a believing Marxist.

Articles of faith as a guide-rope for politics are disastrous to liberty. For the exclusivity of the claim to truth presses toward totality and thereby toward dictatorship, and thereby toward the abolition of freedom. In conditions of political liberty, parties based on a world view are therefore instinctively rejected and factually ineffective. Movements based on a creed and a view of the world are inimical to freedom in politics. For there can be no discussion with men who are fighting for a creed. But in politics the prime necessity is that discussion shall be universal and that everyone shall learn to compound with his fellows for the solution of the problems of existence in which all men can combine all diversities of belief, world views, and interests.

(11) The preservation of liberty presupposes an *ethos of communal life* that has come to be regarded as axiomatic: The feeling for forms and laws, natural modes of human intercourse, consideration and readiness to help, constant respect for the rights of others, unfailing readiness to compromise in questions of mere existence, no oppression of minorities. In this ethos all parties effective in free conditions remain at one. Between conservatives and radicals there still prevails a solidarity in the maintenance of the common element that unites them.

(12) Liberty is safeguarded by a written or unwritten *constitution.* There is no absolutely reliable machinery for the preservation of liberty however. Hence, in free conditions, people are concerned to protect as inviolable something essential, liberty itself, the rights of man, the constitutional State, even against temporary majorities. This inviolable factor must remain beyond the reach of decisions through election or voting. There must be regulations (repetition of a decision after the passage of a sufficient period of time to allow for its reconsideration, plebiscites, a court of justice competent to give a ruling as to whether a decision does or does not accord with the constitution) that can come into operation when a majority momentarily forgets the common fundament of political freedom. Any such regulations, however, can only remain dependably effective as long as they are in harmony with the political ethos of the people. The two together function to prevent the destruction of democracy by democratic means, the abolition of liberty through liberty. The trustworthy road to the expression of the

enduring, authentic will of the people is not, in every case, the absolute validity of democratic techniques, nor, therefore, is it mechanical majority *per se*. Even if these democratic techniques are generally valid, restriction is nonetheless required where, but only where, the rights of man and liberty itself are menaced. In extreme cases of this kind, the principles must be suspended in order to save the principles.

Tolerance must not be exercised toward intolerance, except where the latter can be treated with indifference as a private eccentricity that offers no danger to the community. There must be no freedom for the destruction of freedom.

(13) There is no such thing as a *final state of democratic political liberty satisfactory to all*. Tensions will always make their appearance if the individual is restricted beyond the extent necessary for the guarantee of equality of opportunity, if free competition is curtailed apart from the prevention of clear injustice, if the natural inequality of man and merit through achievement are not rewarded by certain rights, if any number of citizens fail to see in the laws of the State that justice on the basis of which, in their own spheres, they themselves live.

Democracy means that everyone shall win the recognition due to his ability and merit. The constitutional State means the safeguarding of this opportunity and thereby the necessity of transforming this legal safeguard according to circumstances and experience, but without violence and within the framework of juridical forms.

The will to justice is never entirely satisfied. It puts up with a great deal on account of the perils that threaten political freedom. Political freedom always costs something, and sometimes a great deal, in terms of personal renunciation, personal restraint and patience. Liberty of the self is not curtailed by losses of politically determined justice, as long as a struggle for justice is legally possible, even if it should be protracted and frequently unsuccessful.

Elections on the part of the *populace* at decisive points in the course of events are indispensable. *Formal democracy*—free, equal, secret suffrage—is not, *ipso facto*, a guarantee of liberty, but rather a threat to it. Only under the presuppositions set out above—an ethos of communal life, self-education in converse for the mastery of concrete tasks, unconditional defence of the fundamental rights of man, the earnestness of faith as its foundation—is it dependable. Not only may it have ochlocratic consequences with tyranny as an end-result, especially if it is suddenly imposed from above without self-educational preparation, but even before this happens it brings opportunist cliques into power, since the populace does not really know what it is voting for. Parties then prove a failure. Instead of being organs of the people, they become self-sufficient organisations. Instead of an élite they bring to the forefront experts in Parliamentary routine and men of spiritually subaltern nature.

The manner in which democracy is defended against ochlocracy and tyranny, against party cliques and the subaltern mentality, is a question of vital importance to freedom. *Inhibitive regulations* are required to combat the suicidal tendencies of a formal democracy. The absolute sovereignty of every transitory majority requires to be curtailed by something stable, which however, since those who exercise such functions are only human, remains in turn ultimately dependent upon the humanity that grows out of the populace and its genuine will to freedom. The populace must also, in the last resort, choose the inhibitive regulations, but in such a fashion as to short-circuit the parties, so that the risk of their achieving sole dominion is avoided.

(14) Everything depends upon the *elections*. We know the scorn for democracy, the contempt for decisions by vote. It is easy to see the obvious mistakes and aberrations and to declare an election result or a majority decision absurd in individual instances.

In reply to this it must be pointed out again and again: There is no other road to liberty than the one that runs *via* the populace. Only a radical contempt for man, that makes an exception of the contemner and his friends, can prefer the road of tyranny. This latter road leads *via* the self-appointment of individual groups to dominion over slaves, who are kept in tutelage while being led to suppose themselves free, who are moulded by propaganda and surrounded by stage scenery. In the most favourable instance, this may result in the establishment of a benevolent dictatorship.

Both of them, democrat and tyrant, address themselves to the people. The world has entered upon an era in which everyone who wishes to rule is obliged to make use of this form of speech. Both the criminal and fraudulent demagogue, and the noble demagogue in the service of liberty address themselves to the people. Which of them will meet with success can be decided in each instance only by the people themselves; the decision they reach is a decision over themselves.

If the ultimate decision is in the hands of the people, however, then everything possible must be done to assist them to decide aright. Tyranny invents methods by which putting questions to the people becomes a mere sham accompanied by public sound and fury, through which people learn a great deal (so that they may be turned into serviceable instruments) without becoming capable of passing judgement. Democracy, on the other hand, since decision by vote is the only remaining form of legitimacy, seeks to foster the right vote, so that the authentic, enduring will of the people may find expression.

In the long run, the only means of achieving this is to instruct the whole population, to awaken their authentic will by rendering them reflectively conscious of this will.

Men ought not merely to be schooled in technological arts and skills (through which, if it remains their only knowledge, they simply become tools that can be used in servitude in response to the fascist demand: Believe, obey, fight). We humans need education in critical thought and comprehension, we need the world of history and philosophy if we are to become competent to form a judgement and independent. The whole population must be raised to a higher level in a continually intensified educational process; it must be brought from half knowledge to whole knowledge, from the contingent thinking of the moment to methodical thinking, in which everyone can lift himself out of dogmatism into freedom. This is the hope for the evolution of the majority, that in decisions and resolutions by vote it will consciously and deliberately choose that which is better.

A second road is the practical self-education of the people through the participation of the greater part of them in concrete tasks. Hence free and responsible local government is indispensable to the genesis of a democratic ethos. Only that which is practised on a small scale in their immediate surroundings at every moment of their lives is capable of rendering men sufficiently mature for the tasks which they must realise democratically on an increasingly large, and finally vast, scale.

A third road is the organisation of the electoral process itself. The electoral form is of the greatest importance: e.g. the method of voting (votes for personalities or for a list of candidates), the computation of the electoral results (majority or proportional representation), direct or indirect election, etc.

There is far from being one single correct electoral pattern. But the electoral pattern may determine the course of events.

The decisive factor in preserving liberty and legitimacy and preventing despotism and political terror remains the holding of genuine elections. The hallmark of despotism is the abolition of genuine elections and their replacement by sham elections, with which it pays its lying respects to our epoch's will to freedom. Abolition of genuine elections corresponds to the execution of kings in former times; it is an execution of the sovereignty of the people. Annihilation of the source of legitimacy brings the most unrestrained rule of force and the annihilation of liberty.

Tocqueville grasped the profound significance of bowing to the will of the majority in relation to the phenomena of the French Revolution. If prayers were offered to human reason, boundless trust placed in its omnipotence, and laws, institutions and mores refashioned *ad libitum*, it was fundamentally far less human reason in general that the leaders of the Revolution were thinking of than their own reason in particular. 'Never has anyone shown less trust in the wisdom of the community than did these men.' They despised the crowd almost as much as they despised God. 'True and respectful subjection to the will of the majority was as foreign to them as subjection to the will of God. Since that time almost all revolutionaries have exhibited this dual character trait. This is very remote from the respect which the English and Americans evince for the opinion of the majority of their fellow-citizens. With them reason is proud and full of self-confidence, but never presumptuous; hence it has led to liberty, whereas our own has merely invented fresh forms of serfdom.'

There is one very old objection to elections: One vote counts for almost nothing. It is not worth the trouble of voting. The procedure detracts from the pleasure of exercising public will. It diminishes the consciousness of performing a meaningful act. Here there really is a crucial point for the attitude of mind of modern democratic man. If one vote counts for almost nothing, the decision is nevertheless reached through the sum of all the votes, each of which is only a single vote. Hence the contemporary outlook is: I cast my vote with complete earnestness and complete responsibility, and at the same time I know how little the individual means. Humility is necessary to us and in humility the demand to do all that lies in our power. The almost total powerlessness of the vote of the individual is combined with the desire that the decisions of these individuals in their totality shall determine everything.

(15) But suppose the people *do not, in fact, want freedom, justice and democracy?* This does not seem possible in the lucidity of volition, but only where men are befogged by wants and passions.

It is this, however, that places freedom in constant question. *The concern of all for freedom* is necessary. For it is the costliest possession, that never falls to our lot of its own accord, and is not maintained automatically. It can only be preserved where it has risen into consciousness and been accepted into responsibility.

For freedom is always on the defensive, and therefore in danger. Where the populace no longer feels freedom to be in peril, freedom is already lost. Ascendancy slips all too easily into unfreedom and its organisation of force.

(16) Against the political ideal of liberty, as against every ideal, grave contra-indications can be drawn from reality: Liberty is supposed to have proved an impossibility. But the liberty of man is itself the origin which may engender as a reality to experience the very thing declared to be impossible on the basis of previously asserted experiences.

The difference lies in whether, out of belief in God and in the consciousness of the task of realising the dignity of man, we choose the path of freedom and hold firm in boundless patience through all disillusionments, or whether, in the inverted triumph of nihilistic passion, we abandon ourselves to the fate of seeing our nature as humans destroyed by humans.

The crucial hallmark of free conditions is *faith in freedom.* It is enough that approximations to the ideal of political freedom have been attempted and, even though with signal deficiencies, have been successful. This gives us encouragement for the future.

If we look at the course of world history, we see that the political liberty of men is rare, indeed an exception. The majority of men and the greater part of history are destitute of political liberty. Athens, republican Rome, and Iceland were exceptions of this kind. And the greatest, most effectual and most powerful exception of all is England together with America. This was the birthplace of the influence that set free the States of the continent, but only in part and without the vigour of the daily, deliberate assertion of liberty.

Political liberty is a Western phenomenon. If it is compared with Indian and Chinese manifestations, liberty proves in both these realms of culture to be devoid of any basic principle and lacking the continuity of a people, fortuitous and personal. Hence one may ask whether political liberty is a precondition to humanity's attainment of great heights. In view of history this question must be answered in the negative. High spiritual vitality, creativity and a profound psychic life were also possible in political unfreedom. We who regard freedom as desirable, for whom political freedom can never again be divorced from the idea of humanity, see the historical question of whether something like political freedom, having its source in the West, will or will not become a reality for the education of the whole of mankind. And we know how, in the West, political unfreedom has again and again been arraigned as the reason for spiritual decline as well, since Tacitus and Longinus in first-century Rome, at the time of the loss of liberty and the despotism of the Caesarean monarchy, wrote that spiritual life is possible only in political liberty. Nevertheless, the meaning of history for the comparative total conception remains to render evident what man can be, under the most manifold conditions of the ordering of power.

The will to power, and force, are constantly poised to intervene. They begin in situations of helplessness with the demand, first to ease the existence that has been encroached upon from without, then for equality of rights and liberty, then for supremacy, security and sovereignty (always in the name of alleged common interests), and finally for the arbitrary exercise of their own majesty.

In everyday life, force is engaged in a perpetual struggle with free reason. Every imperious word that breaks off discussion—arbitrary disregard of reason, which invites rebellion—unilateral decision—the command that does not keep within the terms of a contract and the particular fields of action pertaining to it—all this begins in the private atmosphere of the home, in the corporate work of an office, the violence which must ultimately break out as war, because in these preliminaries man has factually prepared himself for it and adapted himself to it.

In the face of might and force there must be no self-deception. Theoretical projects of the proper organisation of the world, without a glance at reality, are nugatory. But if we do look at this reality we tend to formulate an erroneous alternative.

Either to live without force, according to the maxim 'do not resist evil'— prepared to accept all the consequences, to endure and perish without a struggle.

Or to recognise force as a *de facto* condition of existence, to have recourse to it as a factor in politics, and thereby to accept the evil of force and affirm the inevitabilities of politics.

Both positions are logically unambiguous and seemingly consistent, and yet, by the touchstone of the task confronting man, an evasion. For the will to use force in the service of the right, to place might under the control of justice, to appeal in politics to the upsurging impulses and not merely to practical interests, to seek the way with the noblest forces of man—this will is not logically unequivocal at all, it cannot be set forth as a perfected project. It can only find its way historically.

Fixed and one-sided viewpoints are always a sign of failure. Truth, however, is not a correct organisation of the world—no such correct, final organisation of the world is vouchsafed to man—but freedom of volition in the open space of endlessly possible world realisation. We may well say there is a deficiency in the spirit that does not become power, and a deficiency in the power that does not combine with the profundity of humanity. The spirit becomes impotent, the power evil. In this tension the historically interminable road is to let might become an element of right, to prove existence to be the foundation of man's freedom.

What we shall discuss in the following section as socialism and world unity, fate has interwoven with the pragmatics of power. Faith has a different meaning. A faith which, as such, allows itself to be caught up in the pragmatics of power, is already lost as faith. It grows as truth only within the area of liberty without force. Then, however, it is the crucial reason for the earnestness with which the practice, and in it the idea, of socialism and world unity are espoused

II. THE BASIC TENDENCIES

A. SOCIALISM

1. *Sources and concept of socialism*

Several sources nourish the socialist idea and have led, for more than a hundred years, to demands that can be successfully fulfilled only in conjunction with one another.

Technology demands the organisation of labour. Machine technology as such calls for the conduct of large-scale enterprises, the community of joint labour.

All men must be supplied with the necessary consumer goods. Every man has the right to expect his existence to be made possible.

All men demand justice and are today able, with awakened consciousness, to comprehend, express and advocate their claim. This claim to justice applies equally to the distribution of the burden of labour and to a share in its disposable products.

No one can evade these demands today. The difficulty does not lie in their justification, but in their implementation.

Today the name socialism is conferred upon every outlook, every tendency and every plan that aims at the ordering of the life and work of the community according to the criteria of justice accompanied by the repudiation of privileges. Socialism is the universal tendency of contemporary mankind toward an organisation of labour and of participation in the products of labour that will make it possible for all men to be free. To this extent almost everyone is a socialist today. Socialist demands figure in the programmes of all parties. Socialism is the basic trait of our epoch.

These statements are, however, quite inadequate to define real modern socialism. Although the latter thinks in terms of the principle of justice, it also, in the shape of Marxism (communism), thinks in terms of a total knowledge of the course of human affairs. The realisation of communism is conceived, by the allegedly scientific method of historical dialectics, as necessary. The communists' own actions take place in the certainty of this necessity, which they only hasten. According to the judgement and intention of its believers, however, the consequence of the realisation of communism will not merely be justice in the ordering of existence for men as they are, but a transformation of humanity itself. Man will emerge from the self-estrangement that he has suffered through class division, and attain his authentic nature in the classless society, with an unprecedented freedom and spiritual fruitfulness, with a happiness springing from the harmonious solidarity of all.

Scientific communism is a typically modern phenomenon, inasmuch as it bases the salvation of man on science as it understands it. It needs nothing else.

On the road to the goal, according to the dialectical view of history, a period of the greatest distress is an inevitable transition. A peaceful realisation through renunciation on the part of the capitalists and through free agreement, achieved in negotiation, as to the structure of the new society is deemed impossible on account of the spiritual make-up of the capitalist holders of power, which is determined by class rule. Dictatorship of the proletariat is the turning-point on the way to the establishment of justice and liberty.

The attainment of this end requires, firstly, the power which, in the crisis of capitalism, falls into the hands of dictatorship, and secondly, planning on the basis of science.

2. Power

Ideas may deceive us into thinking that what is true and just must also come to pass. The belief that an idea is true may fallaciously cause us to suppose that its correctness will, *ipso facto*, compel its realisation. It is true that ideas arouse motives, but they make their influence felt in the real course of events only on condition that they are backed by the solid realities of power. Socialism can only be realised through power that is capable of using force when it comes up against resistance.

The manner in which the energy of the socialist idea combines with power, utilises it, succumbs to it, or masters it, will be decisive for the future liberty of man. To win liberty in justice, socialism must unite with the forces that save man from violence—both from the arbitrary will of the despot and from the arbitrary will of masses in temporary majorities. From the beginning of things this has happened only through legality.

The principles of political freedom evolved in the West are in danger. Only a socialism that makes them its own can remain a socialism of liberty. It alone will be concrete and human; it alone will avoid the abstractions of doctrines, which, as a basis for action, represent the path to unfreedom: in that justice demands the sovereignty of all, it unwittingly places mass sovereignty in the hands of demagogues, who at once become despots, make slaves of everyone and establish a life of fear. It is the path on which growing fear forces the despots to intensify political terror, for they live all the time in distrust, and by their actions they deliver everyone into a life of fear and distrust, since every man is under a continual threat.

The power that becomes master of socialism, instead of socialism making use of it, grows through socialism's basic trait of planning, if it leads to total planning.

Planning is possible only through power, total planning only through total power. As long as the law permits *ad libitum* accumulation of capital, monopoly is possible; monopoly leads to power over consumers, as well as over the workers and employers of the monopoly organisations, because they control the whole of the labour field in question, so that no possibility of employment exists outside them; dismissal means annihilation. Total planning is possible only through the agency of the State that possesses absolute power to start with, or acquires it through its total planning; it is infinitely superior to the power of any monopoly organisation in a capitalist economy, a power of a compass and exclusivity in its hold on private life such as history has never before seen.

3. Planning and total planning

All over the world, people's minds are exercised by the problem of planning. Plans on an immense scale and their implementations are there to be seen.

Planning is any arrangement with a purpose. To this extent, planning has formed an element in human existence from the beginning. Animals live without plan, according to their instincts. In order to find our way about within the multiplicity of planning, we can make certain distinctions:

By *whom* is planning carried out? Planning is either done by private initiative in undertakings competing with other private institutions—the limit is the amalgamation of those whose interests lie in a particular field in trade unions and monopolies, in order to eliminate competition—or else by the State. In its planning the State either confines itself to the ordering of free initiative by means of laws, or it embarks itself upon undertakings that bear a monopoly character *a priori*; in the latter case, the limit is reached when the State, in principle, assumes control of everything in total planning.

What is planned? An individual undertaking—or the economy as a whole—or the overall ordering of human existence in general.

Modern planning began in the economic field, and this is still its proper sphere. Planned economy had its origin in want. To begin with, human collaboration in the economic field arose without any overall plan. Planning was the outcome of a situation of disaster, in which the work process and the whole enterprise were in danger. It was an answer to the question: how can the situation be improved, how can we save ourselves?

World economy came into existence only toward the end of the nineteenth century. In contrast to previous local economies, sufficient to satisfy local needs and therefore autarchic (they included the purveyance through trade of extreme luxury goods of an inessential nature to those few who possessed wealth), all peoples in their growing prosperity were now dependent upon each other through the exchange of mass products and raw materials.

This new interdependence was accompanied by disturbances which were at first incomprehensible to the bulk of the people (as for instance when the price of corn, and with it great fluctuations in the prosperity of agriculture, depended upon the size of the harvest in Canada or Russia). With want came the call for State aid. All interested parties—in many respects at variance with each other—wanted protection by the State. The outcome was the erection of barriers and cordons, beginning with customs and excise regulations, and ending with the desired new autarchy of the totalitarian régime.

All this remained within bounds as long as there was peace, but became total during the two World Wars. Schematically interpreted, the antithesis of possibilities now visible looks like this: World economy, which is as a whole unplanned and within limits rational, which operates through the free market and enriches everyone, presupposes peace and has peace as its goal. The coercion that is planned as a whole, apparently rational but in fact accompanied by growing poverty, that interrupts intercourse or places it under the surveillance of the State, that takes the temporary interests of the individual State as its yardstick, is the consequence of world wars and, in its turn, has a tendency to fresh wars.

Briefly: Some sort of distress is always the source of planning. The most profound distress of all, that caused by war, is the source of total planning.

The meaning and justification of such planning in times of distress are then transformed by the fact that the State's will to power, the will to defence and conquest, reaches the maximum degree of momentary energy through total planning. Concomitant with this is the imposition of the most intense shortages in the interests of armament production. Existence is staked on military conquest, which is alone capable of reversing one's own bankruptcy by the plunder of others. That which is of practical value to military ventures is established as a permanent condition, with a view to a planned or feared war.

Thereupon a fresh motive comes into being. The condition of absolute power, necessitated by war, is to be carried over into the peace as a permanent condition of absolute sovereignty. Whereas the first motive looked upon war as the normal condition, for which peace merely serves to create the preparations, peace may indeed be deemed by this second motive the normal condition. But in peace the greatest happiness of all, justice and the satisfaction of natural needs, is to be realised through the total plan as a permanent condition, and thereby through a concurrent absolute sovereignty. Certain erroneous ideas are involved here.

(1) In the want attendant upon war or some natural catastrophe, total planning is clearly the only means of providing and distributing the necessities of life so that the shortage falls equitably upon all and everyone receives a small but equal share. What is in this case done meaningfully and for limited purposes under abnormal conditions, is transferred onto the totality of the economy, work, production, supply, and above and beyond this onto the whole existence of man. The form of assistance during shortage is made into the form of life in general.

(2) Machine technology is thought, by its nature, to call for direction by an omnipotent State. There are, however, limits to the necessary large-scale organisation of technology, and beyond them its efficiency diminishes. Mammoth organisations become rigid; they desire merely to keep themselves going, and not to transform themselves, and where monopolisation has taken place they become hostile to new inventions. Only in the struggle of competition, unbounded by legal injunctions, can developments and progress, the trying out of the new and the seizing of opportunities be expected with any confidence; here success comes from the full exertion of all the forces of the spirit, because bankruptcy threatens if they fail.

(3) The demand for justice is directed against the misery and crying injustice that arose out of the free trade economy of the liberal era. Here the basic idea of liberalism is reproached with the disastrous confusions which did in fact invade liberalist thinking in the service of egoistic interests. Liberalist theory, as W. Lippmann shows, confused the privileges of corporations (which may indeed be abolished) with the rights of man, which are inviolable—it confused the only limited immunity of juridical persons with the sanctity of natural persons—it confused the possessions of monopolies with private property. The justified struggle against the errors of liberalist thought must not become a struggle against liberality itself.

4. Conception of the economic structure: Free competition or planned economy?

A planned economy exists wherever competition and the free market are restricted or abolished. It began with large-scale enterprises, which, as trusts, established monopolies, and passed from there to State economy.

The question for the economy is whether it should be a market economy or a planned economy. Which is more successful: the reason of all, realised in the play of free initiative in competition, or the reason of a few technical brains, that realise the happiness of all in total planning? Is risk on the market and decision in competition preferable, or direction through commission and the allocation of labour and profits on the part of a bureaucracy? Who is to be the arbiter? The market, on which success or failure takes place in competition, or the unilateral disposition of key men operating through bureaucracy?

Where there is free competition, everyone can win recognition for his products, achievements, ideas or creations, if he can find a public for them. The taste, needs and will of all win recognition for themselves in their multiformity. The whole population decides, and within it also a small minority. In place of monotony there is endless plenty. The particular spirit can fashion its particular environment. Competition provides a spur. *Agon* leads at all times to the highest possible achievements.

Discussion of the question is confined, initially, to the economic field. Here total planning represents elimination of the market in favour of statistical computation and determination of labour, production and distribution according to the knowledge of people employed for this purpose, according to their aims and tastes. The result is extolled as a rational economy for the satisfaction of needs, in contrast to what is characterised as the profit economy of the free market.

The effects of total planning obviously extend beyond the economic sphere, however, to the indirect guidance of the whole of human life, as far as the world of spiritual creation, which, more than any other activity, is dependent upon the freest initiative of individuals and is stifled by any planned direction. In the liberal world it was possible for the taste of Kaiser Wilhelm II himself to remain a fundamentally private reality—despite its inflation through the wealth behind it, and the support of compliant State organs— within a much more comprehensive spiritual life, upon which it made no impression and by which those vacuities were despised or scoffed at. In the totalitarian world, however, Hitler's taste determined who was allowed to paint at all and who was not.

The freedom of individuals to choose what they prefer for the satisfaction of their needs comes to an end; the manifoldness of supply and opportunities of trying things out to see if there are a few people to whom they appeal are at an end. For example, Kant's works are only for a minority, they have no further place in a planned economy in which, in the long run, the sole criterion is the needs of the masses together with the moods of those who hold power or the doctrines of the leaders of the State, who could also, if they wished, order the publication of mass editions of Kant's *Critiques*. The vast multiplicity of free needs makes it possible for the best and still unknown creative workers also to flourish, alongside the trash beloved of the masses, because there are certain groups that respond to their work, desire it and buy it. By contrast, in planned economy a goods-index must be presupposed that is oriented upon the needs of the masses. Instead of man, it is bureaucratic minds that decide what spiritual organism shall be permitted to grow.

Events have proved that economic total planning cannot be confined to the economic sphere. It becomes universal for the life of man. Direction of the economy leads to direction of the whole of life, in consequence of the form of life to which it gives rise.

Whoever desires economic liberty in reliance on the course of affairs when all human energies are aroused by competition, demands the progressive striking of fetters, opening of national frontiers and establishment of universal free world intercourse. He imagines a future in which bureaucracy will grow less and less.

Whoever, confronted by disorder, unpredictable economic crises, the squandering of labour power and over-production, the evils of unemployment and hunger, when technology offers the possibility of wealth, places his hope of salvation in total planning, demands the progressive concentration of power, until everything is directed by a central authority.

It has been said that *both* these alternatives are erroneous, and that truth lies in the middle with the extremes excluded. But the issue is a fundamental decision as to which of the two possibilities is to have pre-eminence. After the fundamental decision has been taken, the other standpoint will certainly be assimilated as a subordinate, but in such a manner as to lose its totality.

In *free market economy* no steps can be taken without far-reaching planning—but in this case it is restricted—and the plan will include the element of *laissez-faire* and the re-establishment of the conditions under which competition remains as a method of selection and confirmation. The planning of non-planning creates a framework and opportunities by means of laws.

In addition, there are certain domains in which planning will be carried out, for restricted spheres, in relative totality, i.e. so as to eliminate competition: thus for example, in public utility undertakings, railways and postal services, in the exploitation of raw materials susceptible of purely quantitative measurement, such as coal-mining, etc. Here freedom is retained through the fact that the acquisition of these raw materials is open to all on terms of equality, and there is no selective allocation to favoured consumers.

The question is—on the pre-assumption that the country is well supplied with the means of production, as distinct from the conditions of shortage prevailing in a war-devastated land—where and to what extent planning through economic guidance exercised by vast organisations becomes reasonable. Maximum practical advantage is by no means the only criterion. In the interests of liberty even the risks of crises and shortages may be accepted as part of the bargain, when distress through the threat to existence becomes absolutely compelling. When there is planning, however, the alternative is between privately organised and State planning. To be sure, monopolies will not be able to dispense with legally restricted State control, if the interests of the nation as a whole are to be protected. In view of experiences of the unprofitability of State enterprises, of the reduced productivity of labour in them, of the risk of red tape that comes with bureaucratisation, there always remains the question of how far planning by private monopolies, controlling themselves through managements drawn from their own factories and offices, is better able to achieve the aim than State planning. The criterion of judgement would be the best way of avoiding the danger of the spur provided by natural competition being lost and replaced by a State terror involving compulsory labour accompanied by liquidation of the right to strike, of freedom of movement, and of all militant initiative on the part of the workers for the advancement of that justice which is never finally attained.

The planning and organisation of the technological apparatus, which is indispensable to its efficient functioning, does not seem incompatible in principle with free competition, the constitutional State and human liberty in general.

Total planning: It dispenses with the incentive of competition, and therefore seeks to establish substitutes, such as output contests. But the principle of free agon is suppressed. The arbiter is appointed, the decision does not spring from the nature of the matter through the agency of unimpeachable experts. Certain qualities that have little to do with the matter play a part in the picking of the winner. Initiative is supposed to be stimulated, but it remains hemmed in by conditions. The whole concern heads toward the sullenness that comes from exhausting work without any hope of carving out a path of one's own by one's own achievements.

We can see before us two major trends, between which we have always had to choose as the origins of our decisions, if we were acting clearly:

Either we stand before comprehensive destiny in free choice. We have confidence in the chances of the free interplay of forces, notwithstanding the frequency with which they give rise to absurdities—for there are always opportunities of correcting them.

Or we stand before the world planned in its totality by man, with its spiritual and human ruin.[2]

5. The medium of planning: Bureaucracy

Where undertakings involving large masses of men proceed in an orderly manner, bureaucracy is needed. Hence the latter arises wherever there are such undertakings. It operated in Ancient Egypt, in the ancient world empires, in the Norse State of Frederick II, but not in the Greek City States. Modern technology, however, furnishes the organisation and effects of bureaucracy with unprecedented scope. It can now become really totalitarian.

Bureaucracy is sovereignty based on regulations and orders issued by officials of the civil service. It functions like a machine, but the implementation of these regulations is determined by the nature and outlook of the officials.

We can draw up a schema characterising the hierarchy of civil services types:

The ideal civil servant, like the artist, thinks almost continually of his vocation—a high government official, a hundred and twenty years ago, asked on his deathbed what he was thinking about, replied, 'About the State'. He obeys the regulations in free understanding, remains bound to the meaning of his occupation, lives in the concrete situations on which he has to decide; he must confine the ethos and activity of bureaucracy to the indispensable minimum, continually ask himself where it can be avoided, and act in such a manner that bureaucracy works rapidly and clearly and remains human and helpful in its operation.

A grade lower we find the officious civil servant, who already takes a delight in bureaucracy as such, zealously strives to expand and complicate its ramifications, enjoys his function, but is trustworthy and upright in his obedience to the regulations.

The third grade has lost the ethos—fidelity to the State and to the service, and trustworthy integrity. Corruptibility and mood become decisive. The civil servant is overcome by an atmosphere of emptiness and senselessness. He gets slack, work is reduced to sitting away the office hours. Anyone who works more zealously is regarded as a disturber of the peace. Instead of immersing himself in the concrete matter in hand, he is left with nothing but a desire to get through the work. Difficulties are settled, not solved. Everything is done in a dilatory fashion, it is postponed and brought into an atmosphere of unclarity. The official enjoys power as one who is powerless in all other respects, but in certain connexions is in a position to decide the fate of individual men. The climate of aridity is galvanised by figures of speech concerning official duty, the interests of the community and justice. He works off his ill-humour on those who cannot defend themselves. In his dealings with the public he shows not the friendly helpfulness that characterises the attitude of an undertaking to its customers, but the attitude of dominion to its object. The bearer of this 'arrogance of the civil servant' becomes rude, inconsiderate in his dealings with the public, sly and patronising, given to procrastination, keeping people waiting, evasion and negation.

Objectively, this degeneration of bureaucracy from an originally meaningful form of sovereignty that kept within bounds and was sustained by human personalities, to an arid apparatus of universal inhibition and oppression, can be characterised in the following manner:

Bureaucracy is a means. But it tends to make itself its own end. The crucial step is the one that leads from bureaucracy as a tool that serves, to bureaucracy that becomes autonomous. In this autonomous bureaucracy, the ethos of self-limitation is replaced by the tendency to boundless self-expansion.

In the first place, this lies in the nature of government by regulation. If the measures taken by bureaucracy bring about disaster and chaos—at the expense of the population—there is no longer any feeling of responsibility to make it reverse its own mistakes. On the contrary, all that happens merely serves as an excuse for the issue of fresh and more extensive regulations. Faith in the panacea of government by regulation seeks to extinguish initiative in the free play of activity and self-help through inventive achievement. There is one remedy for difficulties: fresh regulations. This path represents a levelling down through the subaltern mentality of bureaucrats to the point at which the subaltern mentality is common to all in the absence of any constructive idea. The complication of orders and the disenfranchisement of the populace simultaneously compel this populace to place a greater amount of labour-power at the disposal of bureaucracy for the execution of its orders. Ultimately everyone ends up in the service of the unproductive apparatus.

To this is added the solidarity of interests of all the officials of a bureaucracy. The apparatus must continue to exist and expand, because it is a matter of life and death for the value and status of its bearers. The apparatus, which is supposed to serve the interests of the population, serves itself. It demands stabilisation and security for itself.

This is possible because its very complexity removes it from public control. It becomes opaque and moves continually further out of reach of criticism. Finally no one can see through it, save those who are within it, and even they can only see through their own special field. It becomes immune to attack either from the side of the populace or from the side of the supreme organs of government. It lives from the solidarity of interests of the employees.

This condition persists even when a dictator makes the apparatus his tool with all the means of terrorisation. Then the apparatus is indeed transformed as regards the mental climate of its functionaries; it becomes a means to the implementation of political terror. But the process is one of the favouring or victimisation of individuals and groups, without anyone coming into possession of absolute power. Through its participation in the terror, the apparatus grows anew in its autonomy. Even the dictator who issues the orders must fall in with the solidarity of interests of this apparatus, and permit the corruption he has himself intensified.

6. The limits of meaningful planning

Planning first becomes a problem for discussion at the point where the question arises: Shall planning be confined to palpable individual purposes, and the course of events as a whole be left to the free play of forces—or shall the whole of everyone's activity be ordered by a plan? Shall we confine ourselves to short-term, circumscribed plans, or shall we adopt total planning?

The crucial question is: Is there a dividing-line between that which it is possible to plan, and that which it is impossible to plan with any prospect of success? If such a dividing-line exists, can it be determined?

Total planning would necessarily have to be supported upon total knowledge. Total planning is preceded by the decision as to whether a true total conception, a knowledge of the whole, does or does not exist.

Total knowledge would appear to render possible an adumbration of the future. This adumbration becomes the programme for action. The intention is to foster by one's own actions that which is bound to come, to participate by informed activity in the necessary course of events. The wish is to take an active grasp of the whole, by virtue of one's knowledge of it.

The prerequisite total knowledge does not exist however. This is true even of the economic realm.

No one can oversee the entanglement of economic realities. Our knowledge never extends beyond simplifying aspects. We are already living in an unintentionally created world. If we pursue within it our finite purposes on the basis of our finite knowledge, we bring about with these purposes results that we could not foresee. No will can create this world in its entirety, no cognition can know it. Just as we cultivate organic life, but destroy it by total interventions without being able to reconstitute it, so we do the same to the world of existence historically created by man. A virtually infinite number of factors determine the prosperity of a flourishing economy. No intelligence can calculate them in their totality. The science of economics itself is a means of experiment, not a system for the cognition of the whole.

Now, however, we possess a knowledge of man and of history that is different in character from the knowledge of nature and the interconnexions of economics. It is a contemplative knowledge, of which practical application forms no part. Thus we see the spiritual worlds of a culture, understand them, make them vividly real to ourselves by research and analysis. Thus, further, we see the meaning of human personalities, visualise the possible existence of man in relation to transcendence. But we cannot make it our purpose to become a personality, to create a culture, to produce a spiritual work. What we purpose is at any given time the prerequisite or path to such possibilities, which are realised in the main unintentionally. More than this: We here destroy, if we turn into a purpose the thing—for instance, to become a personality—which, by its very nature, cannot be willed, but must be bestowed upon us, even though our volition and action within a purposive framework, our constant activity, remain a precondition of this bestowal upon us. A fundamental misconstruction is involved if we attempt to act purposefully on the basis of our contemplative or visualising knowledge.

Only in the realm of finite purposes can we reach our goal according to a plan through information and the utilisation of means. In the realm of the living, things are different. To make this a purpose and to plan it simply causes it to disintegrate. That which is possible cannot, on that account, also be purposively willed, without disturbing or even destroying it.

Nietzsche says: 'In any case, if mankind is not to condemn itself to destruction through the agency of a consciously total government, a knowledge of the preconditions of culture, surpassing in extent anything we have acquired up to now, will have to be found as a scientific criterion for ecumenical goals.' This contains a warning for all present abortive endeavours—but at the same time commits the error of supposing such a total knowledge to be a sufficient prerequisite for a total planning that takes its direction from it or employs it as a means. Total knowledge is impossible, on account of the non-objective nature of the comprehensive whole.

Let us convince ourselves. From a rational point of view, total planning is not possible at all. It presupposes illusion as to our own knowledge and ability. In all planning, the crux of the matter is to see, in the concrete situation of the moment, the borderline at which one steps over from reasonable particular planning into the sphere of senseless and destructive planning of the whole. Hence the question arises: What is the extent of a reasonable and beneficial plan? In principle, the limits can be demonstrated by the following facts:

(1) We never know the whole in its entirety, but are always in the midst of it.
(2) Every action produces effects that were not intended and not foreseen.
(3) Planning is possible only in the realm of the mechanical and rational, not in that of the living and of spiritual reason.

The inclination to aim at total plannings, despite their impossibility, has two paramount sources: The model of technology, and the misleading influence of a supposed total knowledge of history.

The source of total planning in technology: Where disturbances appear in technology, the attempt is made to overcome them by means of purposive plans. Technological development itself achieves remarkable things in order to master through technology the damage that technology has wrought. Machines are improved and conditions of work made as favourable as possible. Beyond this reasonable point, however, recourse is had to dubious rational measures.

The dangers of a too rapid switch-over are countered by the purchase and sterilisation of new patents. It is sought to counteract the discontent, exhaustion and emptiness of men by the planned moulding of leisure, by organisation of the home and of private life.

More than this: It is hoped to obviate technology's lack of direction as a whole by the technicisation of its administration. Organisation of the whole in State socialism is intended to enable the correct path to be found, as it were, automatically, through the medium of control and computation on the basis of cogent knowledge.

Since such remarkable things have been achieved through planning within the realm of technology, the road leads from here, in intellectual thoughtlessness attendant upon fascination by technology, to the idea of a technocracy—the administration of technology by technology itself— which will put an end to every evil. It is superstitious belief in the universal constructive ability of science that presses along the road of total planning. The Age of Technology seeks the technological realisation of the idea of the overall reconstruction of human existence.

Attempts to put technology on the road to salvation through technology, however, do not suffice, and are, in fact, bound to make matters worse. In the last analysis, the Devil will not be driven out by Beelzebub.

The reconstruction of human existence cannot be planned and organised in toto. Firstly: Man must go on living all the time, he cannot take a moment off in order to begin the whole thing over again from the beginning. He has always to proceed from the status quo at any given time. Secondly: Dominion over technology is not to be attained through technology, nor its conquest by technocracy, which would rather represent a final levelling down, paralysis and enslavement.

Liberty on the bournes of technology is man himself, who does not allow himself to sink into the constraints of the merely technological, but draws from deeper origins the sustenance to keep alive his powers. The boundary of all planning and fabrication is set where man must give himself freely to his opportunities. Here what he can achieve is essentially incalculable; when purposefully willed it is spoiled or destroyed. It comes toward us from out of the future, astonishing, simple, and overwhelming, beyond and before all technology, including technology within itself. Where man has this openness in front of him and first lives out of and toward it, he is liberated from technicisation of his view of the world, from the technicist forms of the consciousness of being, whose operation is today taken for granted.

The source of total planning in the supposed total knowledge of history: Historical philoso-phy, as a terrestrial total knowledge, developed, through secularisation, from Christian historical thinking—the unique history of mankind made up of Creation, the Fall, the appearance of the Son of God, the end of the world and the Last Judgement. St. Augustine's total conception, based on the re-ligious idea of Providence, was transformed into the idea of the necessity of the concept, which, with Hegel, governs history dialectically, and, as the dialectical idea, enters into an obscure combination with the idea of cau-sality in the necessity of which Marxism thinks. Finally, in the vulgarised interpretation of history, the scientific idea of causality was transferred onto the totality of events, in the shape of beliefs in the knowable necessity of the historical process.

With this spiritual world as its point of departure, it is today an almost natural illusion to suppose it possible to apprehend history *in toto*. In this assumption there prevail the inexact ideas, which do nothing to clarify themselves, that: The total course of events is necessary, is fundamentally already laid down—sufficient investigation will enable it to be recognised in this necessity—the future follows from the past with cogent necessity—the course of the future may be inferred from the past—wrong prognoses do not rest upon a pre-assumption that is erroneous in principle, but upon inadequate insight, which, in principle, can be improved and developed to a point at which it is adequate.

Isolated prognoses that hit the mark seem to substantiate this basic con-ception; for example, Burke's astonishingly accurate prognosis of the further course of the French Revolution, Burckhardt's adumbration of future condi-tions, Nietzsche's prophecy of nihilism. Nevertheless, these were all accurate predictions based on clear discernment of what was already present.

The world of history as a whole, however, is incalculable; in detail it is full of connexions of causality, motive, situation and meaning that are suscepti-ble of investigation. All of them are particular when they become realisable to our perception. Their cognition will never become a proven cognisance of the whole.

The error of the total conception is shown in monocausal thinking that traces everything back to a single principle, either through the absolutisation of a tangible causal factor (e.g. the economic factor in history), or through the totalisation of a single process, which has allegedly been apprehended in its substance (e.g. in the dialectic of the objective spirit in Hegel).

The task is to live in the area of historical possibilities, to see the open world; man lives in the world and not above it. We illumine this area by our hypotheses, by the play of internally consistent images of evolution, by the attempt to draw various lines into the future from the realities of the past and present. But we do not permit such images, ideas and constructions to dominate us. They are orientations and remain questions. To take them for knowledge of reality is deleterious both to truth and to our actions. Only by holding open possibilities do we preserve the meaning of action in the particular.

Interpretation of meaning is, of course, different from causal historical cognition. What happens behind consciousness, and from there furthers or inhibits, we apply interpretively to what constitutes for us the whole issue of history: To be human means to be free; to become specifically human is the meaning of history. It is a European hope that something will come to meet this our meaning, ready to assist it; but it will render us assistance only if we actively lay hold of it. For without freedom, without merit and blame, spontaneously as in nature, nothing of that which constitutes for us the major issue happens in history.

All total planning in the human kingdom operates with man as though he were known, and with expectations based on knowledge of man. In this situation there are two contrary positions:

Man is always the same. The edifice of society is erected with him as he is, in order to provide all, who as humans do not change their nature, with as many goods and as much liberty as possible.

Or else: Man is not always the same, he changes with the conditions under which he lives, through these conditions themselves, along the opaque path of a metamorphosis through which he passes in the course of generations—hence the edifice of society is erected in such a manner as to enable the metamorphosis of man to take place through development of the specifically human element in humanity. An ideal of humanity is the target at which planning is aimed. The new condition of society is possible with transformed man, the new man is possible only through this condition. It is as if the planner were able to oversee man in knowledge, as though he wished to create him as an artist creates the work of art out of the material available to him, a presumption that sets man above man (as in the idea of the young Marx, or in Nietzsche's superman).

Neither of these positions is true, however. Neither shows the right road. Rather can we only live from the decision to work for freedom, and make this decision itself a factor, but in the humility of not knowing the final outcome. That is why the modern question is such a burning one: What is it reasonable to plan, and where does the boundary of planning and fabrication lie?

Thus there arises the necessity of acting without knowledge of the whole, and hence without knowledge of all the consequences of my actions—and at the same time, of these actions becoming a factor in the whole, in which I desire that my actions shall contribute toward the true and the best.

If the right organisation of the world does not exist, either for my knowledge or as the factual pattern of a possible future, then I must relinquish the instinctive touchstone of the understanding, consisting of the right organisation of the world, of perfection and the comprehended whole. Instead of this we must think and act in the totality of the world, each of us at his place. We must plan and purpose, surrounded by the whole, which, however, is present not as something that can be known, but as idea.

For this reason, openness to the future is a precondition of liberty, latitude of interpretation a precondition of the clarity of the present decision. Speculation on the future is precisely not insight into an unequivocal necessity, but into an open space of possibilities and probabilities.

7. Socialism and total planning

Socialism which, as communism, in its enthusiasm for the salvation of mankind that it feels certain of securing, takes steps to mould the future by force in total planning, and socialism as the idea of gradual realisation in the intercommunity of a free democracy, are alien to one another. The former consumes the man who surrenders himself to it in a faith that appears in the guise of a science; it treats the unbeliever as a material available to manipulation by force. The latter casts no spell, lives in the present, requires the sobriety of reason and the humaneness of unceasing communication.

When, in the course of its implementation, socialism comes up against limits, only the calm of reason can be of assistance. An example is the question of how far the planned organisation of work can and must go at any given time, and the way in which it puts an end to liberty when it oversteps this limit. Another such question is how far justice is conditional upon equality, and how far precisely upon the diversity of tasks and the conduct of life determined by them. Justice cannot be achieved solely by quantity and calculation. Over and beyond this, in the realm of qualitative differences, it is a task of infinite dimensions.

Communism may be characterised in contradistinction to socialism as the absolutisation of tendencies which are true in the first place. They then become fanatical through this absoluteness, and in practice cease to operate as a recasting of historical reality, which instead they melt down to a dead level. Some examples:

Firstly: Socialism sets itself in opposition to individualism. It sets community against isolation, against self-will, self-interest and the caprice of the individual.

This opposition, one-sidedly absolutised, means: The individual is denied his rights altogether. Whereas socialism started out with the intention of giving all men the chance to realise their personalities, it becomes, through the levelling down of the individual, the destroyer of personality.

Secondly: Socialism sets itself against capitalism. It desires to substitute common ownership of the means of production for their private ownership.

Absolutised, this has as its result: Instead of the question being confined to the private ownership of the means of production of machine technology—large-scale undertakings—the abolition of private property in general is demanded. Property—the way in which the environment is made up of the objects of daily use, the dwelling and the works of the spirit, that are at the disposal of the individual and that furnish him and his family with the basis of their existence, which is animated by them and in which they mirror their nature—is abolished. This means that man is deprived of his personal world, of the vital precondition of his historically unfolding being.

Thirdly: Socialism sets itself against liberalism. It desires the planning of human affairs, as opposed to preservation of the interplay of forces in competition and the free market, and as opposed to indifference toward the evils that develop out of the free interplay of forces.

Absolutised, this means: Instead of planning for definite purposes, whose effects can be kept under surveillance, planning in toto is desired. Justified opposition complacent to laissez-faire, laissez-passer is transformed into opposition to liberty, which is realised in openness to unpredictable possibilities through experimental initiative in intercourse.

If these examples are compared, one will in every case begin by agreeing with socialism. But in each case, unconcrete hypothesis arises the moment indication of direction changes into absolutisation of a position that excludes alternatives. Instead of succumbing to such an absolutisation we should rather ask ourselves on every occasion:

How far must guidance of the single individual go, how far behest and compliance?—How far common ownership and how far private owner-ship?—How far reasonable and necessary planning, how far trust in the impenetrable course of events through free human initiative?

As long as socialist demands are concretely visualised and thought out they remain within bounds. It is only when concrete reality is lost sight of and a fantastic paradise of man is presupposed as possible, that its demands become abstract and absolute. Socialism ceases to be an idea and becomes an ideology. The demand for complete implementation in fact leads away from its fulfilment. Along the path of coercion it leads to servitude.

There is no such thing as the right organisation of the world. Justice re-mains a never-ending task. It cannot survive violent fixation in human plan-ning as the alleged establishment of the right organisation of the world. For where liberty ceases, justice too is impossible.

Total emancipation of the arbitrary will of all, or of single individuals, on the historical road that remains open, would not accomplish the task either, however. For it would lead to the growth of injustice, and liberty is not pos-sible without justice.

Socialism retains from its origin the idea of liberty and justice for all. It avoids absolutisation. It is accessible to everyone through insight. It can link everyone. This is no longer possible once it becomes a fanatical faith and, through absolutisation, doctrinaire and violent.

Socialism today sees the great task of the common liberation of all through dispositions in which they accept the dominion of necessity, but in such a manner that they thereby enhance their freedom. It is an exceptional situa-tion, in which the laying of fresh foundations in the historical context seems possible to an unprecedented extent. The ordering of existence is the great unsolved task of the epoch. Socialism is the spokesman of all tendencies di-rected toward this ordering. It will approach its goal in the measure in which it attains unanimity without force, moves forward gradually along the route of history and does not, in the will to immediate total realisation, fall into the abyss in which history would come to an end, if man did not, in spite of everything, find new paths again out of the depths of his nature.[3]

We do not know whether political freedom will increase in the world with the advent of socialism, or whether it will be lost. Whoever renounces the presumption of a total knowledge, knows only that liberty neither comes nor remains of its own accord. Because it is in such immense peril, it can flourish only if all who desire it work for it at all times, in word and deed, with their whole beings. Indifference toward liberty, and taking the possession of it for granted, are the beginning of its loss.

The idea of freedom is part of humanity's truth. But we see the strength and self-assurance of the other element in man, the power of the unfree existence. Our understanding may well take fright, and in gloomy moments place a low assessment on the chances of liberty. When we recall our humanity, however, faith comes to life again. We have more confidence in the man who sees the peril soberly—and the free man can see it no otherwise—than the man who sees humanity's incapacity as definitive, without comprehending himself in the barbaric weight of his unillumined vitality or of his doctrines.

8. The motive of total planning and its mastery

Unclarity leads to the need to believe in salvation through total planning. To the superstitious belief in science it seems as though good might be obtained from a superior knowledge, which it supposes to be already in existence somewhere. The yearning for this helping knowledge in the shape of a leader, a superman, whom one can simply obey and who promises to accomplish everything, leads to the self-incurred illusion of the man who gives up enlightenment and ceases to think for himself. All salvation is expected from an impossible source.

Innumerable people regard total planning as the sole deliverance from distress. Unquestioning acceptance of total planning as the best solution has become for many a fundamental viewpoint. Coercive organisation will overcome want and disorder, it will bring happiness.[4]

It seems then that man veils from himself, with Utopian visions of the totality of things, what really happens in the whole, in order to perform, in the narrower area of purposes he can grasp, the tasks imposed on him by power. But some time or other the illusion of this conduct is bound to become manifest to him. For in the service of the veiled powers he has merely worked on his own downfall. Those achievements which, in his illusion, he deemed successes, were merely steps along the road to his ruin. He was not willing to look the Gorgon in the face, but he fell victim to it all the more completely.

It is uncanny how the delusion of total planning, which is not infrequently sustained by manifest idealism, leads man step by step through his own actions deeper and deeper into precisely that which he wishes to overcome, into want, unfreedom, lawlessness. This only happens, however, when that dividing-line is passed at which reasonable planning changes into calamitous planning, and particular planning that can be determined in its entirety into total planning that cannot be determined as a whole.

When man supposes that he can survey the whole, instead of pursuing concrete, tangible aims in the world, he is, so to speak, making himself into God—he loses his relationship to transcendence—he dons blinkers through the operation of which he loses sight of the experience of the origin and fundament of things, in favour of a semblance: mere movement in the world—the establishment of the right organisation of the world for all time—he loses the possibility of upsurge, because he succumbs to an apparatus of terror and despotism—he brings about a perversion of the apparently loftiest idealism of the goal of humanity, into the inhumanity of the squandering of human life, into the transformation of all the circumstances of life into an unprecedented slavery—he annihilates the forces that carry man forward—when he fails, he gives way in despair to the urge to ever more loathsome acts of violence.

No total plan will furnish adequate aid. Another origin, which is possible out of man as man, must be revealed. What is at issue is a metaphysically founded basic attitude, revealed in ethos, that guides the organisational plans. The control of an intrusive conscience, that cannot be objectivised in its entirety, must prevent the will to liberating reconstruction from leading ever deeper into servitude.

Knowledge of the obscurity of the whole may lead to the question: Is not the best thing inaction?

A trivial answer is: I must act in order to live, inaction is an illusion. Action is itself a factor in events.

Above and beyond this, we hear the doubtful alternative: Either total planning of life in the narrowness of the contingent—either participation in the high knowledge and dignity of man in the creation of his own happiness, or the aloofness of nugatory passivity!

Total knowledge, and the total planning founded on it, has in practice a miraculous consequence. It is no longer necessary to enquire and reflect. In time of distress we deceive ourselves: in order to gain false certainty for our actions, because we feel ourselves secure in that which must necessarily come—or in order to give ourselves grounds for despair, so that we can abandon effort and endless patience within the area of the possible—in both instances we are on a false road that will lead to frustration.

To live in the narrowness of the contingent, on the other hand, thoughtlessly robs life of the sense of participation in history, which passes interminably through time—none knows whither.

We are set free from this alternative by humility. Truth and the purity of our volition are determined by our knowledge of the limits of knowledge and ability.

B. WORLD UNITY

Technology has brought about the unification of the globe by making possible a hitherto unheard of speed of communications. The history of the one humanity has begun. A single destiny governs the whole of it. Men from all parts of the world can see one another.

Since the whole sphere of the earth is more accessible to the technology of communications than in former times Eastern Asia was to the Central Empire, or the Mediterranean world to Rome, the political unity of the earth can only be a matter of time. The path seems to lead from national States, via the great continental areas of government, to world empire or world order. It will eventually be enforced by the will to power and dominion which, by all historical analogies, is always there, has as its more or less conscious goal the largest world empire it is possible to attain at any particular time, and then, out of the will to peace, seeks a life free from anxiety in an order of the world.

Thus, in fact, the various local histories have today already become one continental history. To begin with, the universal tendencies proceed toward the structuring of great continental areas of life, which are related to one another. The spheres of the American continent, Eastern Asia, the Russian Empire and the territories of Europe, Hither Asia and Africa cannot continue to live alongside each other without connexions or in mutual indifference. They do not merely observe each other's existence; they either live in de facto material and spiritual exchange, or in a self-enclosure that heightens the tension.

INTRODUCTION

The historical analogy with the end of the Axial Period

Man's self-consciousness developed during the Axial Period. The compelling spiritual images and ideas appeared in the transition to the unmythological or at least no longer naively mythological ages. Endless possibilities were evolved in the free struggle of the spirit of a world rent by power politics. Every force awoke and stimulated the rest.

Through his highest upsurge, however, man first experienced all his distress, the insight into his imperfection and imperfectibility. The goal was redemption.

Rational thinking developed and, in conjunction with it, discussion, in which one throws the ball to the other and a perennially creative growth and deepening of consciousness takes place through generations. To every position there was the counterposition. On the whole, everything remained open. Insecurity became conscious. An unparalleled disquiet took possession of man. The world seemed to consciousness to be growing more and more chaotic.

In the end, the collapse took place. From about 200 B.C. onwards great political and spiritual unifications and dogmatic configurations held the field. The Axial Period ended with the formation of great States, which forcibly realised this unity (the unified Chinese Empire of Tsin Shi hwang-ti, the Maurya dynasty in India, the Roman Empire). These great change-overs from the multiplicity of States to universal empires—world empires in the sense that they embraced the whole of the world process known at the time in the three regions, which at that period were almost completely ignorant of one another—took place simultaneously. The metamorphosis was everywhere remarkable: The free conflict of spirits seems to have come to a standstill. The result was a loss of consciousness. Only a few suitable intellectual possibilities and spiritual figures from the bygone Axial Period were seized upon to impart spiritual community, lustre and concordance to the new State authorities. The imperial idea was realised in forms founded on religion. There arose spiritually stable, long-enduring periods of great empires, attended by a levelling down to mass culture and by the sublime, but unfree, spirituality of conservative aristocracies. It is as though the world fell into a centuries-long sleep, accompanied by the absolute authority of great systems and mummifications.

Universal empires are widely extended empires. Such empires are, for the vast majority of their peoples, foreign dominations, in contrast to the Greek City States and limited, self-governing tribal and national communities. The latter's self-government rested on active participation in political thought and action in the aristocratic form of democracy as it existed, in a different shape, in Athens and Rome. This democracy vanished with the transition to the equalising pseudo-democracy of extensive empires (to a great extent in Athens with the end of Pericles, totally in Rome with the transition to Caesarism). Where participation in political activity finally gave way to mere obedience and subjection, all sovereignty per se became foreign domination to the consciousness of the individual, at least for the greater part of the population of the empire.

Hence a profound transformation of man accompanied the transformation of his conditions into those of extended empires. Political impotence altered consciousness and life. Despotic forces, which seemed to be inseparable from the extended empire, threw the individual back upon himself, isolated him, levelled him down. Where no real share in responsibility and no intervention in the whole were possible, all were slaves. This slavery was veiled by figures of speech and sham contrivances from the free past. There was hardly ever so much talk of Greek liberty, which was again and again guaranteed by the victors, as when it was finally destroyed in favour of an imperial régime. That which took place in men who asserted their existence in community, to the accompaniment of a continual outer and inner fight for a better order, from out of the existing de facto orders in the Greek City States, was now lost. Something quite different then constituted a bond between the powerless: membership of a divine kingdom, belief in resurrection and redemption (the Christians). On the other hand, there developed magnificently in the rulers (the Romans) an all-embracing consciousness of responsible guidance of the State in the universal interests of mankind, a high art of government, of the construction of a world-spanning authority.

The analogy may, perhaps, cast some light on our future, despite the fact that this will look quite different. It is, at the same time, a warning for all who desire the liberty of man.

What will unity look like? If the first termination of the present development, which may not be so very far off, is the World State, this may appear either as an empire won by conquest and subject to a unified rule (perhaps in the form of a government which is in actual fact centralised, but which recognises the sham sovereignty of many States), or—the outcome of agreement and treaty—as a world government of united States which have renounced their individual sovereignty in favour of the sovereignty of mankind, that is seeking its way with legal order as the sovereign authority.

Motives on this passage to world unity are, for one thing, the will to power, which is no less alive today than at any other time, and which knows no bounds until it has subjugated everything, and, for another, amongst powers none of which dare risk a decision by force in view of the monstrous perils, the great planetary distress that presses toward agreement—and above both these, the idea of human solidarity.

All the phenomena of the present have the appearance of a preparatory struggle for the points of departure of the final battle for the planetary order. Contemporary world politics are seeking a basis for the ultimate settlement, whether this is to be reached by military or peaceful means. Until this has been achieved, all conditions and power relationships are temporary. Hence the present appears as a transition to this final planetary order, even if the exact opposite develops first: e.g. the radical interruption of communication on earth for the majority of people by totalitarian regimes. We shall now proceed to a more detailed analysis of the tendencies which are leading out of this transition period into the future.

1. World empire or world order

The question is, along what path will the unitary world order be attained. It might take place along the desperate road of force, as, in the words of Bismarck, the unity of Germany could be achieved only by 'blood and iron'. Or it might take place through an order arising by negotiation out of maturing understanding in mutuality, in the same way as, in the eighteenth century, the States of North America found their way to union at the cost of abrogating an essential part of their particular sovereignty in favour of the sovereignty of the whole.

The shape of the order would, in the first case, be the static peace of despotism, in the second case, a peaceful community of all subject to transmutation in perennial democratic unrest and self-rectification. Reducing the possibilities to a simple antithesis, therefore, the issue is between the path to world empire or the path to world order.

World empire. This is world peace through a single power, which coerces all from one point on the earth. It maintains itself by the use of force. It moulds the levelled masses by terror and total planning. A uniform world view is forced upon all, in simple outlines, by propaganda. Censorship and direction of spiritual activity compel the latter to play its part in the plan of the moment, which may be modified at any time.

World order. This is unity without unifying force other than that afforded by common decision in negotiation. Orders agreed upon can only be altered along the legally fixed path by new decisions. The supremacy of this procedure and of majority decisions has been accepted in common; it guarantees the common rights of all, which also protect those who are for the time being in a minority; these rights remain an order of mankind in movement and self-rectification.

The enslavement of all from one point stands in contrast to the order of all attendant upon renunciation by each single State of absolute sovereignty. Hence the road to world order leads *via* the voluntary renunciation of those with power as a precondition of liberty.

Where a sovereignty remains which is not that of mankind as a whole, there also remains a source of unfreedom; for it must assert itself by force against force. The organisation of force, however, conquest and empire-building by conquest, lead to dictatorship, even if the starting-point was free democracy. So it happened in Rome in the transition from the Republic to Caesarism. So the French Revolution changed into the dictatorship of Napoleon. Democracy that conquers abandons itself. Democracy that lives on good terms with others lays the foundations for the union of all with equal rights. The demand for full sovereignty is rooted in the energy of self-assertion destitute of communication. In the age of absolutism, when the concept of sovereignty was defined, the consequences were ruthlessly made conscious in word and deed.

Where the right of veto remains in decision by vote taken in common by the great powers, the claim to absolute sovereignty is maintained. If men assemble with peace, which is unconditionally desired by all, as their aim, they will be bound by agreement to accept the decision of the majority. There remains the possibility of further work to convince the rest that the decision was wrong and to have it rescinded by a fresh decision. Neither veto nor force is permissible however.

The motives for renouncing veto and sovereignty spring from the humaneness that desires peace—shrewd foresight that sees one's own power coming to grief unless there is unison with all the rest—the prospect of losing so much in a war, even in the event of victory, that this disaster outweighs everything else—the pleasure of mutual acceptance in spiritual conflict and the building up of the world—pleasure in life with men of equal status, and unpleasure in dominion over the vanquished and over slaves.

World order, with the abolition of absolute sovereignty, would mean the abolition of the old concept of the State in favour of mankind. The outcome would not be a World State (that would be a world empire), but an order, perennially re-established in negotiation and decision, of States governing themselves within legally restricted domains: an all-embracing federalism.

World order would be the continuation and universalisation of internal political freedom. Both are possible only through restriction of the political order to questions of existence. On the plane of existence, the issue is not the development, moulding and fulfilment of humanity *in toto*, but that which is or may be common to all men by nature, that which links men together above all diversities, above divergences of faith and world view—that which is universally human.

Natural law has, since early times, sought to give prominence to this common bond. It is the foundation of the rights of man, and in world order would erect an authority that would also protect the individual person from acts of violence on the part of his State, through the possibility of effective legal action under the sovereignty of mankind.

It is possible to evolve principles which are judicious for man as man (such as Kant's principle of perpetual peace). The concepts of the right of self-determination, equality of rights, the sovereignty of the State, retain their relative, but lose their absolute significance. The total State and total war can be demonstrated as contradictory to natural law; because in them the means and prerequisites of humanity become the final goal, or because through absolutisation of the means the meaning of the whole, the right of man, is destroyed.

Natural law is confined to the ordering of existence. Its end-purpose is always a relative one, that of the ordering of existence, but from the motive of the absolute end-purpose of authentic and complete humanity in the world.

The age of world unity cannot be adumbrated in advance, however fervent our interest in it may be. It is perhaps possible, however, to discuss the possibilities and limits of what will be:

(1) All happening will now be from 'within'. It will no longer be possible for any foreign powers, any barbarian peoples, such as have always existed for the universal empires of the past, to break in from outside. There will be neither limes nor Chinese wall (except that during the transition period the major areas will be divided off against one another). World unity will be single, all-embracing, enclosed, and hence not directly comparable to earlier empires.

If there is no further menace from without, there will no longer be a foreign policy, there will be no further need to adjust the order to the needs of defence against outside attack. The maxim of the primacy of foreign over domestic policy will have lost its meaning, as the validity of this maxim always has diminished when the threat from without was slight (for instance in England), and in the times of the great empires, at least for short periods (in Rome and in China).

The whole of production can be for the benefit of existence, and not of military destruction.

The necessary interconnexion between military organisation (against a threat from without or for purposes of conquest), total planning, force and unfreedom will break down. There remains, however, the possibility of the same interconnexion in a State based on terror and playing the role of a world empire. In the event of a general disintegration of human life, however, and of hidden anarchy, the whole will not, as heretofore, be galvanised into activity by a threat from without.

(2) A coming world order could not arise as a finished whole, but in numerous gradations of freedom. There will be stages in the evolution of the order. That which holds all men together as their common concern may be confined to a few factors, but it must under all circumstances take sovereignty away from all in favour of one comprehensive sovereignty. This sovereignty can be restricted to the elementary power-problems— the military, the police, the creation of laws—and in this sovereignty the whole of mankind can participate by voting and collaboration.

The order of human life, however, would be much richer than the all-embracing legality of mankind. What it will be like in universal peace must depend upon the various orders with their origins in history; the manifold pattern of life will be determined by the remoulding imposed upon it by technological conditions.

Restricted orders on the way to this final world order will become points of departure for the formation of a public spirit of mankind based on ethical considerations.

All this will take place only in the absence of total planning—if the sole plan consists of the laws and agreements that are valid for all—in a free market economy that is still decisive in essential domains—in free competition and in the rivalry of the spirit, in free intercourse, especially in the realm of the spirit.

(3) The metamorphoses that will overtake the soul and spirit of man in a *world empire*, as opposed to a world order, can be conjectured by analogy with the Roman and Chinese Empires. An unparalleled levelling down of humanity is probable, an ant's life in empty industriousness, a stiffening and desiccation of the spirit, a conservation in hierarchies of power through authority that is losing all trace of spirit. Yet these perils cannot become absolute in man. In imperial world unity there will be new modes of movement, fresh possibilities of individuation, of revolution, of the bursting apart of the whole into new parts, which will once again be in conflict with one another.

(4) Is a legal world order through a political form and a binding ethos possible to mankind at all? This question can only be answered in the future, by ages of fulfilment that have enjoyed peace and creativeness for a time in great orders. To seek to anticipate it would mean to create it out of thought. That is impossible. The expectation that primordial truth will play a part in the reality of the new world order tells us nothing about the content of this new order. For the common ethos which will in the future become the public property of mankind cannot arise in the re-establishment of vanished realities, but must consist of unpredictable constructions kindled afresh from the contents of the old.

The question of whether a world order based on converse and joint decision, as the precondition and consequence of liberty, is possible must be answered by saying that it has never before existed. This is no contra-indication of its possibility, however. It is analogous to the evolution of bourgeois liberty in a democratic order, to that conquest of force by law and justice, which, although seldom and never more than imperfectly, has nonetheless in fact been successful in exceptional instances. That which happened in circumscribed States, and therefore became real at some point, is not, in principle, impossible to mankind as a whole. But even if the idea is easily grasped, its realisation is immensely difficult, so difficult that there will always be many who are disposed to consider it impossible.

In any case, the way leads historically *via* the *de facto* political powers.

2. The political powers

(1)   The road to world order runs solely *via the sovereign States*, whose forces are organised for immediate military action in the event of conflict. The manner in which they escape from this state of tension, through negotiation or war, and find their way to one another, will decide the destiny of mankind.

A picture of the States as they actually are will give us a picture of the political situation of the world. There are the Great Powers—America and Russia—then the allied European nations, then the neutrals, and then, in stages, the vanquished. The complete powerlessness of the latter corresponds to the complete sovereignty possessed by the first alone. In between lie those who are autonomous, but yet more or less dependent and not infrequently compelled to make their decisions at a sign from the Great Powers.

Looking at the situation as a whole, it is obvious that the day of national States is over. The world powers of today comprise several nations. The nation, in the sense of the European peoples, is too small to be a world power as such.

The issue today is the fashion in which nations come together to constitute a world power: whether they are subjugated by one nation, or whether they find their way to each other as living nations of equal status in a community of States, to which they have sacrificed their particular sovereignty. This community of States may in turn call itself a nation, out of a political principle of the life of the State and of society, in which the members of several different peoples find their way to each other. The meaning of national consciousness has been transformed from an ethnic to a political one, from something naturally given to a spiritual principle. Yet today, by virtue of the survival of spectres from the past, there is still, and even increased, talk of nationalism, whereas it has already ceased to be a factor in politically decisive events.

Alongside the existing Great Powers of today, which industrial development has made mighty, there are the powers of the future; above all, China, which through its raw materials, human masses, aptitudes, cultural heritage and geographical position may perhaps become a key to political events at a not too distant date; in addition, there is India, which like a separate continent, on the fundament of a unique spiritual heritage handed down by its various peoples, presents the possibility of a power developing which, despite all movements of liberation, is still in fact slumbering there.

Seen within the totality of history, the two most powerful contemporary States, America and Russia, are historically quite young formations. It is true that the culture that took thousands of years to evolve has become theirs. But it is like something thrust upon them from without. Christianity came to Russia, Europe is spiritually present in America. Both America and Russia, however, measured against the primordial, world-creating cultures, are characterised by a lack of roots and thereby, simultaneously, by a magnificent open-mindedness. To look at them is singularly instructive and liberating for us, but also frightening. It is only to us in Europe that our cultural heritage is exclusively valuable, as, in a different fashion, their heritage is to the Chinese and Indians. To us and to them, in every situation, it gives a feeling of provenance, security and demand upon ourselves. By contrast, it is astonishing how those who are today the mighty of this earth are often oppressed by a slight feeling of inferiority, which they veil in a peculiar childishness and in the anger of their demands.

To see through the manner in which the play of political forces takes place, changes with the manoeuvres of the States in the confused maze of the chances of power, and how, nonetheless, certain great basic trends are preserved, would be of the greatest interest. For intellectual ideas of political order will come to realisation only on the road via the power that is to be won in this interplay of forces.

In the foreground of everyday life there is a great deal that looks fortuitous. Harm is wrought by everything that stands in opposition to organisation in larger contexts; such, for instance, as national claims that are made absolute, all particular artifices intended to gain special advantage for oneself, all attempts to play the Great Powers off one against the other in the hope of profiting by it.

(2) The whole population of the globe, more than two thousand million people in all, is drawn into the interplay of these powers. But guidance and decision is in the hands of the peoples who, comparatively, constitute no more than an infinitesimal fraction of this total mass. The majority is passive.

There is a *primal distribution of the world* which has existed since the dawn of history. Only once since the sixteenth century has this primal distribution been changed on a grand scale in relation to large areas that were unpopulated or settled by primitive peoples incapable of resistance. The white race took possession of the regions of America, Australia and Northern Asia as far as the Pacific Ocean. This established a new distribution of the earth.

A coming world federation will have to start from this distribution of the world as a reality, if the road to a forcible world order is to be avoided. On the path of violence the extermination of peoples, deportations, the annihilation of whole races, and thereby the negation of humanity, seem possible. It will not be possible for the Europeans permanently to dominate, or even merely to guide, the great human masses of China and India, which have stood firm, nor the peoples of the Near East. The prodigious difficulty is, however, that all these population masses must first reach the political maturity which will render them capable of emerging from the estate of violence into that of mutual agreement, and of grasping the nature of political freedom as a life-form.

These mighty, but still largely passive powers give rise to the question: Will the peoples conscious of liberty, numbering at most a few hundred millions, be able to bring conviction to the spirits of more than two thousand million others, and enter with them into a free, legal world community?

(3) The road to world unity starts from *a few historical origins* and from a quantitatively infinitesimal minority of man. World order springs from the same motives as the order of bourgeois society. Since bourgeois liberty was won at only a few places on the earth in historical processes unique to each, and since these constitute, as it were, the school of political

liberty, the world will have to accomplish on a large scale what was there exemplified on a small one.

The classical development of political freedom, which gives at least an orientation to all and is for many exemplary, occurred not more than seven hundred years ago in England. On this spiritual political fundament, liberty was created afresh in America. Within a very small area Switzerland realised this freedom in its federalism, which may appear like a model of possible European and world unity.

Today political freedom has almost disappeared amongst the defeated peoples. Here it had already been destroyed when the apparatus of a terrorist order declared that it was defending it.

The road to world order leads *via* the awakening and self-understanding of political liberty in as many countries as possible. This situation is without analogy in the conditions of transition to earlier world empires after the Axial Period. The idea and the task were scarcely conscious at that time; the reality of free States did not exist amongst the powers that were coming to sovereignty.

World order today, if it is realised at all, will start from the federalism of the States which are already free. It will be successful only if it exercises a sufficiently strong attraction to lead others to follow it out of conviction, and peacefully to join in with the world order which brings liberty, wealth and spiritual creativeness, the potentiality of humanity in its plenitude and multi-formity.

(4) If the unity of the earth is forced upon us by communications, a crucial factor will be the *sense of the earth and of power* imparted by the perspectives of travel.

For centuries England, through its domination of the ocean, saw the world from the sea as coasts which all lay as though enclosed within the private empire of dominion over the waves.

Today air-traffic has been added; although it is not yet equal to sea-traffic in its performance in transporting goods and travellers, it is nevertheless such an important extension that, to the politically seeing eye, the world becomes a whole from the air as well.

Power on the water and in the air seems more essential to the unity of the earth than power on land, even though in the last resort the latter must everywhere accompany the final act of decision in war.

The omnipresence of the legally directed world police would probably be most rapidly and safely implemented in the air.

3. The perils on the road to world order

Before the constitution of a dependable world order, there lies the transition period, which is full of perils. To be sure, all human existence is at all times a transition. But now the very foundations of humanity are tottering, the elementary groundwork of the future must be laid down.

We should like to be able to characterise this transition period that lies before us. It is our immediate future, whereas everything that will begin with world order or world empire will take place only in succession to it.

World order cannot be realised directly. Hence the nugatoriness of the enthusiasm, the invective, the projects, which are supposed to contribute immediately to its achievement, as though they represented the philosopher's stone.

Much more clearly than world order itself, we can see the perils that threaten on the way thither. Every peril bears within itself, through the fact that it is known, an element of surmountability. In human affairs there is no intrinsically mortal danger, if man can be free in accordance with his nature.

(1) *Impatience:* The road will reach its destination only if the active participants are possessed of infinite patience.

It is fatal, in the desire to force through that which one has recognised as right, to let failure cause one to refuse further collaboration, obstinately to break off converse, and to have recourse to violence or the preparation of violence.

The momentary supremacy of the one who holds the trump card, threatens force, or blackmails, proves in the long run to be weakness, and is in any case to blame for the lengthening or blocking of the road. The exceptionally difficult task is, without becoming weak, not to forget force when confronted by force, but to postpone its use until the very last moment. For the responsible statesman there is no prestige reason for the use of force, no reason for a preventive war, no reason for breaking off negotiations. In every situation there remains human speech—until one party, possessing sufficient force to do so, breaks off and is now a criminal in the measure in which all the rest had, and still have, patience.

It is impossible to assess what will, in the future, aid this process and what will hinder it. Situations continually change. The attempt must not be abandoned, even in relation to the malevolent and underhand. Intolerance must be patiently led to tolerance. We must relegate to the final stage the goal of rendering all force harmless as criminality by means of the one legal force of humanity. Until then the possessor of great force (the magnitude of which alone distinguishes him from the criminal, if he makes use of it) must be treated with the circumspection and patience that may win his friendship. If this is to succeed at all, it can do so only if the rest remain calm and do not throw away the slightest opportunity for reconciliation.

An example of the fact that the craving after immediate realisation of the right may be a mistake is perhaps provided by the following: The right of veto is in itself an evil. But its abolition would presuppose that all the interested parties were ready, even in a serious instance, to bend their wills to the majority decision, that in their ethos they had really renounced sovereignty, in the same way as the citizens within a State. This calls for essential human community realised in every phase of intercourse. Before this has been attained, abolition of the right of veto would be fruitless. For if a Great Power were to oppose a majority decision and its execution, this would mean war.

It is stimulating to see how, in participation in political negotiations, in so far as they are made public, this patience finds a language, seeks paths, and evokes intercommunity again through repeated new flashes of inspiration. It is disheartening to see how, against all reason, ignoring all facts and motives, in perpetual disruption of converse, the sovereignty of the veto smashes what all the rest sought to build up.

And it is magnificent to see from a study of history—particularly the history of the English, Americans and Swiss—how man had patience, overcame himself, and even in hatred, came to terms with his opponent at the dictate of reason—and how ways were found of carrying out peaceably the revolutionary changes for which the times were ripe.

Patience—obduracy—steadfastness—these are indispensable to the politically active man. This patience consists in the ethical attitude that does not succumb to personal mortifications, that keeps the objective whole always in view, that appraises and distinguishes the essential from the inessential. It consists in the watchfulness that remains undiminished in waiting and in apparent fruitlessness: comparable to the huntsman at his station, who waits for hours, but at the instant when the fox leaps across the woodland path, has to raise his gun, take aim, and fire in the fraction of a second. This untiring alertness that misses nothing and is watchful, not for one single thing, as for a wild animal, but for all unforeseeable favourable opportunities, is indispensable to the active statesman. The great danger to human activity lies in impatience, exhaustion and the climate of fruitlessness.

(2) *Once a dictatorship has been set up it cannot be got rid of again from within:* Germany and Italy were set free from without. All attempts from within came to grief. This might be a coincidence. But if we call to mind the way in which a terrorist regime operates with the means of total planning and bureaucracy, it becomes evident how fundamentally insurmountable is the machine that maintains itself almost automatically, and in which everything that appears to oppose it from within is obliterated. The means of modern technology give the *de facto* ruler a tremendous preponderance of power, if he makes ruthless use of all the means at his disposal. There is just as little chance of overthrowing such a regime as there is of the inmates of a penitentiary overthrowing the governor and his staff. The machine reaches the peak of impregnability when the terror includes all, in such a manner that those who do not wish it become terrorised terrorists, killing in order not to be killed themselves.

Hitherto such despotic terrorist regimes were local. Thus they could be annihilated from without, if not from within. If, however, the peoples should fail to absorb this into their consciousness and into their concern for the future, if they should all slip unawares into such a dictatorship in the shape of a world dictatorship, there would be no further prospect of liberation. The danger of this state of affairs coming about is all the more acute when people feel safe from it, and suppose, for example, that only the servile Germans could find themselves in such a situation. If the same fate befalls the rest of the world, there will be no more outside. The rigidification of the whole in total planning, stabilised by terror, would annihilate liberty and mean the road to increasing ruin for all.

(3) *The danger of absolute destruction:* On the road to the order of the World State events might take place which, before the goal had been reached, might inflict such destruction upon mankind that we can hardly imagine the continuation of history. A miserable remnant would be left

living scattered over the surface of the earth, to start all over again as thousands of years ago. The links between men would have been torn apart, technology would be at an end and life dependent upon the local possibilities of the moment, which would just suffice to maintain it in extreme want to the accompaniment of exhausting effort demanding vital force and youthfulness. This end would arise if a war resulted in the demolition of the structure of technology, if raw materials were used up without the discovery of a substitute, if war did not cease but crumbled, as it were, into more and more circumscribed local hostilities—a state of perpetual warfare such as existed prior to history.

The meaning of warfare has undergone a metamorphosis in the course of history. There were wars that were the chivalrous sport of aristocrats and conducted according to the rules of the game. There were wars whose purpose was the decision of a question, and which came to a timely end before all organisable forces had been thrown in. There were wars of extermination.

There were civil wars and ministerial wars between nations, which nevertheless retained some sort of solidarity, through the fact that both parties were European. There were more pitiless wars between cultures and religions alien to one another.

Today war seems transformed by the extent of its means, the magnitude of its consequences. It has acquired a different meaning:

(1) All the most extreme elements foreshadowed during historical epochs seem to have combined to such a degree that there are absolutely no moderating tendencies left in war. Hitler Germany was the first country in the Age of Technology to embark in principle on the path which the rest then followed of necessity. Now we are threatened by a war which the Age of Technology and the abolition of all restraints will make so different that extermination and deportations, which to a certain extent also occurred in earlier times—with the Assyrians and the Mongols— do not suffice to characterise the disaster.

This uncontrolled totality of war, with no moderation of its means, is due in part to the interrelationship between total planning and war. The one lends impetus to the other. Power that seeks to reach absolute ascendancy is bound to tend toward total planning. Since, however, this reduces economic prosperity, there comes a point at which the optimum of armament has been reached. War is forced on the country by its inner development, which, with the continuance of peace, would lead to its growing weaker.

In the long run wealth, progress and vigour are attendant upon liberty; for a short time, however, and transitorily, supremacy comes with total planning and terrorist force, with its organisation of all the energies of a population for the destructive gamble, into which everything is thrown without reservation.

The way of the world seems to lead to such catastrophes, whose consequences in anarchy and misery beggar description. The only salvation is a world order based on the rule of law and possessing the power to preserve peace, by meeting every act of violence with superior force that robs it of all chance of success, and by punishing it as a crime.

(2) If war cannot be avoided, the crucial thing for world history is what manner of men emerge victorious; whether they are the representatives of naked force, or a human type that lives by the spirit and by the principle of freedom. The factor that will decide the issue of war is technology. And here we come face to face with an ominous fact: Technology can be used by everyone. Not everyone can discover it, but once it has been discovered even primitive peoples can learn its ways, can learn to serve machines, to fly aeroplanes and drive tanks. Hence technology in the hands of the peoples which did not invent it, becomes an immense danger to the spiritually creative peoples. If it comes to war, the only chance is that the inventive peoples will gain the military advantage by means of new inventions.

It is true that decisions on the nature of the new world order will not be wrested from the struggle of spirits alone. If, however, decisions are reached on the way to this new order through the agency of technology, which, at the last moment, is carried to fresh heights by free, creative spirits, its victory might be of spiritual significance also. What will to free order prevails in the warring powers might, through this new order, lead simultaneously to liberation for the world, if the sense of freedom is assimilated by men who are becoming more and more awakened, while, at the same time, it is fostered by the victors themselves.

(3) In the shape of the atom bomb as a means of destruction, technology opens up a completely different vista. Today everyone is aware of the threat to human life represented by the atom bomb. On its account there must be no more war. It becomes a motive—though up to now only a weak one—for the preservation of peace, because of the immense danger with which this kind of war threatens everyone.

In very truth, technology may cause destruction on a scale which it is still impossible to predict. If it is reproached with having set free the elemental and brought it to destructive effectiveness, this has been its nature since the beginning, when man learnt to kindle fire. Today the Promethean idea does not bring with it anything new in principle, but quantitatively it increases the peril beyond all measure, to the point at which we contemplate the possibility of pulverising the globe in space—with which the Promethean idea becomes something qualitatively different as well.

With the atom bomb, a piece of solar substance has been brought to the earth. The same thing happens to it on the surface of the earth which has hitherto happened only in the sun.

Up to the present, the application of nuclear chain reactions has been confined to those substances extracted with great difficulty from uranium ores. The fear that this type of atomic fission might spread to other elements, to matter itself, as fire spreads to all inflammable material, is stated by physicists to be groundless. Nevertheless, there is no certain limit valid for all time. Giving oneself up to the play of fantasy it is possible to imagine:

It is uncertain beyond what dividing-line the explosion will lay hold on further elements and terrestrial matter as a whole, like a conflagration. The whole globe would explode, whether intentionally or unintentionally. Then our solar system would be temporarily lit up, a *nova* would have appeared in space.

We can pose a singular question. Our history has lasted some six thousand years only. Why should this history occur just now, after the immeasurable ages of the universe and of the earth that have preceded it? Do not humans, or at all events, rational beings, exist anywhere else in the universe? Is it not the natural development of the spirit to extend its operations into the universe? Why have we not long since had news, through radiations, from the universe? Communications from rational beings infinitely further advanced in technology than ourselves? Can it be because all high technological development has so far led to the point at which the beings have brought about the destruction of their planet with the atomic bomb? Can some of the *novae* be end-effects of the activities of technological rational beings?

Is the progidious task then to recognise the gravity of this danger, to take it really seriously, and to introduce a self-education of mankind which, despite the constant danger, will avert such an end? The peril can be overcome only if it is consciously seen, if its menace is consciously prevented and rendered impossible. This will only happen if the ethos of man is equal to the task. It is not to be accomplished technologically: man as such must become trustworthy in the preservation and effectiveness of the institutions he has created.

Or are we confronted by a necessity before which there is nothing left but capitulation—where sentimental visions and unreal demands become unworthy of man, because they deprive him of his veracity? No, and even if it had happened in the world a thousand times—which is in any case pure fantasy—each fresh instance would present afresh the task of preventing the catastrophe, and that by means of every conceivable direct measure. Since, however, all such measures are unreliable in themselves, they require to be founded in the ethos and religion of all. In this way alone can the unconditional no to the atom bomb provide support for those measures which will be effectual only if they apply to everyone.

Anyone who regards the terrestrial catastrophe, whatever its nature, as inescapable, must see his life against this background. What is a life that must come to such an end?

All this is the play of ideas, however; its only meaning is to bring the factual danger into consciousness and to call up a vision of a world order based on the rule of law, which, in its all-decisive significance, evokes the whole earnestness of man.

4. Ideas opposed to the possibility of world order

The idea of world order, this European idea, is disputed. It is supposed to be Utopian.

Men are supposed to be incapable of communal order. World order is supposed to be possible only through the power of an ordering dictator. The national socialists' plan of subjugating Europe and then, with the combined force of Europe, of conquering the world, in order to Europeanise it, is supposed to have been good and workable as an ideal; only the bearers of the idea were evil.

This is not so. These basic ideas of contempt for man and of force, which, in the last resort, is always terrorist, are inseparably bound up with men of just this type.

But, the thesis goes on, the world dominion which will naturally arise out of the quantitative preponderance in territory, population and raw materials will, in the last analysis, be just as much a rule of force, as far as the less fortunate peoples are concerned, as a dictatorship. Along a seemingly peaceful road, certain men will enforce their will on all the rest through economic expansion.

This is an exaggeration if the situation is compared to the ruin of war. And it is a mistake to forget that there are, in principle, peaceful means of redressing injustices arising out of economic power. There is here, however, a real question for the success of true world order. Economic power must also be prepared to accept self-limitation under laws, and to subject itself to conditions; it too will have to serve the idea of world order, if the idea is to become a reality.

World order—the thesis continues—is not a desirable goal at all. If it were once stabilised, it would probably result in a totality of knowledge and valuation for all, a complacency, and an end of humanity, a new sleep of the spirit in the tranquillity of recollection that understands less and less, a state of fulfilment, a universality of that desired by all, while their consciousness diminishes and they undergo a metamorphosis into creatures that are hardly human any more.

All this might apply to the subjects of a world empire, if it lasted for hundreds and thousands of years. It certainly does not apply to world order. In the latter the elements of unrest remain. For it is never perfected; it is always in mutation. New decisions and enterprises are called for. The manner in which the position reached will give birth to fresh situations requiring mastery cannot be foretold. Discontent and insufficiency will seek a new break-through and upsurge.

World order—this thesis finally states—is impossible because of what man is and because of the situations in which, by the nature of the matter, agreement is out of the question, and decision by war—the 'appeal to heaven'—is inescapable. Man is inadequate. He falls short of what is required of him in possessiveness—in disregard of others—in the flight from order into confusion, and then into the spiritless struggle for power—in self-assertion through the breaking-off of communication with 'irreducible' demands—in the urge to destruction.

5. *The idea of world order*

In opposition to all denials of the possibility of a just and legal world order of peace, observation of history and our own wills again and again gives rise to the question: Will this new order not one day become possible, this convergence of all into a realm of peace? The trail toward it was blazed at the very beginning, when men founded State communities for the creation of order among themselves. The only question was the size to be attained by these communities of peace, within which the settlement of conflicts by force became a crime and hence punishable. In such large communities there already prevailed, even if only for limited periods and under a constant threat, dependability and the outlook that sustains legal order. There is, in principle, no boundary to the endeavour to expand such a community, till it becomes the community of all men.

Hence the readiness to renunciation and compromise, to mutual sacrifice, to the self-limitation of power not only from considerations of advantage, but also from the recognition of justice, has been as perennial a feature of history as the urge to force. The greatest proclivity to such an attitude was perhaps to be found in aristocratic, moderate, inwardly cultured men (like Solon); less in the average man, who is always disposed to consider himself right and the other in the wrong; none whatever in men of violence, who are not prepared to come to terms at all, but want to hit out.

In view of this human diversity, doubt will be justified: In world unity—whether it is a unity of world order or world empire—there will be no permanent calm, any more than within the State formations we have seen up to now. Jubilation at the attainment of *pax aeterna* will prove illusory. The forces of remoulding will assume fresh shapes.

In his finitude, man is left with basic instincts and resistances which render it improbable that we can expect a condition of the world in which the liberty of all is so integrated as to become an absolute power capable of finally exorcising everything that threatens freedom, including finite aspiration to power, finite interests, and self-will. We have rather to reckon that the wild passions will be re-established in new forms.

Above all, however, there is an essential difference between what the individual can at any time become through his own agency, and what the community of political order can become in the course of history. The individual can become existence that is capable of finding its own eternal meaning in the manifestation of the epoch; the human group and mankind, however, can become an order that is a communal product of history only through generations and that gives scope to the potentialities and limitations of all individuals. But order only exists through the spirit with which individuals animate it and which gives individuals their stamp in the sequence of generations. All institutions are dependent upon men, who are individuals. The individual is here the crucial factor—in so far as it takes many or the majority of individuals to sustain the order—and yet, at the same time, as an individual, he is powerless.

The singular fragility of all orders, with the spirit that bears them, is reason enough to regard the future with uncertainty. Illusions and Utopias are certainly powerful factors in history, but not of the kind that create order for liberty and humanity. Rather is it of crucial importance to liberty that, in thinking out the possibility or impossibility of a world order, we should not lay down any picture of the future, any devised reality, as the goal toward which history is of necessity steering, which we ourselves assimilate as such into our fundamental wills, and with the attainment of which history would be consummated. Never shall we find a fulfilment of history, save in every present as this presentness itself.

The limit of historical possibilities has its deep foundation in humanity. No perfect end-state can ever be attained in the human world, because man is a creature that constantly strives to thrust out beyond itself, and is not only imperfect, but imperfectible. A mankind which desired only to be itself would, in restricting itself to itself, lose humanity.

In history, however, we may and must lay hold of ideas, if we want to gain a meaning for our life in community. Projects of perpetual peace, or of the prerequisites for perpetual peace, remain true, even if the idea is incapable of realisation as a concrete ideal, but remains rather an infinite task beyond the possibility of being fashioned into a reality. An idea can be brought into congruence neither with the anticipated image of a possible reality, nor with the reality itself, even though it is the meaning implicit in planning for it.

Its basis, however, is an inexplicable confidence, namely the certitude of faith that everything is not null and void, not merely a senseless chaos, a passing from nothing into nothing. The ideas that guide our passage through the world are revealed to this confidence. For this confidence, truth consists in the vision of Isaiah, in which the idea becomes a symbolic image, this vision of universal concord: 'And they shall beat their swords into plough-shares, and their spears into pruninghooks: nation shall not lift up sword against nation, neither shall they learn war any more.'

C. FAITH

Introduction

The task of mastering the Age of Technology in favour of the specifically human element in humanity has become conscious in the major tendencies of this age, socialism and world order.

It is not enough, however, to found them on science, technology and civilisation. These do not afford a reliable foundation. They are in the service of evil as well as good. Man himself must live from a different origin. Hence flaws have today appeared in our trust in science. Superstitious belief in science, enlightenment that has proved deceptive, and the disintegration of its contents bear witness against it.

Even the great spiritual powers handed down to us no longer support life. There is no longer any complete trust in humanism: it seems to stand aloof, as though it were not there at all.

It is no longer possible for the masses to place entire trust in the Churches as such; they were too impotent when evil triumphed.

Science, humanism and the Churches are too indispensable to us, we shall never relinquish these powers. They do not suffice, they conceal in themselves evil aberrations, but by virtue of their potentialities they are indispensable preconditions for the whole of man.

Today the situation demands: We must return to a deeper origin, to a fountainhead from which all faith once welled forth in its particular historical shapes, to this wellspring which can flow at any time man is ready for it. When trust in that which is manifest and given in the world no longer supports life, then trust in the origin of all things must lay the foundations. Up to now we have hardly got further than feeling the task to exist. So far, it seems, we have all failed to accomplish it.

The question is: How will the content of our cultural heritage be preserved under the conditions of the Age of Technology and the reorganisation of the whole human community? How shall we preserve the infinite value of the individual, the dignity and rights of man, the freedom of the spirit, the metaphysical experiences of the millennia?

The specific question of the future, however, which conditions and includes everything, is how and what man will believe.

Faith cannot be discussed in the same terms as those in which we spoke of socialism and the trends and counter-trends of total planning, of world unity and the trends to world empire or world order. Faith is not a matter of the goals of volition, nor of the contents of reason that become purposes. For faith cannot be willed, it does not consist in propositions, between which one has to choose, it evades the programme. But it is the Comprehensive, by which socialism, political freedom, and world order must be borne along their path, because it is from faith alone that they receive their meaning. Without faith there will be no guidance from the fountainhead of humanity, but a falling prey to that which has been thought, conjectured and imagined, to doctrines, and then, as a result, to chaos and ruin. At no point is it possible to discuss faith in tangible terms, but perhaps something can be said about it. One can circle round its potentialities. We shall attempt this.

1. Faith and nihilism

Faith is the Comprehensive that holds the reins even when the understanding seems to be autonomous. Faith is not a particular content, not a dogma— dogma may be the expression of an historical shape assumed by faith; but it may also be a delusion. Faith is the fulfilling and moving element in the depths of man, in which man is linked, above and beyond himself, with the origin of his being.

The self-evidence of faith is achieved only in historical patterns—no truth may regard itself as the sole and exclusive truth for all men, without becoming intolerant and at the same time untrue—but between all believers there exists a hidden common element. The only antagonist, the antagonist that lurks in readiness in every one of us, is nihilism.

Nihilism is the sinking down into lack of faith. It may seem as though man, as an animal species in the realm of the living, could live in his immediacy from his instincts. But he cannot. He can only, as Aristotle said, be more or less like an animal. If he denies this and seeks to live self-evidently from nature like the beasts, he can follow this path only in conjunction with the consciousness of nihilism, and therefore only with a bad conscience or with the presentiment that he is lost. In nihilism he shows himself to be still a man and not a beast by cynicism and hate, by negative thinking and acting, by a condition of chronic indignation.

Man is not merely a creature of instinct, not merely a point of understanding, but also a creature that is, as it were, above and beyond itself. He is not exhausted by that which he becomes as an object of physiology, psychology and sociology. He can win a part in the Comprehensive, through which he first becomes authentically himself. This Comprehensive we call idea, in so far as man is spirit; we call it faith, in so far as he is existence.

Man cannot live without faith. For even nihilism, as the opposite pole to faith, exists only in relation to a possible, but denied, faith.

That which is happening today in the direction of socialism, planning and world order will never become real and find its meaning solely and decisively through rational cognition, nor through the instincts of man, but essentially through the way in which men believe and through the content of their faith—or how they stand nihilistically at the opposite pole to faith.

The important thing for the course of events is what ethical standards we recognise factually in our practical activity, from what origin we live, what we love.

2. The aspect of the present situation

When Rome drew the whole of the ancient world into its empire, it completed the levelling which had been going forward since the time of Alexander. Links of national custom were weakened, the local historical heritage ceased to sustain the proud life of autonomous energies. The world was levelled off spiritually into two languages (Greek and Latin), into a shallow ethical system which, because it was without effect on the masses, made room for enjoyment for its own sake and for the desperate sufferings of slaves, of the poor, and of the vanquished. The ultimate wisdom of the individual lay in shutting himself off from the wicked world. A philosophy of personal steadfastness—based either on dogmatic doctrines or on scepticism, it made little difference which—afforded an escape to many, but could not permeate the masses. Where nothing is really believed any more, the most absurd beliefs gain the upper hand. Superstition in manifold guises, doctrines of salvation of the most extraordinary kinds, circles gathered round peripatetic preachers, therapists, poets and prophets, in an endless confusion of vogue, success and oblivion, present a garish picture of narrow fanaticisms, wild adorations, enthusiastic devotion, and also of opportunism, imposture and knavery. It is wonderful to see how, in the midst of this chaos, Christianity ultimately gained paramountcy—this spiritual organism which, although it is by no means unequivocal, is yet of all faiths the one with the incomparably most profound implications, which was then, and for all time continued to be, typified by an absolute earnestness, before which all other species of faith vanished. This was not planned and not fabricated. When plan and purpose become involved in Christianity, which they did finally after Constantine— when it was misused, it was already there out of its deep origin, and its links with this origin held fast through all distortions and perversions.

We find in our own period much that is analogous to this ancient world. But the great difference is that contemporary Christianity has no parallel there, and that nothing corresponding to the Christianity which, at that time, was new and world transforming, is in any way visible today as a solution. Hence comparison is relevant only in respect of particular phenomena, for instance in analogy with the workers of magic, the communities formed around them, and doctrines of salvation of an absurd kind.

The picture of the modes of faith current in our era may be seen in a totally different light. To statements regarding the age's loss of faith, the factual impotence and ineffectiveness of the Churches, and nihilism as the basic feature of our world, the reply is made: This picture of ruin emanates from false standards derived from the past and from that which is outmoded beyond recall. Today, it has been said, there are mighty faiths, capable of moving mountains, derived from a new origin. This was already said of the Jacobins of the French Revolution and their faith in virtue and terror, reason implemented by the most radical force. Similarly, the great liberal movements of the nineteenth century have been called a religion of liberty (Croce). Thus, finally, Spengler asserted the appearance of fundamental conceptions with a religious character and an irresistibly cogent power of conviction as the end-stages of cultures; thus the end for the West is socialism as for India it was Buddhism, and for the ancient world stoicism. The religion of socialism moves the human masses of our era.

Total planning, pacifism and so forth seem, as it were, like social religions. They have the appearance of being the faiths of men without faith. Instead of living in faith, man lives in illusions concerning realities in the world, concerning the future and the course of events, which, in his faith, he thinks he knows.[5]

The thesis that justifies this out of nihilism runs: Man always lives on illusions. History is the course taken by changing illusions. In contradiction of this it must be said that history is traversed not only by the many illusions, but also by the fight against them for truth. Admittedly, the man without power is particularly disposed to illusions, and today the individual is perhaps more powerless than ever before. But he can also lay hold of the only chance open to powerlessness, unconditional striving for truth.

The nihilist declares this in turn to be illusion. For there is no truth. Hence he finishes up with the thesis: One must believe, no matter what—the necessary illusion will be extracted from one's own energies, which can say: I do not believe it, but one must believe it.

If we are speaking of faith psychologically, and do not enquire into the content, the truth and objectivity, we are dealing here at all points with analogies to religious faith: Claim to the exclusive validity of one's own truth, fanaticism, lack of understanding for anything else, absoluteness of the postulates, readiness for sacrifice and for devotion of one's life to the cause.

Images arise with the appeal of religious symbols, as for instance when the young Marx thinks in his writings of a new man, the truly human man, who has never before existed, who will now awake, the man who will divest himself of his self-estrangement. Or when today the new man of machine labour, the hard man with masklike features, reliable in his service and impersonal, is glorified in his sovereignty.

Psychological features cannot, however, impart to a faith the character of religious faith. These features are characteristic rather of substitutes for religion and of anti-philosophy. In the medium of rationality, in the misuse of science for the establishment of a superstitious belief in science, a demonstrably fallacious idea of the possible perfection of the world, of the right organisation of the world, is perverted into the content of a faith. But these perversions are powerful; they are at work throughout the world, and impel the course of events into the danger of intensified ruin. In actual fact, no fresh content of faith exists, the emptiness of this faith seems rather to be a correlate of man's loss of himself. It is typical that the advocates of such faiths respect nothing save force and power. They can no longer listen to reason, an origin of truth with its provenance in the spirit has no validity for them.

Let us pose the question once more in principle: Is faith possible without transcendence? Can man be taken possession of by a goal belonging to the inner world, that has the character of faith, because its content appertains to the future and is therefore, so to speak, transcendent to the present and in contrast to the suffering, discordancy and self-contradictory reality of the present?—a goal which, like so many religious faiths, has the tendency to delude us concerning the present, to console, to find a substitute in something non-existent, non-present?—and is nevertheless capable of successfully calling for self-sacrifice and renunciation in the interests of this illusory future?

Will the consequence of such a faith, in which all enchantment is lost, and in which, with transcendence, the transparency of things is also extinguished, be a decline of the human spirit and creativeness? Will there remain only skill, intensity of labour, and an occasional striking of the right solution, a Promethean enthusiasm for the technological, for the learning of manual dexterity? Or will the road lead here into fresh depths of being, which are not yet visible to us because, as yet, no language speaks to us from out of them?

We deem it improbable. It is more likely that to all this is opposed the consciousness of man's eternal origin, the consciousness of man who, in manifold historical garbs, is essentially the same through the content of his faith, which links him to the matrix of his being. Man can veil himself and his origin, he can let it slip from consciousness, he can invert himself. But he can also re-establish himself.

This is at all times possible to him. From the mystery of self-discovery in existence the profound consciousness of being grows in him—it requires thought and finds communicability in the products of thought—his consciousness of being becomes sure of itself in love—out of love the content of being is revealed. Out of the attitude of man to man in the acceptance of concern for others, in converse, in communication, there grows up the perception of the true, and the absolute is aroused.

Notions and ideas come and go, and the language in which we call to mind the eternal. The latter itself cannot undergo mutation. It is. But no one knows it as such. If we now attempt to call to mind eternal faith, we do not cease to be aware of the fact that such abstractions are almost empty indications, and that these abstract formulations also wear an historical garb.

3. The basic categories of eternal faith

We shall venture to formulate the nexus of faith by a few propositions: Faith in God, faith in man, faith in possibilities in the world.

(1) Faith in God. The notions of God produced by man are not God Him-
    self. But we can bring the Godhead to consciousness only through the
    medium of mental images that operate like a language. These mental
    images are symbols, are historical, are always inadequate.

In some way or other man becomes certain of transcendence—it may be the
space of nothingness in which everything is, this nothingness which may
then suddenly become plenitude and authentic Being.

The Godhead is origin and goal, it is peace of mind. There is security.

It is impossible for man to lose transcendence, without ceasing to be man.

Negative speech relates to mental images. It is founded on the presence of
a profound idea of God, or on the remoteness of endless longing.

Always we live with symbols. In them we experience and apprehend transcendence, authentic reality. Loss of this reality occurs both in making this
symbol a real existence in the world, and in aestheticising the symbol into
an optional guide for emotions.

(2) Faith in man. Faith in man is faith in the possibility of freedom; the image
    of man remains incomplete if it lacks this basic feature of his existence,
    which does not take shape as an image: that he, bestowed upon himself
    by God, shall thank or blame himself for what becomes of him.

The echo from history, that which lends wings to our intercourse with our
ancestors as far back as the origin of the human race, is their quest for freedom, the fashion in which they realised freedom, the forms in which they
discovered and desired it. We recognise ourselves in what men were capable
of, and what they say to us out of their historical reality.

To freedom pertains authentic communication, which is more than contact, compact, sympathy, community of interests and enjoyment.

Liberty and communication, both of them evade demonstration. Where
demonstration by experience begins, there is no liberty and no existential
communication. Both of them give rise to that which then becomes the object of experience, without being adequately explicable as a phenomenon,
and to that which is then a pointer to the processes of liberty, which in itself,
where we gain a share in it, is understandable and compelling.

Faith in man is faith in his potentialities arising from liberty, not faith in
a man in the sense of the deification of that man. Faith in man presupposes

faith in the Deity through whom he is. Without faith in God, faith in man degenerates into contempt for man, into loss of respect for man as man, with the final consequence that the alien human life is treated with indifference, as something to be used and destroyed.

(3) *Faith in possibilities in the world.* Only to fallacious cognition is the world self-enclosed, does it contract into an allegedly knowable mechanism, or into an indefinite, unconscious all-life.

What critical cognition reveals at its limits, and what corresponds to the immediate experience of self-discovery in this enigmatic world, is the openness, the incalculability of the whole, the inexhaustible possibilities.

Faith in the world does not mean faith in it as a self-sufficient entity, but holding fast to the fundamental enigma of self-discovery in the world with its tasks and possibilities.

The world is a place of tasks, is itself derived from transcendence; in it befalls the language to which we listen when we understand what we really want.

The consequences of faith (in God, in man, in possibilities in the world) are essential for the paths of socialism and world unity. Without faith we are left with the understanding, mechanistic thinking, the irrational and ruin.

(1) *Strength from ruin:* Faith alone sets in motion the forces that master man's basic animal instincts, deprive them of overlordship, and transform them into motors of upsurging humanity: the brutal force of the desire to dominate—delight in violence, in cruelty—the empty will to prestige—the desire for wealth and pleasure—the erotic instincts, which force themselves to the front wherever they are given the opportunity.

The first step toward the taming of the naked instincts is external force accompanied by terror and the engendering of anxiety, then the already indirect force of the *tabu;* then adaptive conquest takes place through the faith of the man who masters himself through the meaning of his actions out of his faith.

History is man's advance toward liberty through the cultivation of faith. Out of faith are devised the laws that subjugate force, legitimacy is constituted, without which there can be no reliance on anything, man becomes himself through his subjection to absolute imperatives.

(2) *Tolerance:* The road to world order can only reach its destination if tolerance prevails. Intolerance means force, repulsion and conquest.

Tolerance does not imply indifference, however. Indifference is born rather of the arrogance of one's own truth and is the mildest form of intolerance: secret contempt—let others believe what they like, it doesn't concern me.

Tolerance, by contrast, is open-minded; it knows its own limitations and seeks to integrate them humanly into diversity, without reducing the notions and ideas of faith to an absolute common denominator.

It may be that every human contains all potentialities, but only a restricted reality is ever sure. It is restricted firstly by the finitude of existence. Secondly because in the origin of manifestation there is a manifoldness of historicity, through which we not only remain differentiated, but at the same time acquire our natures and our unconditionality. Man in his manifestation should certainly not be of one single type, but he should be concerned with himself in all his multiformity. For our roots extend beyond our historically particular origin to the one origin that comprehends us all. This origin is the source of the demand for boundless communication, which, in the manifest world, is the path along which truth is disclosed.

Converse is therefore the indispensable path not only in questions of existence for our political order, but in every aspect of our being. But the impetus and content of this converse are furnished by faith alone; by faith in man and his potentialities, by faith in the One that can guide the association of all, by the faith that I myself only become with the becoming of the other self.

The bournes of tolerance lie at absolute intolerance. But every living man, however intolerably he may behave, must bear within him the possibility of tolerance, because he is human.

(3) *The animation of all activity:* Whatever becomes a reality on the roads of socialism and planning, on the road of world order—institutions, works, regulations governing human intercourse, and behaviour-patterns—will undergo metamorphoses according to the kind of people involved in them. Their ways of thought, their faiths, and their characters will determine the mode of realisation and the further consequences.

Everything which the understanding devises, sets as its aims, or introduces as a means, because it is done and suffered by men, is ultimately guided by motives of which the understanding did not think; these motives may be either instincts and passions, or the impulses imparted by faith, or ideas.

Hence it is fatal for consciousness to seek to devote itself entirely to the realm of understanding. In so doing it succumbs in an all the more veiled fashion to the elemental.

In the critical consciousness, faith leads to the self-regulation of finite things: of power and force, of the plans devised by the understanding, of science, of art. Everything is situated within its frontiers, and over all extends a guidance which is not a plan. Guidance stems from a more profound order that becomes conscious of itself in the illuminations of faith. The finite is thereby given a soul, as it were, and is the manner in which the infinite becomes present. The finite becomes, so to speak, a vessel or a language, and through its effects the bearer of a presence of the infinite, when it does not forget its finitude.

Hence also the possibility of an appeal to men in institutions, in bureaucracies, in science and technology: from the idea of faith, at all small and great turning-points, to find the way to bring the spirit of the whole to manifestation, in self-limitation to bring forth meaning and humaneness out of the unending. Statesmen, civil servants, scientists—they all gain status and meaning by testifying to guidance from the Comprehensive through the self-limitation of their power.

4. The faith of the future

The aspect of the present and the categories of eternal faith seem so totally disparate as to be mutually exclusive. The diversity between them adds poignancy to the question of the future: In what shape will man's faith manifest itself?

For a start we hear radical pessimism: In the immensity of distress everything will disappear, faith along with culture; nothing will be left but lack of reflection, paralysis of soul and spirit; for this distress is the decline on the way to bodily destruction. Such statements contain a pitiless truth. For the moments of revelation from the depths of the soul in the greatest distress remain—so it seems—without effect on the world, without communication; or they vanish for the world in the most intimate communication between those nearest to each other. Once distress had been overcome, the question of the faith of the future would be almost due for an answer.

Beyond annihilation lies silence, the horrible silence out of which something like a mirage advances upon us, and yet nothing more is said to us.

If in the future, however, faith is going to exist, communicate itself, and link
men together, one thing is certain: We can do nothing to plan the future
realities of faith. We can only be ready to receive it, and live in such a manner
that this readiness increases. We cannot make our own transformation the
goal of our wills; it must, rather, be bestowed upon us, if we live in such a
fashion that we can experience the gift. With this, it seems proper to keep
silent about the faith of the future.

But if it is true that faith is present at all times, even a public opinion
which accepts the proposition 'God is dead' as a believed truth cannot completely extinguish that which exists always. Then this residue, or the germ
of this faith, will seek its language. And philosophy can conceive the area
within which such a language is possible. It springs from two motives:

(1) He who believes loves the believing man, wherever he meets him. Just
     as freedom strives that all around it shall become free, so faith strives
     that all shall come to their historical faith. It is not compulsion that is
     meaningful, and not enforcement, but to arouse attention through a
     language in which, no matter how, transcendence is testified to. It is
     true that we cannot render each other decisive aid in the province of
     faith, but only meet one another. If transcendence helps, it helps only
     the individual by his selfhood. In converse we can, however, encourage
     and unfold one another out of that which is innate in each individual.
(2) If the work that plans can never engender a faith, it can nonetheless
     excogitate, and perhaps create, possibilities out of faith for faith.

This fact is inescapable for the future: The way of the spirit and the fate of mankind pass through all men. What they do not absorb has little chance of survival.
As ever, sublime unfoldment and creation will become aristocratic. But the
substratum of these and the simple fundament, to which everything brought
forth by the spirit is related, must have become a reality in the consciousness
of the majority, or it must meet it half-way as an unexpressed yearning.

In this process, it is today more crucial than ever what the people who
have learnt to read and write—prior to this they were slumbering and ineffectual masses—now really do read. For many centuries the Bible was the

book which every reader contemplated from childhood to old age. Today this method of passing on the cultural heritage and of education seems, in a large section of the population, to be disappearing in favour of sporadic reading, Newspapers, including those of high intellectual quality and written by the best brains of the day, indispensable to every contemporary person, become a danger when they remain the only reading matter for the type of person who skims through his paper and quickly forgets what he has read. It is impossible to predict what reading that dominates his life will operate for the education of man in the future.

Because it depends upon all men, those endeavours have pre-eminence for the determination of the future that are addressed to the whole population, if they really succeed in piercing the hearts of men and do not merely produce factitious constructs. The latter, because they have not taken root in men's hearts, break down at once in the face of real catastrophe, as happened with the sham constructs of fascism, that had been affirmed, known and lived with such a paralysing effect.

No one can foretell what might be possible through the rejuvenation of the Churches. We can see forces emanating from ecclesiastical faith which, in their personal shape, are of poignant absoluteness. But today we do not see the great, widely effective manifestation as a whole.

Ecclesiastical faith is expressed in notions, ideas, dogmas and becomes creed. It is capable of forgetting its origin, and identifying itself with these particular contents and objectifications, and must then lose its strength. But it also needs this integument for the preservation of its heritage.

The majority of people seem bound to faith in some kind of palpable reality. In their shrewdness, institutions that desire power over the people and, at the same time, to help everyone, therefore always address themselves to the craving for sensible reality and definite religious dogmas, when everything else seems unable to strike roots in the masses.

Opposed to this is a metamorphosis of the mode of faith which is foreign to the Churches. Man, aware of his liberty, leaves his faith in suspension in an inexpressible general implication, and is decisive in his historicity, in the decisions of his personal life; he tests and holds himself open, and takes as his foundation the authority of the whole heritage of history. The question is whether the epoch, which has taught whole populations to read and write for the first time, does not by this very fact afford new possibilities for a free faith that is undogmatic in its tenets, without diminution of earnestness and unconditionality. Up to the present such a mode of faith has at all times failed to arouse any response in the mass of the population.

Hence it is despised as private and powerless by the functionaries of dogmatic, doctrinaire, institutional modes of faith, secure in the sense of power they derive from membership of mighty organisms, that are effective in the world and at times omnipotent on a broad front. Since however, in the last analysis, the mass consists of separate individuals, so that the elements of private life have an ubiquitous influence, it is crucial for the course of events whether these tangible aids to faith, even if they are forms of superstition, bear in themselves that which can be recognised in sublime unfoldments and from the origin in man as an individual, in his manner of living directly to God.

If doubt concerning the contemporary Churches and their capacity for transformation is not inclined to give them a favourable prognosis—possibly quite erroneously—this doubt need by no means apply to the Biblical religion. It is probable that the faith of the future will continue to move within the fundamental positions and categories of the Axial Period, from which the Biblical religion stems: because for our overall view of history, the spiritual paramountcy of those centuries of origin is so great—because science and technology, with the contents arising out of them, cannot hold out against the lofty contents of the faith and humanity of that origin—because the dissolution of modern thought has not been able to offer anything of real content out of its own origin to overcome it—because the simplicity of depth does not exist in any new shape, and could hardly assert its new shape, if it were to come into being, without having preserved the former content.

What seems probable today, therefore, is a transformation wrought by re-establishment of the Biblical religion. In opposition to the tendencies of the age to severance, enclosure and fanaticism in groups (corresponding to the enclosing boundaries arising out of the outlook of total planning), stand the tendencies to amalgamation on the basis of a great, simple truth.

But who could disclose in the individual instance what today is fundamentally extinct, what represents a vain clinging to lost causes, and what is original and capable of supporting life!

That in the last resort the decision on the future of our Western humanity lies in the relation of our faith to the Biblical religion seems, however, to be certain.

We may consider a transformation of the Biblical religion to be no longer possible, that it is likely to die out in benumbing creeds (instead of being carried alive through the ages in these protective integuments), and hence may simply be extinguished in the coming political catastrophes; in this event, because man cannot cease to be man, something different in its origins is bound to appear. This new manifestation, of which we can form no notion, would cause the Biblical religion to vanish into a mere recollection, such as the Greek myths are for us; even this recollection might be lost. The religion of the Bible would have had a long run, as long as Confucianism, which is today in the same uncertain situation, but not yet as long as the ancient Egyptian religion.

This new manifestation would not come to life through an act of establishment which, in correlation to the rule of force of a world empire, would have outward chances only. If it is really to take hold of men, something like a new Axial Period would have to come to pass. Then the loosening up of mankind would show what is developing in the communication of spiritual conflict, in the harnessing of spiritual unconditionality, in the beatitude of knowing the new process of revelation to be borne by the Godhead.

We may think further: In coming centuries men will perhaps arise who, sustained by the sight of the origin of the Axial Period, will proclaim truths replete with the knowledge and experience of our era that will really be believed and lived. Man would once more experience in full earnestness the meaning of the fact that God is, and once more know the *pneuma*. that sweeps life along

To expect this in the shape of a fresh revelation from God, however, would seem to be mistaken. The concept of revelation belongs exclusively to the Biblical religion. The revelation has taken place and is complete. The idea of revelation will remain inseparably bound up with the Biblical religion. In the lucidity of our world, a prophecy that made its appearance with the claim to a fresh divine revelation would perhaps always give the impression of madness or false prophecy, of superstition, that collapses before the one great, true prophecy which occurred thousands of years ago. And yet, who knows?

At all events, any such new revelation would become untrue in a merely usurped and enforced exclusivity. For that the truth of faith lies in the multiplicity of its historical manifestations, in the self-encountering of this multiplicity through ever deeper communication, is an insight and experience of latter centuries which cannot be reversed. This experience cannot be fallacious in its origin.

In view, however, of the possibility of a totalitarian world empire and a totalitarian doctrinal truth corresponding to it, the only hope left is for the individual, for innumerable individuals, as they have lived from the Axial Period until today, from China to the West, to preserve the stream of philosophy, however narrow it may become. The independence from both Church and State of the deepest inner being of the man related to transcendence, his liberty of soul, that draws courage from discourse with the great cultural heritage, this remains the last refuge, as it has been so often before in evil periods of transition.

If it be deemed improbable that a world order will develop without unity of faith, I venture to assert the reverse. The universality of a world order obligatory to all (in contrast to a world empire) is possible only when the multiple contents of faith remain free in their historical communication, without the unity of an objective, universally valid doctrinal content. The common element of all faith in relation to world order can only be that everyone desires the ordering of the foundations of existence, in a world community in which he has room to evolve with the peaceful means of the spirit.

So we do not expect a fresh revelation from God in the exclusivity of an annunciation with validity for the whole of mankind. Something else is possible. Perhaps we may expect something resembling a revelation through a prophecy (in using this word we are speaking imprecisely of a future phenomenon in a category belonging to the past) credible today, which would then assume manifold shape, or else, through sages and lawgivers (speaking again in categories of the Axial Period), make possible an ascent to high-minded, devoted, penetrating, pure humanity. There is in us an insufficiency, something resembling waiting, resembling readiness. Philosophy is incomplete and must remain aware of the fact, if it is not to slip into fallacy. We are wandering in the obscurity of the future, on guard against the enemies of truth, incapable of relinquishing our own thinking nescience in obedience to an imposed knowledge—but above all ready to hear and see when fulfilling symbols and profound thoughts once more illumine the path of life.

In this process, philosophising will in any case accomplish an essential task. It will repay us thoughtfully to resist the absurdities, falsifications and perversions, the claim to exclusive possession of historical truth, and blind intolerance. Philosophy leads us along the road to the point at which love acquires its depth in real communication. Then in this love, through the success of communication, the truth that links us together will be disclosed to those who are most remote in the diversity of their historical origin.

Today individuals are palpable. He who would like to live in the unclosed and unorganised and unorganisable community of authentic human beings—in what used to be called the invisible Church—does in fact live to-day as an individual in alliance with individuals scattered over the face of the earth, an alliance that survives every disaster, a dependability that is not fixed by any pact or any specific imperative. He lives in complete insufficiency, but in a communal insufficiency, and obdurately seeks with others the right road within this world and not outside it. These individuals meet one another, exhort and encourage one another. They repudiate the modern combina-tion of eccentric faith contents with the practice of a nihilistic realism. They know that the task imposed upon man is to realise in this world that which is possible to man, and that this possibility is not a single and solitary one. But every individual must know where he stands and for what he will work. It is as though everyone were charged by the Deity to work and live for boundless openness, authentic reason, truth and love and fidelity, without the recourse to force that is typical of the States and Churches in which we have to live and whose insufficiency we should like to oppose

NOTES

1   (Page 165): The views put forward in the text would not have become clear to me without the brilliant insight of Hannah Arendt ('Organised Guilt', *Die Wand-lung, Jahrgang* I, p. 650, reprinted in Six Essays by Hannah Arendt, Heidelberg 1948—'Concentration Camps', *Die Wandlung, Jahrgang* III, p. 309).

2   (Page 200): Concerning total planning: Walter Lippmann, *The Good Soci-ety*, 1938. F. A. Hayek, *The Road to Serfdom*. J. Wilhelm Röpke, *Die Gesell-schaftskrise der Gegenwart, 4. Aufl.*, Zurich 1942.

3   (Page 210): Walter Lippmann and F. A. Hayek have provided a fundamental elucidation of the problem of total planning. According to Lippmann the con-sequences of total planning can be formulated in a few sentences:

   The extended compass of the plan is accompanied by a reduction in mo-bility and capacity for adaptation.

   The road to mastery of want and disorder through total planning in fact intensifies both. The coercion that is intended to overcome chaos evokes chaos in real earnest.

   The coerciveness of organisation is heightened to the point of terrori-sation. For the growing dissatisfaction under compulsion can only be pre-vented from breaking out by the continual increase of compulsion.

   Total planning goes hand in hand with armament and war; it is cold war through the breaking off of free intercourse.

Total planning is carried over onto the smallest of groups. There develops a tendency to erect barriers, ruthlessly to force through particularisms of all sorts with the aid of political power.

These tendencies of planned economy force themselves through even without the wish of the active participants; they grow because they are in the nature of the matter. Beyond them, planned economy contains tendencies to the modification of the whole of human existence, including its spiritual conditions, tendencies which the idealistic champions of planning conceal from themselves. Hayek has convincingly characterised them:

(1) Planned economy destroys democracy. If democracy is government and government control through Parliament, discussion and majority decisions, it is possible only where the tasks of the State are confined to provinces in relation to which decision can be reached along the path of free discussion and by majorities. But a parliament can never control total planning. It rather dismisses itself through so-called delegation of authority.

(2) Planned economy destroys the constitutional State. The constitutional State lives by laws that remain operative even *vis-à-vis* the dictatorship of majorities, because a majority cannot abolish them immediately, but only in a legal procedure that takes time and enables majorities to be controlled by other majorities. Total planning, however, requires sovereignty through dispositions, regulations, delegations of authority, that represent a so-called legality, but rest upon the uncontrolled arbitrariness of bureaucracy and those to whom authority is delegated, and can be altered at will.

The constitutional State affords a safeguard against the arbitrary dominion of majorities whose only claim to absolute validity rests upon the fact that they are the product of a democratic electoral procedure. Such majorities, however, may be as arbitrary and dialectical as individuals. It is not the origin, but the limitation of government power that preserves it from arbitrariness. This limitation is provided by orientation by fixed norms, which, in the constitutional State, are valid for the power of the State as well. Total planning, however, leads to direct appeals to the majorities of the mass, who vote without having any idea of the issue upon which they are deciding.

(3) Planned economy tends towards absolute totality. It is an illusion to suppose that authoritative direction can be confined to economic questions. There are no purely economic goals. At the end of total planning stands the abolition of money, that instrument of freedom. 'If all

rewards, instead of being paid in money, were distributed in the form of public distinction and privileges, of positions of power over others, better living conditions and better food, in the form of travel or educational facilities, this would mean no more and no less than that the recipient would be deprived of choice and that the person responsible for fixing the reward would decide not only its level, but also its concrete form.' The question is 'whether it is to be we who decide what is more important and what less important to us, or whether this is to be decided by the planning authority'.

(4) Total planning produces a selection of leaders in which low characters gain the upper hand. Totalitarian discipline demands uniformity. This is most easily achieved at the lower spiritual and moral levels. The lowest common denominator contains the greatest number of people. Paramountcy is in the hands of the malleable and the credulous, whose vague notions are easily led, and whose passions are easily whipped up. Unity is most simply attained in hate and envy.

Particularly serviceable are the industrious, disciplined, energetic and ruthless, who possess a sense of order, are conscientious over their work, remain absolutely obedient to the authorities, and are characterised by a readiness for sacrifice and by physical courage. Unserviceable, on the other hand, are the tolerant, who respect others and their opinions, the spiritually independent, who stand up for their convictions even against a superior, people possessed of civil courage, who are inclined to consideration for the weak and the sick and who repudiate and despise mere power, because they live by an ancient tradition of personal liberty.

(5) Total planning requires propaganda and causes the disappearance of truth from public life. Men who serve as tools must believe in the aims for which they are being used. Hence directed propaganda is a vital necessity to the totalitarian system. News and opinions are prepared. Respect for truth, indeed the feeling for truth, must be destroyed. Conducted doctrines aimed at perpetual self-justification, and denying a hearing to other doctrines, are bound to paralyse spiritual life. The thinking of total planning begins with reason, with the aim of elevating it to absolute sovereignty; but it ends by annihilating reason. For it has not grasped the process upon which the growth of reason is dependent: the interplay of individuals with various knowledge and various opinions.

(6) Total planning destroys liberty: 'Market economy resting on competition is the only economic and social system calculated to reduce to a minimum, through decentralisation, the power of man over man.'

'The transformation of economic power into political ends by transforming a power that is always limited into one from which there is no escape.' Total planning, in order to maintain itself on its disastrous course, has to destroy everything that threatens it: Truth, i.e. free science and the free word of the writer—just legal verdicts, i.e. the independent judiciary—public discussion, i.e. the freedom of the press.

Interrelationships appear to have been demonstrated by Lippmann and Hayek, whose inevitability it is not easy to meet with effective counterarguments. This conception, which every actively engaged person ought to visualise, at least as a possibility, is compounded out of experiences of our era and ideal-typical constructions.

4 (Page 211): The attempt at a direct realisation of justice by force leads to conditions in which not even the most elementary justice is fulfilled. Trotsky (quoted by Hayek) shows that the differences of income in Russia and America are by no means favourable to Russia from the point of view of justice: Between the lowest and the highest salaries, the ratio, in Russia as in America, is in the neighbourhood of 1 : 50. In Russia the upper 11 or 12 per cent of the total population receive some 50 per cent of the national income; in America approximately 35 per cent of the national income goes to the upper 10 per cent.

5 (Page 238): Concerning Marxism, psychoanalysis and racial theory, cf. my *Geistige Situation der Zeit*, Berlin 1931, Sammlung Göschen *Band 1000, 6. unveränderte Aufl.*, Berlin 1948, pp. 135 ff.

I consider this earlier work supplementary to the present one. The earlier was conceived unhistorically, this present historically. Both relate to the present.

PART 3

THE MEANING OF HISTORY

INTRODUCTION

THE MEANING OF CONCEPTIONS OF HISTORY

What does a universal view of history mean to us? We wish to understand history as a whole, in order to understand ourselves. History for us is the memory which is not only known to us, but from which we live. It is the groundwork which is laid down and to which we remain bound, if we do not want to melt away into nothing, but desire to win a part in humanity.

A view of history creates the area out of which our consciousness of humanity is aroused. The picture we form of history becomes a factor in our volition. The manner in which we think of history sets limits on our potentialities, or sustains us by its implications, or lures us away from our reality. Even in unimpeachable objectivity, historical knowledge is no mere indifferent factual content, but an active element in our lives. The use of this knowledge for purposes of propaganda in the interests of a power amounts to a lie about history. The task of ascertaining history as a whole is one of grave responsibility.

We can either know of our historical fundament through the contemplation of the greatness that lies close to our hearts. We raise ourselves up on that which was, through which we became, which is an exemplar to us. When a great man lived is then of no consequence. Everything then lies, as it were, on a single, timeless plane of the valid. The historical heritage is then unhistorically present to us, so to speak.

Or we can view greatness consciously historically, in the temporal sequence of events. We enquire as to the when and where. The whole is a passage through time. Time is subdivided. Everything does not exist at all times, but every age has its own greatness. The past has peaks and valleys in its significance. There are tranquil ages, which seem to contain that which will last for ever, and which feel themselves to be final. And there are ages of change, which see upheavals that, in extreme instances, appear to go to the roots of humanity itself.

Hence, along with history, the historical consciousness itself changes. In our era it is determined by the consciousness of crisis, which has been growing for more than a hundred years, and has today become universal as the consciousness of almost all men.

Already to Hegel, the European world showed its sunset glow. 'Only at dusk does the owl of Minerva begin its flight'—it was thus that he understood his own philosophic activity, not yet in the consciousness of decline, however, but of consummation.

Intellectually, the consciousness of crisis reached its zenith with Kierkegaard and Nietzsche. Since their time the knowledge that we are at a turning-point in history, at the termination of history in the existing sense, that we are witnessing the radical metamorphosis of humanity itself, has been gaining currency.

After the First World War, it was no longer the sunset glow merely of Europe, but of all the cultures of the earth. An end of mankind, a recasting from which no people and no man was exempt—whether it was to annihilation, or to rebirth—could be felt. It was still not the end itself; but the knowledge of its possible imminence became prevalent. The anticipated end was either experienced in fearful horror, or cold-bloodedly interpreted—on the one hand naturalistically-biologically or sociologically, on the other as a metaphysico-substantial process. The atmosphere is totally diverse as between, say, Klages or Spengler or Alfred Weber. But there can be no doubt that the reality of crisis, on an historically unparalleled scale, underlies all of them.

In this crisis of consciousness, the contemplation of history may help us to understand ourselves and our situation.

One thing, it seems, is always able to stand firm: humanity as such, and its self-reflection in philosophic activity. Even in periods of disintegration, so history shows us, high philosophy was still possible.

The will to self-understanding on the basis of a universal view of history is perhaps an example of this philosophic activity that stands firm and, seeking its fundament, looks into the future, not prophetically but in faith, not dishearteningly but encouragingly.

We cannot push our historical memory deep enough nor far enough. It may be that we hear what history means as a whole most readily from the margins. These margins are experienced by contrast with that which is not history, by contrast with the before and the beyond, and in the process of penetrating into the concretely historical, so as to apprehend it more profoundly, more clearly, and on a broader front.

Enquiry into the meaning of the whole of history leaves us without the final answer, however. Yet this enquiry, and the critically intensified endeavours to find an answer, help us against the short-circuits of facile pseudo-knowledge that vanishes as quickly as it comes—against the inclination merely to traduce one's own epoch, which it is so easy to discredit—against the declarations of total bankruptcy, which to us today sound almost old-fashioned—against demands to bring into being the entirely new, the originating, which will now save us, and which is set in opposition to the whole line of development from Plato to Hegel or Nietzsche, as its invalidation. A marvellous enhancement is imparted to one's thinking, to the accompaniment of a poverty of content (in mimicry of an extreme, but well-founded, state of consciousness in Nietzsche). The pompous comportment of the no and the affirmation of nothingness is not a reality of one's own, however. It is possible to lead a spiritual sham life on the sensation of combating something only so long as one's capital holds out.

The unhistorical element in history consists of the simple physical substratum and the identically recurrent, the regular causalities.

In the flux of mere happening, the specifically historical possesses a unique character. It is the heritage through authority and, within this, a continuity through reminiscent relationship to the past. It is the transmutation of phenomena in consciously achieved connexions of meaning.

Historical consciousness registers the presence of something irreplaceably its own, something individual, whose validity for us cannot be adequately explained by any universal value, an entity possessing a temporally evanescent shape.

The historical is that which comes to naught, but is everlasting in time. It is the hallmark of this Being that it is history, and thereby not permanence through all time. For in contradistinction to mere happening, in which, as matter, the universal forms and laws simply repeat themselves, history is the happening which in itself, cutting across time, annulling time, lays hold of the eternal.

Why is there any such thing as history? Because man is finite, imperfect and unperfectible he must, in his metamorphosis through time, become aware of the eternal, and he can do so only along this path. Man's imperfection and his historicity are the same thing. Man's limitations exclude certain possibilities. There can be no ideal state on earth. There is no right organisation of the world. There is no perfect man. Permanent end-states are possible only as a regression to mere natural happening. In consequence of perpetual imperfection in history, things must perpetually become different. History cannot be brought to a conclusion through its own agency. It can come to an end only through an inner breakdown or cosmic disasters.

But although the question of what in history is the specifically historical, in its fulfilment from the eternal, impels us to descry it, it nevertheless remains impossible for us to judge an historical phenomenon *in toto* and definitively. For we are not the Deity, who sits in judgement, but men, who open their senses in order to gain a share in the historical, which we therefore seek with all the greater concern the more we comprehend it.

History is at one and the same time happening and consciousness of this happening, history and knowledge of history. This history is, so to speak, encompassed by abysses. If it falls back into one of these, it ceases to be history. To our consciousness, it is to be merged in itself and picked out:

Firstly: History has boundaries that divide it off from other aspects of reality, from nature and the cosmos. Around history lies the boundless space of the existent in general (§1).

Secondly: History possesses inner structures through the transformation of the mere reality of the individual thing and of the purely transient. It becomes history only with the unity of the universal and the individual, but in such a way that it exhibits the intrinsic individuality of irreplaceable significance, an unique-universal. It is transitionality as the fulfilment of being (§2).

Thirdly: History becomes the idea of a whole, through the question: In what does the unity of history consist? (§3).

The abysses: Nature outside history and as the volcanic matrix of history—the reality that appears within it as its ephemeral transitionality—endless dispersal, out of which the always dubious unity seeks to achieve itself—to see these abysses consciously heightens our feeling for the specifically historical.

12

BOUNDARIES OF HISTORY

A. NATURE AND HISTORY

We have the notion of the history of mankind as a minute part of the history of life on earth. The history of mankind is very short (at the very most it dates from the tertiary formation, and is probably later) in comparison with the history of plants and animals, which completely dominate the historical picture of the earth from a temporal point of view. The six thousand years of recorded history known to us is in turn a very short happening in comparison with the long, unhistorical history of mankind, that lasted for hundreds of thousands of years.

This notion is not incorrect. But it contains no hint of what constitutes history proper. For history is not itself like nature, but exists on the groundwork of nature, which was in the immeasurable aeons before history, is today, and sustains everything that we are.

To be sure, we speak of the history of nature and of the history of man. Both together constitute an irreversible process in time. But the two of them are disparate in nature and meaning.

The history of nature is not conscious of itself. It is mere happening that does not know itself, but is first known by man. Consciousness and purposiveness are not a factor in this happening.

By human standards, this history is of very long duration. Its foreground aspect, by the criterion of human life, is the repetition of the same. Nature is in this sense unhistorical.[1]

Hence we are being misled by our habit of thinking in the categories of nature, when we look at history itself on analogy with natural processes:

(1) We have a picture of endless coming and going, of extinction and repetition—in endless time there is an opportunity for everything, but no meaning that runs through time. In such a picture there is no true history.

(2) The life process causes the genesis of man as a species of animal. Man spreads over the face of the earth as do some other forms of life, but not all.

(3) Mankind as a whole is a life process. It grows, blossoms, ages and dies. This is pictured not only as an unique process of mankind, but as a repetitive, multiple process of human cultures, in succession to and concurrently with one another. Out of the amorphous material of natural mankind, cultures grow as historical bodies whose course is subject to laws, with life-phases, with a beginning and an end. Cultures are, so to speak, organisms, drawing their life from their own sources, unconcerned with one another, but modified or deranged by contact with each other.

Such views, shackled by the categories of natural processes, do not reveal what is specifically historical, however.

B. HEREDITY AND TRADITION

We humans are, at one and the same time, nature and history. Our nature is disclosed in heredity, our history in tradition. Stability through heredity, which shows us, as natural creatures, the same for thousands of years, stands in contrast to the imperilment of our tradition. Consciousness may sink away, the spiritual acquisitions of millennia are not a dependable possession.

The historical process may come to an end through forgetting, through the disappearance of what has been acquired historically. Even the almost unconscious stability of the mode of life and thinking arising out of habit and unquestioned faith, which is formed daily in the overall condition of communal circumstances and is seemingly fixed in the depths, becomes insecure the moment this condition is altered. Then everyday life breaks loose from tradition, the historically evolved ethos ceases, the life-form crumbles, absolute undependability develops. Atomised man becomes the indeterminate mass of an unhistorical agglomeration of life, which, however, as human life in turmoil and anxiety, whether open or concealed, lives on, veiled by the vital force of its existence.

In short, it is not heredity that makes us human, but always the content of a tradition. In heredity man possesses something virtually indestructible, in tradition something that may well get lost.

Tradition leads back into the matrix of prehistory. It comprises everything which is not biologically inheritable, but an historical substance of humanity.

Long prehistory, short history—what can this difference signify?

At the dawn of history, acquired from prehistory, there stands as it were humanity's capital, which is not a biologically inheritable, but an historical substance, a capital that may be increased or squandered. It is something that is real prior to all thought, that cannot be fabricated or intentionally created.

This substance first becomes mature and clear through the spiritual movement that takes place in history. In this movement the substance passes through metamorphoses. Perhaps new origins make their appearance in history, which as realities—the prime example is the Axial Period—are in turn presuppositions. All this does not occur in the whole of mankind as such, however, but only at the heights attained by individuals, who flower and are forgotten again, misunderstood and lost.

There is in history a trend toward liberation from the presuppositions of substance, away from tradition and toward the point of mere thinking, as though something could be brought forth out of this insubstantial work of reason. It is enlightenment, which, inverting itself, no longer enlightens anything, but leads into nothingness.

C. HISTORY AND COSMOS

Why do we live and accomplish our history in infinite space at precisely this point, on a minute grain of dust in the universe, as though in an out-of-the-way corner? Why just now in infinite time? What happened to cause the commencement of history? These are questions whose unanswerability makes us conscious of an enigma.

The fundamental fact of our existence is that we appear to be isolated in the cosmos. We are the only articulate rational beings in the silence of the universe. In the history of the solar system there has arisen on the earth, for a so far infinitesimally short period, a condition in which humans evolve and realise knowledge of themselves and of being. Only here is this inwardness of self-understanding to be found. At least we do not know of any other reality of inwardness. Within the boundless cosmos, on a tiny planet, for a tiny period of a few millennia, something has taken place as though this planet were the all-embracing, the authentic. This is the place, a mote in the immensity of the cosmos, at which Being has awakened with man.

But this cosmos is the obscurity of the comprehensive existent, in which, from which, and through which that happens which we are, and whose provenance is itself uncomprehended. This obscurity as a whole only shows us the foreground aspect of the inert processes investigated by astronomy and astrophysics, which, in their fantastic magnitude, are suddenly hardly more to us than a cloud of dust in the room lit up by the rays of the sun. The cosmos must be infinitely more than this foreground aspect of investigable facts, something deeper than that which has begun to unveil itself, namely that to which our human historical manifestation gives birth.

For our terrestrial existence, however, another abyss has been reached. With the accessibility of the planet as a whole, the road of space is closed. Up till now, man was able to roam, to move into unknown distances, and to live in the background of those distances, which remained boundlessly accessible to his foot when it drove him forth. Now the house of our existence is closed up, its size is known exactly; it can be pictured as a whole for purposes of plan and action. But this whole is radically isolated in the universe. Through the actuality of this situation the human world condenses, as it were, on earth. Outside it is a universe which seems, spiritually, to be entirely empty and into which it appears as though the human world will never be able to enter. In this isolation all that remains to it is the reality of self-understanding related purely to itself. This isolation in the cosmos is a real boundary of history. Up to the present, nothing but empty notions and unfulfillable potentialities have crossed it with the vain question: Are there life and spirit, are there rational beings, elsewhere in the universe?

Negative replies are given to this question:

(a) The indispensable preconditions of life are a coincidence in the almost empty, frozen universe sprinkled here and there with incandescent masses at great distances from one another. On the other planets of our solar system life is either not possible at all, or possible only in the shape of low forms of plant-life. It is not absolutely beyond the bounds of possibility that other solar systems may contain planets of the same type as the earth, but it is improbable on account of the number of chance circumstances which would have to coincide to produce such a result (Eddington).

(b) The specific characteristics of man, according to the profound conception arising out of the Judaico-Christian revealed religion, possess uniqueness; God's creation is a single one, and man is the likeness of God; there cannot be many 'worlds' (so says Christianity and so says Hegel). Both revelation, through which man comprehends himself in his nullity and grandeur, as well as the natural tendency through which man feels himself to be the centre and unique, lead to this conclusion.

Positive answers are also given:

(a) It may be a coincidence, but there is plenty of room in the infinite world for this coincidence to take place contemporaneously, or in the sequence of time. In fact it is extremely probable that, amongst the thousands of millions of suns in the Galactic System, and amongst the innumerable galactic systems besides our own, the coincidence in its conjunction of circumstances might occur several times.

(b) Man has at all times assumed the existence in the world of other rational beings besides himself: demons, angels, star-gods. In this manner he surrounded himself with mythical relations. The world was not empty. With the transformation of the world into a mechanism of mere inert masses, this emptiness has become complete. It seems impossible that alone in the world man possesses consciousness and thinks, once we visualise this in all its implications. Is this vast world only there for man? We cannot even comprehend all life on the earth as being in relation to man. Everything exists for itself, and the long history of the earth was life without man.

(c) If man were not alone, one might perhaps say that there has been plenty of opportunity during infinite ages for any creatures with spirit in the world to give evidence of their presence: the world would long since have been 'discovered' from somewhere, and any newly evolving rational life would immediately have been assimilated into a continually existent community of communication in the cosmos.

To this we might perfectly well reply, however: We are perpetually encompassed by the beams of this communication, as by radio beams, which we do not observe if we have no receiver. We have not yet progressed far enough to perceive the beams which are continually diffused through the cosmos and emanate from a cosmic community that has long since been realised. We on the earth are only just starting. The moment of awakening has begun. Why should we not one day discover the language that does in fact pervade the world, first of all picking it up without understanding it, and then, so to speak, deciphering it like the Egyptian hieroglyphics? Until we incessantly hear the messages communicated by rational beings in the world, and until we become capable of replying?

All further picturing of this idea is objectless, like the idea itself—such things, for instance, as the consequences which the distance of light years might have upon possible exchanges.

Up to the present all speculations of this kind have only the one meaning of holding potentiality open, and making papable the isolation of man's position on earth. No sort of consequences arise for us as long as there is no real trace of rational beings in the cosmos. We can neither deny the possibility, nor reckon with the reality. We can, however, become conscious of the astonishing and always disquietingly poignant fact that man, in the infinite spaces and aeons, upon this small planet, has only during the last six thousand years come to himself in the enquiry and knowledge that we call philosophising.

The prodigious historic phenomenon of this thinking consciousness, and of the humanity in it and through it, is, in its entirety, an evanescent event in the universe, entirely new, entirely of the present instant, just beginning in fact—and yet, for itself and seen from within, as old as if it comprehended the universe.

NOTE

1   (Page 262): But even that which, in the history of nature, is reversible, definitive, unique, does not possess what in man we call 'historicity'.

Human history first acquires an essential meaning from the 'historicity' of 'existence'. No doubt its fundament is a process analogous to the processes of nature. This fundament is not its essence, however.

The objectivising categories of a natural process do not apply to the being of man, which is made up of spirit and existence, for the understanding experience of which radically different objectifying categories are requisite.

Concerning 'historicity' cf. my *Philosophie*, Berlin 1932, *Bd. II*, pp. 118 ff. *Zweite Auflage* 1948, pp. 397 ff.

13

BASIC STRUCTURES OF HISTORY

The history of man stands out from the rest of the world through its possession of a mode of being all its own. Within the sciences, a peculiar cognition corresponds to it. We will pick out two fundamental characteristics of history.

A. THE UNIVERSAL AND THE INDIVIDUAL

If we apprehend history in universal laws (in causal relationships, morphological laws, dialectical necessities), this universal never gives us history itself. For history in its individual occurrence is something *ipso facto* unique.

What we call history is external, that which happens in space and time at a particular place. This is true of all reality, however. Although in principle the natural sciences possess knowledge of the universal laws underlying all natural happening, they have no knowledge of such things as, for example, why accumulations of sulphur are found in Sicily, and none whatever concerning the reason for the *de facto* distribution of matter in space. The limit of natural scientific cognition is individualised reality, which can only be described, not comprehended.

But to be localised in space and time, to be an individual—these hallmarks of all reality—do not suffice to distinguish individuality in history.

That which is repeated, that which as an individual is replaceable by another individual, which amounts to an instance of a universal, none of this, as such, amounts to history. To be history the individual must be unique, irreplaceable, single.

To us, this mode of uniqueness exists only in man and his creations, in all other realities only in so far as they are related to man and become his means, expression or purpose. Man is not history as a natural being, but only as a spiritual being.

In history we are accessible to ourselves as ourselves, but in that which is our essential feature we are not accessible to ourselves as an object of investigation. It is true that we can also become an object of investigation to ourselves as nature, as an instance of a universal, as real individuals. In history, however, we encounter ourselves as freedom, as existence, as spirit, as the earnestness of decision, and as independence from the whole world. In history we are addressed by that which does not address us in nature, the mystery of the leaps into liberty, and the manifestation of Being in human consciousness.

Our understanding is inclined to regard that which is thought and imagined particularly as Being itself, and, as it were, to possess Being in this excogitated thing; so it is in history with the individual, which is thought only in respect of the universal.

The individual is not historical by the mere fact of being called by name as a reality in its place in space and time, however; nor is the universal that appears in such individuals as universal law, as typical shape, as universally valid value. We fall into a trap every time we suppose ourselves to see the historical itself in this universal.

The historical is rather the single, the irreplaceable—not the real individual, which is, rather, permeated, consumed and transformed by the specifically historical individual—not the individual as a vessel for the universal or as the representative of a universal, but rather the reality that first animates this universal. It is the self-existent which is bound up with the origin of everything existent, sure of itself in this matrix in its consciousness.

This historical individual is disclosed only to love, and to the power of intuition and clairvoyance that grows in love. Entirely present in love, the single individual becomes endlessly open to the desire for knowledge that is guided by love. It is revealed in phenomena which also become unpredictably different. It is real as an historical individual, and yet to mere knowledge it is, at the same time, non-existent as such.

To love of the historical individual, the matrix of Being to which it is attached becomes simultaneously perceptible. In the infinitude of the loved individual, the world becomes manifest. Hence genuine love experiences expansion and intensification through itself, spreads to everything historically existent, becomes love of Being itself in its origin. Thus it becomes manifest to loving intuition how Being, this one single vast individual, is historical in the world. But it is revealed only in the historicity of the love of an individual to an individual.

To the Being of history corresponds the particularity of historical cognition. Historical research creates the prerequisites in real insight, through which and on the margins of which there may dawn upon us that which is no longer accessible to research itself, but from which research is guided in its choice of themes and in its differentiation between essential and inessential. On the road via the always universal object of our cognition, research shows at its margins the irreplaceable individual of history as that which is never universal. To catch a glimpse of this individual links us with it on a plane that lies above and beyond cognition, but is attainable only through cognition.

That which we make our own in the shape of the historically particular enables us to go forward to total history as to a single individual. All history is rooted in the matrix of this one comprehensive historicity.

B. THE TRANSITIONALITY OF HISTORY

In history nature is still present at every moment. It is the reality that supports, the repetitive, the enduring, that changes only very slowly and unconsciously like all nature. But where spirit appears there is consciousness, reflection, incessant movement in work with oneself, on oneself, in an interminable openness of the possible.

The more decisive the uniquely single, the less identical repetition there is, the more authentic is history. Everything great is a phenomenon in transition.

If history is the manifestation of Being, then truth is at all times present in history, never consummate, however, but always in motion. It is lost where it is believed to have become a final possession. The more radical the movement, the greater the depth out of which truth may appear. Hence the greatest spiritual works are those of transition, at the boundary of epochs. Some examples:

Greek tragedy stands at the transition from myth to philosophy. Still creating myths out of the primeval substance of tradition, and rendering them more profound in the image, the tragic poets, despite the fact that they drew their intuition from original sources, lived by questioning and interpreting. They heightened the content and were on the road to its dissolution. They were the creators of the most profoundly significant configurations of the myth, and at the same time of the end of the myth as all-embracing truth.

The mysticism of Eckhart was so uninhibitedly audacious because it was in line with the creed of the Church and the origin of new, free reason. It had not yet slipped into the noxious play of irresponsible paradoxes, had no destructive impulse, and, because it lived from the potentialities of the man with the broadest outlook, who set no bounds to thought, it opened the path to the most profound insight as well as to the decomposition of tradition.

The philosophy of German idealism, from Fichte and Hegel to Schelling, stood at the transition from faith to godlessness. The age of Goethe lived an aesthetic religion in the radiant lustre of the understanding of all the depths of the spirit, nourished by the bygone substance of Christian faith, which was then lost by its successors.

Analogously, Plato or Shakespeare or Rembrandt are to be understood in terms of transition. Transition in this sense applies to whole epochs—above all, the centuries of the Axial Period from 600 to 300 B.C.

But there is always transition. The depth of the movement of a transition brings the highest clarity of Being and truth. The weakening of transition to an apparently permanent set of circumstances causes consciousness to decline along with the sense of time, and man to fall into the sleep of external repetition, into habituation and nature.

The greatest phenomena in the history of man's spiritual evolution are, as transition, simultaneously conclusion and commencement. They stand between the old and the new as truths that are originally valid only at their particular place in history, and which then remain to memory as irreplaceable figures, which are also, however, unrepeatable and inimitable. Human greatness seems to be conditional upon such a transition. And therefore its work, although it surmounts time in the timeless construct, is yet never for posterity the truth with which we can become identical, if we too kindle ourselves at it and are set in motion by it.

We should like to see consummate truth and lucid life springing from the depths of Being somewhere in history. But when we believe we can see it, we are falling prey to illusions.

Romanticism imagined a remote antiquity in which the zenith of humanity was a life with God, of which we have no record beyond interpretable traces, and which is for us a poignant silence. Then there was truth. We snatch at a last spark as it goes out. From this vantage point, the whole of history looks like the loss of an initial capital. Where empirical research uncovers remote antiquity in the shape of remains, however, it finds no corroboration of such dreams. The primeval ages it discloses were harsh, and man infinitely helpless and dependent. Humanity is first apprehensible to us through that which becomes spirit and communicable.

Even in the sequence of phenomena of which we have historical information and real cognisance, however, we never find absolute consummation (save in art, but here in play and symbol). Everything great is transition, even and precisely that which, in its meaning and purpose, records everlasting permanency. The spiritual creation of the Middle Ages, which reached consummation in the system of St. Thomas and the poetry of Dante, and was still the product of faith, was the picture of something which, at the moment at which it was thought, was already over and irrecoverably lost. During the transition, men who still lived in the dying world, but stood under the threat of a new epoch, set down their idea of this world—for it was never a reality in this form—and secured it for ever.

There is no human permanency of duration, and perhaps least of all where it is desired. The truth through which Being becomes conscious appears in time. Temporality acquires content through this appearance, in impermanence and evanescence. Essential repetition is therefore life out of present origin in communication with that which is past—as the road to the one origin of everything. Empty repetition, on the other hand, is the mere repetition of a phenomenon in imitation, without metamorphosis out of one's own origin. Progress exists only in the knowledge of the understanding—a movement which, in itself, is mere opportunity that may equally well have the result of deepening man or of rendering him shallower; it too is an element in the incessant movement in time, not the meaning of this movement itself.

All that is essential in history is that in it men are able to remember, and thereby to preserve what has been as a factor in what will be. For man, time acquires the unique meaning of historicity, whereas the nature of existence is the perpetual repetition of the same, which changes over very long periods of time, but only unconsciously—for what reason, we have only an ink-ling or no idea at all.

The enduring—whether it is order or anarchic chaos—that lasts through time, to which time is of no significance, immediately loses historic import.

Every phenomenon of authentic truth, however, is related in its origin, in that permanency which is not duration in time, but time-effacing eternity. This truth I meet only in the present, only in my own transition, but in understanding, not in imitation, and not in the identical repetition of a phenomenon that has occurred before.

Historically every transition is also a particular one. The question is: What transition makes possible precisely this mode of the manifestation of being? It is only to such processes of making possible that we can refer in relation to the great transition periods of the past.

The basic feature of history therefore is: It is *ipso facto* transition. It is not typified by that which is essentially enduring—everything enduring is its groundwork, its material and its means. Concomitant with this is the notion: Sometime or other there will be an end of history, of mankind, as there was once its beginning. The latter—the beginning as well as the end—is in practice so distant from us that it is not perceptible to us, but from out of it comes an all-overshadowing criterion.

14

THE UNITY OF HISTORY

INTRODUCTION

Man's historicity is, from the outset, multiple historicity. But the multiple is subject to the imperative of the One. This is the exclusivity of the demand of an historicity to be the only one and to dominate all others, but it must develop for consciousness in the communication of the multiply historical as the absolute historicity of the One.

It is the unity of the history of mankind, to which everything that has value and meaning seems to be related. But how are we to think of this unity of the history of mankind?

To begin with, experience seems to testify against unity. Historical phenomena are immeasurably dispersed. There are many peoples, many cultures, and in each of these again an endless multiplicity of peculiar historical facts. Everywhere on the face of the earth where there was any possibility of gaining a livelihood, man has settled and brought himself to particular manifestation. There appears to be a multiplicity which develops and passes away concurrently and successively.

To regard man in this light means to describe and classify him as is done with the multiformity of the vegetable kingdom. It is the fortuitousness of a many, which, as the genus 'man', exhibits certain typical basic features, and therein, like all living things, deviations within an area open to the play of possibilities. Any such naturalisation of man, however, causes the specifically human in man to vanish.

For in all the dispersion of the phenomenon man, the essential is that men are concerned with each other. Wherever they meet they are interested in one another, confront one another in antipathy or sympathy, learn from one another, exchange. When they meet it is as though each recognised himself in the other, and at the same time made himself independent of the other, whom he recognises as himself. In this meeting man learns that, however he may be in his particularity, he is related to all others on the basis of the one thing which, though he neither possesses nor knows it, imperceptibly guides him or, at moments, seizes him with an all-pervading enthusiasm.

Seen thus, the phenomenon of man in the dispersal of history is a movement toward the One—perhaps it is provenance from a single matrix—in any case, it is not an existence that shows its ultimate nature in the dispersion of the multiple.

A. FACTS THAT POINT TO UNITY

1. Unity of the human make-up

We have some such trivial notion of humanity in history as this. Man is a totality of innate tendencies. At any given moment, under the particular conditions, parts of his energies, gifts and impulses are realised, whilst others slumber unawakened. Since, however, man is always the same potentially, everything remains possible at all times. The varying unfoldment of his parts does not mean a difference of nature, but a difference of manifestation. In the collation of all manifestations, as the development to varying degrees of common potentialities, the totality of humanity is first disclosed.

The question of whether man's make-up has been transformed during the few millennia of history, or whether the nature of man has remained the same throughout this period, must be answered by saying that no facts are available in evidence of any such transformation. Any changes that have taken place are rather to be understood in terms of the selection of that which was already present. That which is given in the basic make-up as permanent and unchanging appears at different times, through the agency of varying selection, in quite different directions. At any given time those men become visible, successful, and then numerically preponderant whose personal qualities satisfy the particular conditions of the current society and its situation. Conditions may be characterised by the type of human make-up they fostered. With the alteration of conditions, selection changes, and previously hidden types of make-up, which have long been suppressed and reduced to a small number by negative selection, now come to the fore. The varying manifestation of the same nature under ever diverse preconditions, with a diverse selection, is disclosed.

Nevertheless, to this train of thought the rejoinder must be made that the whole of humanity can in no wise be pictured as the totality of innate human tendencies. There is no man who is or can be everything human, neither in reality nor in the projection of an idea of him.

The further objection must be made that the essential variation of the make-up with which an individual is naturally endowed is elemental. Especially when we look at the personal qualities and character traits which already make their appearance in earliest childhood does the ineluctable course taken by the innate disposition become visible. These qualities and traits create a gulf of difference between the make-up of one man and another.

These ideas, and the objections to them, all contain an element of truth, but they do not go so far as to explain man.

To reach the unity of humanity which is revealed in history, we must pass beyond the biologico-psychological plane of consideration.

In what does the enduring nature of man consist, which alone makes understanding between us, and our solidarity, possible at all? Again and again unity is doubted. For in all history there is a mutation of human knowledge, consciousness and self-consciousness. There is a coming into being and a dying away of spiritual potentialities, an estrangement, and finally an incomprehension. Is there unity in this notwithstanding? At all events, as the unrestricted will to comprehension.

If this unity cannot be understood as being derived from the biological scaffolding, because we cannot approach its meaning in the biological sphere, it must have some other basis. What is meant by this origin is not a biological make-up, or derivation from one root, but humanity as a unity from a higher origin. This can be visually imagined only in a symbol: in the idea of the creation of man by the Deity after His image, and of the Fall.

This origin—which links all us humans together, impels us toward one another, causes us to presuppose unity as well as to seek it—cannot, as such, be either known or contemplated, nor does it stand before us as an empirical reality.

The objection to the idea of unity, based on the indication of the signal innate diversities between the make-up of individuals and peoples, which in life cause mutual repulsion and are seemingly the source of radical divisions, is fallacious if it is intended to assert the existence of a diversity of the inner being of man down to his ultimate roots, of such a kind as to create an unbridgeable gulf between man and man. Greatly as we experience, in their manifestation, the separating chasms, and great as is the conflict between those of disparate natures, or the indifference with which humans pass one another by, the factors that potentially link together, which slumber in the depths and which cannot be overlooked, are equally great. The Comprehensive remains the reality over and above all reality that has become particular. One can never foretell what may be aroused under new conditions in new situations. No one can draw a line under a man as though he could calculate what would or would not be possible for him. Still less can peoples or epochs be finally determined. The characterisation that can be made of peoples and epochs is never absolutely valid. For at all times there are other possibilities. What the individual, or small circles, succeed in doing need by no means be universally adopted and become a character of the people and its culture as a whole, and yet it forms part of it. Aristarchus' astronomy (the Copernican universe) was without effect in Greece, as were the wisdom and divine faith of Amenemhope in Egypt, So often have the highest achievements stood on one side, uncomprehended and isolated, and either attained an ineffectual prestige for particular contingent reasons of the moment or taken effect through being misunderstood and distorted. It can be doubted whether Plato had any real effect in Greece, or Kant in Germany, outside a narrow, though magnificent, spiritual current.

Thus the unity toward which man lives, if he becomes authentically historical, cannot have its basis in a unity of biological derivation, but only in the higher origin that causes man to become directly out of the hand of the Deity. This unity of origin is not the continuance of a *status quo*. It is rather historicity itself. This is evident from the following:

(1) The unity of man in the movement of his metamorphoses is not a static unity of persisting, and merely alternately realised, qualities. Man has become man in history through a movement that is not a movement

of his natural make-up. As a natural being he is given his make-up in the area open to the play of its variations, as an historical being he reaches out beyond this natural datum. From this origin he must press on toward the unity that links all. This is a postulate: Without this unity understanding would not be possible, there would be a chasm between those of disparate natures, an understanding history would be impossible.

(2) The manifestation of individual men is of a self-exclusive character in its particular reality. Man as an individual cannot unite what he realises out of essentially disparate origins, for instance, the hero and the saint.

Man, even the individual man, is from his origin potentially everything, but in reality a single thing. In this he is not a restricted part, however, but historical, an origin of his own, turned to the other historical origin in the consciousness of the one historical fundament that links all.

The individual man is never a complete, never an ideal man. The complete man cannot, in principle, exist; for everything which he is and realises, can be, and is, broken through again, is open. Man is not a finished and not a perfectible being.

(3) In history, that which is unrepeatable and irreplaceable comes to light in unique creations, break-throughs and realisations. Because these creative steps cannot be in any way conceived causally, nor deduced as necessary, they are like revelations from some other source than the mere course of happening. But once they have come into existence, they lay the foundations of the humanity that comes after. From them man acquires his knowledge and volition, his prototypes and antitypes, his criteria, his thought-patterns and his symbols, his inner world. They are steps toward unity, because they appertain to the one self-understanding spirit and address themselves to all.

2. *The universal*

The unity of mankind is impressively evident in the fact that similar basic traits of religion, forms of thought, implements, and social forms recur all over the earth. The simplicity of man is great, despite his diversity. Psychological and sociological facts are such that comparison is possible everywhere, and a multitude of regularities can be noted, which demonstrate fundamental structures of humanity in the psychological and sociological provinces.

Precisely through observation of the common element, however, does that which is divergent become clear, whether it is to be comprehended from specific types of human make-up, or from historical situations and events. If we turn our gaze upon the universal, we shall find congruence in that which is essential, and comprehend particularities as local, attaching them to place and time.

It is precisely this universal, however, which cannot constitute the true unity of mankind. Just the reverse. If we turn our gaze upon the depths of the truth that is manifested, we shall find the historically great within the particular, but in the universal the commonplace, the unhistorically constant, which is, so to speak, the fluid medium of the factual and the correct.

If, between the most distant cultures, a common possession forms the substratum of humanity, it is quite especially surprising and important to note that there are always divergences as well, where we thought we had found an absolute universal—that somewhere something is missing which is otherwise typical of man, and also that the absolutely universal always possesses an abstract character, a uniformity.

That which, by the yardstick of the universal, is a mere particularisation, may be precisely the fulfilment of true historicity. The unity of mankind can take root only in the relationship of these historical particulars to one another, which is not essentially divergence, but rather a positively original content, not the instance of a universal, but a link in the one comprehensive historicity of mankind.

3. Progress

The road leads forward in knowledge and technological ability, one step succeeds the other, that which has been acquired may be passed on in the identical shape and become the property of all. As a result, there passes through the history of individual cultures, and of all cultures, a line of growing acquisitions, which is, however, confined to the impersonal, universally valid knowledge and ability of consciousness in general.

In this domain, world history may be conceived of as a development in an ascending line, with retrogressions and standstills it is true, but on the whole with perpetual augmentation of the possession to which men and peoples make their contribution, and which, by nature accessible to all men, also becomes the possession of all. Historically we see the stages of this advance, and in the present we stand at the highest point. This is only a line in the whole, however. Humanity itself, the ethos of man, his goodness and wisdom, make no progress. Art and poetry are indeed comprehensible to all, but not typical of all; they are bound to peoples and their epochs, each one at a unique and unsurpassable height.

Hence there is progress in knowledge, in technology, in the prerequisites for new human possibilities, but not in the substance of humanity. Progress in substance is refuted by the facts. The peoples which had reached the highest levels perished, succumbing to those inferior to them. Cultures were destroyed by barbarians. The physical annihilation of the highest types of men by the oppressive realities of the mass is a fundamental phenomenon of history. The average that multiplies the most, the growth of the thoughtless populace, triumphs without a struggle through mere existence *en masse* over that which is spiritually higher. There is a constant counter-selection of those who are inferior, e.g. in conditions under which cunning and brutality promise lasting advantages. One inclines toward the proposition: Everything exalted perishes, everything inferior endures.

Against such a generalisation, we can point to the recurrence of the great, even if it remains silent for centuries and longer. But how fragile, how dubious and uncertain is this endurance!

These are said to be only setbacks, only contingent ruin. In the long run there is reason to believe in substantial progress. But precisely these contingencies, these destructions are, at any rate in the foreground, the overwhelming basic happening of history.

It is said things need not continue to be as they have been till now. It is up to us to guide the course of events better. But this is the Utopian idea that everything can be fabricated, the principle of 'breeding' applied to the realm of man, where the object can never be known, surveyed and manipulated.

It is said ruin is the consequence of guilt. If we only expiate our sins and prove ourselves in a pure life, things will be different. Indeed, this has been the exhortation since the ancient prophets—but we do not know upon what route, when or how, the good of a world order will follow from the ethically pure life. We may not deny the reality that the ethically good as such is by no means crowned with success—nor is it done for the sake of success. But the ethically good that assumes responsibility for success and the consequences remains the one great chance.

Progress will indeed bring a unity of the knowable, but not the unity of mankind. The unity of universally valid truth which, wherever it is found, remains the same in its unending advance, appears only in science and technology. This universally communicable and transferable truth, which addresses itself to the understanding alone, is not the unity of mankind. This progress brings a unity of the understanding. It links men in the understanding, so that they discuss rationally with one another; but it leaves them capable of annihilating each other with the same weapons of technology. For the understanding only links understanding as a whole, not men. It brings no genuine communication and no solidarity.

4. Unity in space and time

The unity of man springs from life on the common natural soil (unity of the planet), and from existence in the one common time.

In the course of history intercourse developed—with setbacks. The multiplicity of the naturally given, the manifoldness of peoples and countries, existed for a long time in unrelated contiguity. The path of intercourse linked them, caused tribes to amalgamate into peoples, peoples into groups of peoples, countries into continents, and then to fall apart again. It enabled men of different peoples to catch sight of one another and then forget each other again, until the moment of conscious and factual connexion of all to all began, and intercourse became uninterrupted—either in real consummation, or in the rupture of warfare. The history of mankind as perpetual mutual exchange in the unity of intercourse commenced.

Men had long ago taken possession of the surface of the earth, with the exception of the polar regions, deserts and high mountain-chains, in the course of many thousands of years of migration. Mankind was always mobile. Amazing journeys were made at the threshold of history. The Northmen came to Greenland and America, the Polynesians crossed the whole Pacific, the Malays reached Madagascar. The languages of Negro Africa and of America are each so closely related amongst themselves as to indicate continual intercourse within these continents. Inventions, tools, ideas, legends travelled long distances across the earth in primeval historical times, always in short stages, as though passed from one hand to the other. Only Australia, and perhaps America, remained in isolation for a long time; but even they were not absolutely isolated (there are striking parallels between Eastern Asia and Mexico). Isolation does not mean that no man of another country was ever carried to their shores, but that they were never subjected to any perceptible foreign influence.

In the course of history great empires were formed, which, for a while, increased the contact between men within their domains. Then they disintegrated again, the highways of intercourse were interrupted, relations broken off, knowledge of the existence of the others forgotten. There were peoples which, from time to time, shut themselves off from the outer world—such as Egypt, Japan and China; but every wall erected was ultimately broken through again.

During the last five hundred years, the Europeans have drawn the whole earth into their communications net. They have carried their civilisation to all parts of the world and have taken for themselves goods of civilisation which they did not possess. They brought their domestic animals, useful plants and weapons, their manufactures and machines, their customs and their beliefs and all the evils of their world; they fetched potatoes, maize, quinine, cocoa, tobacco, the hammock, etc. It was they who first made the unity of the earth conscious, intercourse systematic, lasting and reliable.

This intercourse between peoples has meant a continual growing together of mankind, the creation of unity through the planet's becoming one to the consciousness, and ultimately to the actions, of men.

There is no sign of a unity of the most ancient history of cultural evolution as radiating out from one point on the earth. As far as empirical vision can see, there is rather a dispersion of men; we see the many endeavours and then the stimulus afforded by contacts between men and cultures, development resulting from the superimposition of various cultures and peoples ensuing upon conquests, and the significance of racial mixture, which either had a levelling effect or brought about exceptional achievements. Always happening is rendered historical by intercourse; it is a thrusting toward unity, not procedure from an originally given unity.

Unity through the one terrestrial soil, through common enclosure in space and time, is nevertheless the most superficial unity, which is certainly not identical with the unity of history. It is common to all reality and not the portion of man alone. The mere co-existence of men on the closed surface of the earth, which they fill, does not of itself constitute the unity of mankind. This unity is made possible by intercourse. It is by no means this intercourse *per se*, however, but only the outcome of that which takes place in this intercourse.

A glance at the globe shows the narrow strip, which is furthermore interrupted at several places (it runs from the Mediterranean region to China), that gave birth to everything spiritual which is valid today. There is no geographical right to historical equality.

5. Particular unities

In the movement of human affairs there are, to our cognition, many lines which run separately from one another and subsequently meet—or particular lines which, although they recur typically, represent only features of the whole, not the whole itself.

Thus there is the circumscribed sequence of a particular set of cultural phenomena. A few generations cohere in typical stylistic sequences or developments of thought, from their origin to their disintegration.

There are unities of cultures as *de facto* common worlds of life-forms, dispositions, ideas, units of faith, the peoples in their provenance, their language, their destiny—the religions as 'world religions', which disseminate transcendentally procured attitudes to life in ethos, faith and outlook over wide areas—the States as power units which mould everything else.

These unities lack universality. They are individual unities alongside others, cultures alongside cultures. There are many peoples, religions, States. These stand in relation to one another, cultures in silent exchanges, States in warfare and the mutual acceptance of politics, religions in mission and disputation. All of them undergo transformation, are not finally fixed, run into one another.

History shows the great factual unities in their powerfulness, the spheres of culture as, so to speak, subterranean dissemination that forms men without the use of force, the peoples as unconscious, pre-historical movements, the religions as 'world religions', though always within limits, the States as empires.

All these unities are wont to intersect and overlay one another. The coincidence of all unities reached its peak in China after the founding of the United Empire. Culture, religion and the State all coincided. The whole was the one world of man, the one empire, beyond which, to the consciousness of the Chinese, there was nothing except the primitive barbarians on the frontiers, who, as a potential component of the empire, had mentally already been incorporated into it. If the 'Central Empire' is compared with the Roman Empire the difference is considerable. The Roman Empire was a relatively transient phenomenon, although in the sequel the idea of this empire cast a spell that lasted for a thousand years. Beyond its frontiers there were Teutons and Parthians as real forces which were never vanquished. Despite the cosmic-religious unity of paganism, it was unable to permeate its peoples with this unity, as happened in China; its genesis rather caused the simultaneous growth of Christianity, which broke through it.

B. UNITY THROUGH MEANING AND GOAL

If the manifold facts which represent a unity, or point to unity, do not suffice to constitute the unity of history, a different starting-point is perhaps possible. Unity is not a fact, but a goal. The unity of history is perhaps produced by men's ability to understand each other in the idea of the One, in the one truth, in the world of the spirit, in which all things are meaningfully related to one another and belong together, however alien to each other they may be at the outset.

Unity springs from the meaning in the direction of which history occurs, a meaning that lends significance to that which, without it, would remain nugatory in dispersion.

This goal may appear as a concealed meaning, which no one intended, but which the observer tries out interpretively, or then apprehends as conscious purpose, as will to unity. The meaning is expressed as the goal of history:

(1) The goal is taken to be *civilisation* and the *humanisation* of man. What this may be, beyond the ordering of existence is, however, by no means clearly determined, but itself historical. As the ordering of existence, however, the goal is legal world order. The path of history leads out of dispersion *via* merely *de facto* contact in peace and war to cohabitation on earth in a real unity achieved through the rule of law. This unity would, through the ordering of existence, give scope to all the potentialities of the human soul and spirit.

(2) The goal is taken to be *liberty* and the consciousness of liberty. Everything that has happened up to now is to be construed as an attempt to attain liberty.

But the process that will reveal to us what liberty is has no end.

The will to a world order of law does not make its immediate goal liberty, but only political liberty, which gives human existence scope for all the possibilities of genuine liberty.

(3) The goal is taken to be the *noble man* and the creation of the spirit, the production of culture in communal conditions; it is taken to be the genius.

The urge is to the most lucid consciousness. The unity of meaning originates from the point at which man becomes most decisively conscious of himself in extreme situations—where he puts the most profound questions—where he finds the creative answers by which his life is guided and which give it its characteristic stamp. This unity in the nobility of humanity does not consist in the diffusion of implements and knowledge, not in the extent of conquests and imperial jurisdiction, not in extreme formations such as killing asceticism or the sort of training imposed on the Janizaries—not in the permanence and stability of institutions and fixations—but in the radiant moments of the most profound lucidity of consciousness, of essential revelations.

This most essential element may then be a minute speck in the stream of history. But it may begin to work like a ferment in the totality of events. Or it may remain ineffectually in memory, ready to take effect, a question put to the future. Or it may find in the world no echo to its unique nobility, vanish without recollection, and exist only for transcendence.

That such peaks appear irreplaceably valuable to us, rests upon the fact that they fall within the province of a unity which we have always presupposed and never really known, a unity without which, as its goal, origin and justification, there would be no history.

(4) The goal is taken to be the *manifestation of Being in man*, the perception of being in its depths, that is, the manifestation of the Godhead.

Such goals are attainable in every present, and indeed are attained—up to a point; they are regained in a perennial process of loss and devaluation. They are realised by every generation in its own way.

This does not mean that the single, overall goal of history is achieved, however. The imaginary goal of the future tends rather to turn our attention back to the present, which must not be let slip.

The unity of history *per se* is not laid bare by any interpretation of meaning. Every formulation, even if it hits the highest target, remains at a goal which is not the Comprehensive, at least not in the sense that all other goals could be derived from one particular concept, so that the unity of the goal would lay open to view the one meaning of history. Hence all supposed goals do indeed become factors within history, if they are desired or if faith is bestowed on them, but they are never anything that covers the whole of history.

Every meaning is present to the consciousness of men as an intended meaning in manifold shape. Within it we humans raise ourselves aloft to the One, without having it at our disposal as a content of knowledge.

At all times, however, the craving to know and believe one meaning as single and all-embracing is satisfied. And if every meaning that is absolutised is bound to come to grief, new generations in their turn immediately seek, through their philosophers, an all-embracing meaning that has governed, and is governing, history, and which, once it has been conceived, can also be assimilated into their own will as an intended meaning and taken as a guide (as in the Christian philosophy of history, as in Hegel, in Comte, etc.).

This unity is brought into view in an interpretive total conception of history.

C. UNITY FOR THE THINKING TOTAL CONCEPTION

To comprehend the unity of history, i.e. to think of universal history as a whole, is the urge of historical knowledge in search of its ultimate meaning.

Philosophical consideration of history has therefore enquired after the unity that holds mankind together. Men settled the globe, but they were scattered and did not know of one another, lived in the most diverse guises and spoke thousands of languages. In earlier times, anyone who thought of universal history, because of the narrowness of his horizon, constructed a unity at the expense of restriction; amongst ourselves, for instance, he restricted himself to the West, in China to the Central Empire. That which lay beyond had no part in it and was regarded as a life of barbarians, primitive peoples, which were certainly an object of ethnological interest, but not of history. Unity consisted in the presupposition of the tendency to cause all the still unknown peoples of the earth to participate, stage by stage, in the one— namely, one's own—culture, to bring them into one's own sphere of order.

If faith presupposed one fundament and one goal, the idea sought to recognise these in real history. Assumptions of a knowledge of unity, either given by divine revelation or intelligible to reason, were attempts at constructing the one history of mankind.

God's passage through history became visible in the West in the succession of His acts running from Creation, via expulsion from Paradise, announcement of His will through the prophets, redemption through His appearance in person at the turning-point of the ages, to the end in the anticipated Last

Judgement. That which was first thought of by the Jewish prophets, then assumed Christian form through St. Augustine, which was repeated and inflected from Joachim Fiore to Bousset, secularised from Lessing and Herder to Hegel, was always this knowledge of the one whole history, in which everything has its place. A series of fundamental principles of human existence made their appearance which, apprehended in their depths, taught what truly is and happens.

Such a construction, however—magnificently as it has been believed and expressed throughout two millennia—breaks down:

(a) If I know the whole, every human existence has its place in the whole. It is not for itself, but serves a path. It is not immediate to transcendence, but through the medium of a position in time, which narrows it and makes it a part. Every human existence, every period, every people, is mediatised. Against this the original relationship to the Godhead, the infinitude of the Comprehensive, which can be whole at any time, revolts.

(b) In the knowledge of the whole, the greater proportion of human reality, whole peoples, epochs and cultures, fall to one side as of no account. They are no more than chance and incidental products of natural happening.

(c) History is not closed and does not reveal its origin. For this construction, however, it is closed. The beginning and end are invented as an addition in the shape of an alleged revelation. In fact, two mutually exclusive fundamental conceptions of history confront one another.

Either history is visible as a whole, and as the unity of a knowable evolution with a beginning and an end. I myself with my period stand at the particular point, thought of either as the lowest or the highest point yet reached.

Or history is actually, and for my consciousness, unclosed. I hold myself open to the future. It is an attitude of waiting and of seeking the truth, of not yet knowing even that which already is, but which will be fully understandable only from the vantage point of the future. In this basic attitude even the past is unconcluded: it still lives, its decisions are not totally, but only relatively, final; they can be revised. That which was is still capable of reinterpretation. That which seemed to have been decided becomes once more a query. That which has been, has still to reveal to us what it is. It does not lie there as an inert residue. There is more in the past than what has so far been objectively and rationally extracted from it. The thinker himself is still standing in the evolution that is history; he is not at the end, and hence— from his position on a hill with a restricted view, not on the world mountain from which everything is visible—he knows the directions of possible ways, and yet does not know the origin and goal of the whole.

Hence history may appear to us as a field for experiment, unity vanishes in the infinitude of the possible. The permanent basic attitude is one of questioning. The calm of a great symbol of the whole, of an image of the unity of everything, that erases time and with it past and future, is only a halting-place in time, not the finality of a known truth.

If history is not to disintegrate into the dispersion of the fortuitous, into a coming and going without direction, into the pathlessness of many sham paths, then the idea of the unity of history is inescapable. The only question is the manner in which it is apprehended.

We have drawn up a long list of negations: The unity of history is not to be apprehended by knowledge. It cannot be construed as the unity of man's biological origin. As the unity of the earth's surface and as common enclosure by real time it is a purely external unity. The unity of the all-embracing goal cannot be demonstrated. The idea of a world order of law is directed toward the substrata of human existence, not toward the meaning of history in toto, and is itself still a query. Unity cannot be comprehended by reference to the identity of a universally valid truth, for this unity relates only to the understanding. It is not progress toward a goal or in a process that goes on into infinity. Unity does not consist in the most lucid consciousness, nor in the nobility of spiritual creation. It is not contained in a meaning toward which everything happens or ought to happen. Nor is unity to be discerned as the articulated organism of a totality of mankind. The totality of history is not truly present in a visual image either as reality or as meaning.

He who does not fall in with the arrogant assumption of an all-embracing comprehension of history as a unity, will nonetheless see in all these strivings for unity a dash of truth. This becomes fallacious if the particular is carried over onto the whole. It remains true as an indication and a sign.

Every line of development, every typical form, all facts of unity are simplifications within history that become fallacious when they are used as a means of seeing through history in its totality. The important thing is to apprehend the manifoldness of these lines, forms, unities, but to remain open to that which lies beyond them, in which these phenomena occur, to remain open to man and to the always present whole of humanity; this humanity embraces everything and bears within itself that which, despite all its magnificence, is never more than one phenomenon amongst others.

There remains the demand constituted by the idea of unity. We are confronted by universal history as a task.

(a) At the least, there remains the scanning of all human happening in the whole world. In the alternative between dispersed isolation and essential centralisation, neither of the two extremes is accepted; instead a pertinent, constructive classification of history is sought. Even if every construction of the unity of history will always make abysmal nescience felt in knowledge, the way of classification under the idea of a unity is nevertheless possible.

(b) This unity is then supported by the closedness of the planet, which, as space and soil, is entire and susceptible of control; furthermore, by the exactitude of chronology in the one time, even if it is abstract; in addition, by the unity of the root of the human race, which is of one species, a biological fact which points to common derivation.

(c) The principal basis for unity is the fact that men meet each other in the one spirit of a universal capacity for understanding. Men find one another in a comprehensive spirit, which, although no one sees it as a whole, nonetheless contains all. Unity finds its most decisive expression in relation to the one God.

(d) The idea of unity is concretely present in the consciousness of universal possibilities. The openness with which things are looked at increases the claim that everything can acquire importance for everything, and is of concern to everything through the mere fact of its existence. We live in the consciousness of a space in which nothing is indifferent, which opens up distant vistas as concerning us, and which at the same time indicates the current present as a decision over the road that will be taken. With our eyes on the earliest beginnings, which never go as far back as the origin, and with our eyes on the future, which is always unconcluded, possibilities become known in an incomprehensible whole, so that the unity of the whole is manifested in the decisiveness of the present fulfilment of the task.

(e) If a tenable and finished picture of the whole is out of reach, there remain forms in which images of the whole are from time to time disclosed. These forms are:

History is seen in hierarchies of value, in its origins, in its crucial stages. The real is divided up into the essential and the inessential.

History stands under a whole that was called Providence, and was later conceived of as a law. Although the concrete shape it has taken is erroneous, this idea of the whole will remain an extreme notion of that which is not seen, but within which we see, which cannot be planned, but within which planning must be carried out. History as a whole is unique, is specifically historical and not merely natural happening. There remains the idea of an order of the whole, in which everything has its proper place. It is not mere fortuitous multiformity, but all the features of the fortuitous are merged in the one great basic feature of history.

As an interpretation of unity we, for our part, have projected a schema of world history which seems today in the closest accord with openness and unity and empirical reality. Our exposition of world history sought to derive historical unity from the Axial Period, which was common to the whole of mankind.

The word axis was not intended to convey the concealed interior, round which the foreground of phenomena at all times revolves, that element which is itself timeless, but which extends through all ages and is enveloped by the dust-clouds of the solely present. The appellation axis was bestowed rather upon an era around the middle of the last millennium B.C., for which everything that preceded it would appear to have been a preparation, and to which everything subsequent actually, and often in clear consciousness, relates back. The world history of humanity derives its structure from this period. It is not an axis of which we might assert a permanent absoluteness and uniqueness. But it is the axis of the short world history that has taken place up till now, that which, in the consciousness of all men, might represent the basis of the historical unity they recognise in solidarity. This real axis would then be the incarnation of an ideal axis, around which mankind in its movement is drawn together.

SUMMARY

We seek to apprehend the unity of history in images of the whole, which demonstrate the historicity of mankind per se in an empirically founded structure—wherein the fundamental fact remains the boundless openness into the future and the short beginning: we are just starting. Into the future in fact, and as the past in interpretation, history is an open, infinite world of relationships of meaning, which, at any rate from time to time, seem to flow into one growing common meaning.

The theme is: not one of those universal categories, not historical laws, but enquiry after the unity of history in its factual, perceptibly given, unique shape, which is not a law, but the historical arcanum itself. This shape we call the structure of history. It must be construed, in its spatial-temporal localisation, as the spiritual reality of humanity.

The interpretive contemplation of history becomes a determination of man's will. Unity becomes his goal. Contemplation of the past is related to this goal. It becomes conscious, for example, as world peace in world order through a legal order aimed at the liberation from want and the bestowal of happiness upon, as nearly as possible, everyone.

This goal relates, however, only to the substratum of existence, which it is possible for all to attain in common. It is true that this unity in the preconditions for all human possibilities would be of immense importance; it is not the final goal, however, but in turn a means.

Unity is sought at a higher level in the totality of the world of human being and creating. With this in view, the unity of past history is derived from the emphasis of that which concerns all men, of that which is essential to all.

What this is, however, can become manifest only in the movement of living together. The demand for boundless communication testifies to the solidarity of all men in potential understanding. But that which is known, fashioned, aimed at does not, in itself, constitute unity, nor does the image of a goal; all these constitute unity only when they enter into the communication of man with man. The ultimate question is then:

Does the unity of mankind consist in unification on the basis of a common faith, in the objectivity of that which is thought and believed in common to be true, in an organisation of the one eternal truth by an authority that spans the earth?

Or is the only unity truly attainable to us humans unity through communication of the historically manifold origins, which are mutually concerned with one another, without becoming identical in the manifestation of idea and symbol—a unity which leaves the One concealed in manifoldness, the One that can remain true only in the will to boundless communication, as an endless task in the interminable testing of human possibilities?

All assertions of absolute alienness, of the permanent impossibility of mutual understanding, remain the expression of resignation in lassitude, of failure before the most profound demand of humanity—the intensification of temporary impossibilities into absolute impossibilities, the extinction of inner readiness.[1]

The unity of history will never be consummated in the accomplished unification of mankind. History lies between origin and goal, the idea of unity is at work in it. Man follows his great highway of history, but never terminates it by realising its final goal. The unity of mankind is, rather, the bourne of history. That is to say: Achieved, consummate unity would be the end of history. History remains movement, under the guidance of unity, accompanied by notions and ideas of unity.

Unity is contained in such notions as these: Mankind stems from one origin, from which it has evolved in infinite division, and strives toward the re-unification of that which has been split up. Complete obscurity surrounds the one origin, however. Wherever we come across man he is already in the dispersion and differentiation of individuals and races; we see several cultural evolutions, manifold beginnings, which must have been preceded by an already human evolution that we do not know. Unity guides us as the notion of an organism which is reaching perfection in the mutuality of the many. All such notions are vague, however.

Notions of unity delude us, if we take them to be more than symbols. Unity as the goal is an unending task; for all unities which become visible to us are particular, are only preconditions for a possible unity; or they are levelling processes, behind which abysmal alienness, repulsion and conflict lie concealed.

It is not possible to formulate a clear and consistent picture of perfect unity, even in the realm of ideas. This unity cannot become real, either as the complete man, or as the right organisation of the world, or as final, penetrating and open mutual understanding and agreement. The One is rather the infinitely remote point of reference, which is origin and goal at one and the same time; it is the One of transcendence. As such it cannot be, so to speak, taken captive; it cannot become the exclusive possession of an historical faith that could be enforced upon all as truth *per se.*

If universal history as a whole proceeds from the One to the One, it does so in such a way that everything accessible to us lies between these ultimate poles. There is a becoming of unities, an enthusiastic seeking of unity; and then again a passionate smashing of unities.

Thus this deepest unity is elevated to an invisible religion, to the realm of spirits, the secret realm of the manifestation of Being in the concord of souls. Historically, however, there remains movement, which, always between beginning and end, never attains to, nor continuously is, what it really signifies.

NOTE

1   (Page 291): It is a question of a great polarity: catholicity and reason, cf. my book *Von der Wahrheit,* Munich 1948, pp. 832–68.

15

OUR MODERN HISTORICAL CONSCIOUSNESS

We live in a great heritage of historical knowledge. The great historians since antiquity, historico-philosophical total conceptions, art and poetry fill our historical imagination. To this has been added during recent centuries—in a thoroughgoing fashion in the nineteenth century—critical historical research. Never did any age possess so much information concerning the past as our own. That which the generations before us did not possess at all is at our finger-tips in the shape of publications, reconstructions, collections and classifications.

Today a transformation of our historical consciousness seems to be in progress. The great achievement of scientific historical research is being preserved and continued. But now we have to see how this material is to be given a fresh shape, how, after being refined in the melting-pot of nihilism, it can serve to become a single, marvellous language of the eternal origin. History will cease to be a mere field of knowledge, and become once again a question of the consciousness of life and of existence; it will cease to be an affair of aesthetic culture, and become the earnestness of hearing and response. The way in which we look at history is no longer harmless. The meaning of our own lives is determined by the manner in which we know ourselves in the whole and obtain from this whole an historical fundament and goal.

Perhaps we can characterise a few features of the historical consciousness which is coming into being:

(a) New is the *many-sidedness* and *precision* of the *methods of research*, the feeling for the infinitely complex tissue of causal factors, as well as for objectification in categories quite other than causal, in morphological structures, in laws of meaning, in ideal-typical constructs.

To be sure, we still take pleasure in reading simple narrative expositions. We seek with their aid to fill the space of our inner intuition with images. But intuition first becomes essential to our cognition with the analyses that are nowadays comprised under the term sociology. This is represented by Max Weber and his works, with his clear and multi-dimensional conceptuality in this widest of all the horizons of historical interpretation, which he keeps free from fixation in a total conception. Today anyone acquainted with such thinking reads many pages of Ranke's with reluctance, on account of the vagueness of his concepts. Penetrating comprehension demands a wide variety of specialised knowledge and its combination in the formulation of questions which are illuminating in themselves. In the process, the old method of comparison, through its newly acquired acuity, causes the unique to stand out all the more clearly. Engrossment in the specifically historical brings the enigma of the unique to more lucid consciousness.

(b) Today the attitude to history that knows it as an *overseeable whole* is being surmounted. No exclusive total outline of history is still capable of satisfying us. We do not obtain a final, but only a currently possible, integument for the totality of history, which breaks up again.

Furthermore, we find no historically localised revelation of absolute truth. At no point is anything to be found which it would behove us to repeat identically. Truth lies in the never known origin, from the vantage point of which everything particular is circumscribed in its manifestation. We know: Wherever we find ourselves on the way to historical absolutisation, fallacy will one day be revealed and the painful recoil of nihilism will set us free for fresh original thinking.

Nevertheless, we do not possess, but we at all times seek, a reminiscent knowledge of the totality of history in which we are situated at a unique instant. It is the total conception which gives our consciousness its horizon at any given moment.

Today, in the consciousness of calamity, we tend not only to discern a relative closedness in individual developments of the past, but also to see the whole course of history up to the present as being rounded off. It seems to be concluded and irretrievably lost; something new must take its place. We have grown used to statements concerning the end of philosophy, that takes leave of us in the persons of elaborators of the ideas of their predecessors and historians—concerning the end of art, that behaves with the desperation of approaching death in the repetition of bygone styles, accompanied by caprice and private longings, and the substitution of the functional forms of technology for art—concerning the end of history altogether in any hitherto accepted sense. At the eleventh hour, exercising the power of understanding, we can form a picture of that which is already growing strange to us, that which no longer is, and never again will be; we can once more put into words that which will soon have been completely forgotten.

Such propositions carry no convictions at all; their consequence is always a nihilism that makes way for something about which we can make no clear statement, but about which, perhaps for that very reason, we speak in all the more fanatical terms.

In contrast to this, the modern approach is to render all total conceptions, including negative ones like the foregoing, provisional, to present all possible total conceptions to our imagination in order to test how far they fit the facts. This process will sooner or later result in a comprehensive conception, in which the rest are individual elements; with this conception we shall live, make our present conscious to ourselves, and illumine our situation.

In actual fact, we are at all times formulating total views of history. If these develop into schemata of history as possible perspectives, their meaning is distorted as soon as a total conception comes to be taken for real knowledge of the whole, whose course is apprehended in its necessity. We attain the truth only so far as, instead of total causality, we investigate particular causalities extending into the infinite. To our contemplative gaze, however, there are in history the leaps of human creation, the revelation of unexpected contents, and self-transformation in the succession of generations.

Of every construction of a total conception we say today: it must be empirically proven. We reject conceptions of events and conditions which are
only conjectural. We search hungrily in all directions for the reality of tradition. That which is irreal can no longer survive. What this means can be
seen from the extreme example that Schelling still clung with complete conviction to the theory that the creation of the world took place six thousand
years ago, whereas today no one doubts the bone finds which prove man's
life on earth to have gone on for more than a hundred thousand years. It
is true that the resulting chronological criterion of history is purely external, but it cannot be forgotten and has its effects on consciousness. For the
ephemeral briefness of the history that has passed is clear.

The totality of history is an open whole. *Vis-à-vis* this whole the empirical
approach, conscious of the small extent of its factual knowledge, is ever
ready to assimilate fresh facts; the philosophical approach discards all totality
of an absolute mundane immanence. If empiricism and philosophy mutually aid one another, the thinking man is left with the area of possibilities,
and thereby with freedom. The open whole has for him no beginning and
no end. No termination of history can enter his ken.

The method of the total thinking that is still possible, and that sees through
itself, contains the following elements.

Facts are taken up and, so to speak, tapped to hear what sound they emit
and to get a hint of the meaning they may possibly have.

At all points we are led to the frontiers, in order to obtain the most extreme horizons.

From out of these horizons demands come to us. A reaction throws the
viewer of history back upon himself and his presentness.

(c)   Mere *aesthetic consideration* of history is *done away with*. If, *vis-à-vis* the endless material of historical knowledge, it is deemed worthwhile recall-
ing everything, simply because it was—in a spirit of detachment that
merely ascertains actual facts without end—this unselectiveness arises
out of an aesthetic attitude, to which everything can in some way be
considered as a means to the stimulation and satisfaction of curiosity: one thing is beautiful and so is the other. This historism devoid
of obligations, whether it be scientific or aesthetic, leads to a state of
mind in which, after everything has become of equal value, nothing has
any longer any value at all. Historical reality is not free of obligations,

however. Our true approach to history should be to wrestle with it. History concerns us; that in it which concerns us is continually expanding, which makes it a question of immediate importance to mankind. History acquires increasing immediate significance, the less it is an object of mere aesthetic enjoyment.

(d) We are attuned to the unity of mankind in a more comprehensive and concrete sense than previously. We know the deep satisfaction that comes when we gaze into the origin of the one mankind, from the wealth of its ramifications in manifestation. It is from this area that we are first thrown back upon our own historicity, which becomes, through consciousness, both more profound to itself and more open to all others and to the one comprehensive historicity of man.

It is not a question of 'mankind' as an abstract concept in which man disappears. Rather is the abstract concept of mankind dropped from our historical consciousness. The idea of mankind becomes concrete and perceptual only in real history as a totality. There, however, it becomes a refuge in the origin, from whence come the right standards, after we have become helpless in bewilderment amidst catastrophe and the destruction of all the habits of thought which previously gave security. The origin brings the demand for communication in an unrestricted sense. It imparts the satisfaction of affinity in the midst of the alien, and of the community of the human running through all peoples. It shows the goal that leaves a possibility open to our longing for and our will to life in community.

World history may look like a chaos of chance events—in its entirety like the swirling waters of a whirlpool. It goes on and on, from one muddle to another, from one disaster to another, with brief flashes of happiness, with islands that remain for a short time protected from the flood, till they too are submerged; all in all, in a metaphor of Max Weber: World history resembles a street paved by the devil with destroyed values.

Seen in this light, history has no unity and hence no structure, and no other meaning than that contained in the incalculably numerous causal concatenations and constructions, such as also occur in the processes of nature, save that in history they are much more inexact.

But historical philosophy means the search for such a unity, such a meaning, for the structure of world history—and this can concern only mankind as a whole.

HISTORY AND THE PRESENT BECOME INSEPARABLE TO US

(e) Historical consciousness is situated in a polarity: I step back before his-
     tory and see it as something confronting me, like the whole chain of a
     distant great range of mountains, in its general outline and in its details.
     Or I become aware of presentness as a whole, the Now, which is and
     in which I am, in the deepening of which history becomes to me the
     present that I myself am.

Both are necessary, the objectivity of history as the other, that exists even
without me, and the subjectivity of the Now, without which no other has
any meaning for me. The one comes really alive through the other. Each one
by itself renders history ineffectual, either as the unending content of the
knowledge of that which is open to indifferent choice, or as oblivion.

But how are the two to be linked? Not by any rational method. Rather does
the one control the movement of the other by simultaneously stimulating it.

This fundamental situation in historical consciousness determines the
manner in which we are convinced of the structure of history as a whole.

To forgo the latter is impossible; then it would simply take unconscious
and uncontrolled possession of our outlook. To formulate it, however, renders it provisional as a piece of knowledge, while it remains a factor in our
consciousness of Being.

While research and existence with their consciousness of Being attain
consummation in mutual tension, research itself lives in the tension between
the current whole and the smallest detail. Historical total consciousness, in
conjunction with loving nearness to the particular, visualises a world in
which man can live as himself with his matrix. Openness into the breadth of
history and self-identity with the present, perception of history as a whole,
and life from present origin, these tensions make possible the man who, cast
back upon his absolute historicity, has come to himself.

A universal view of history and consciousness of one's present situation
mutually sustain one another. As I see the totality of the past, so I experience
the present. The deeper the foundations I acquire in the past, the more outstanding my participation in the present course of events.

Where I belong and what I am living for I first learn in the mirror of
history. 'He who cannot give himself an account of three thousand years is
left without landmarks in the dark, and can live only from day to day'—this

represents consciousness of meaning, then consciousness of place (orientation) and, above all, consciousness of substance.

It is an astonishing fact that presentness can vanish from us, that we can lose reality, by always living elsewhere, so to speak, by living in fantasy, in history, and avoiding complete presentness.

It is, however, wrong to contrast this with the presentness of the mere instant, life in the Now destitute of recollection or future. For such a life is the loss of human potentialities in a Now that is becoming more and more empty, in which there is nothing left of the plenitude of the Now drawn from the everlasting present.

The riddle of the fulfilled Now will never be solved, but deepened, by historical consciousness. The depth of the Now becomes manifest only hand in hand with past and future, with memory, and with the idea of that toward which I am living. Therein I am certain of the everlasting present through the shape of history, through faith wearing the garb of history.

Or can I elude history, escape from it into the timeless?

16

OVERCOMING HISTORY

We have called to mind: History is not completed—happening conceals in itself infinite possibilities—whenever history takes shape as a known whole this shape is broken through, that which is remembered discloses, through fresh data, hitherto unobserved truth; that which was discarded as inessential acquires overriding essentiality. The conclusion of history seems impossible; it proceeds from the endless into the endless, and only an external disaster can break off the whole process in a fashion alien to its meaning.

We are seized by a feeling of dissatisfaction with history. We should like to force our way through history to a point before and above all history, to the matrix of Being, before which the whole of history becomes a phenomenon that can never be 'right' in itself, to the point at which, sharing knowledge with creation so to speak, we are no longer entirely at the mercy of history.

But for us the known Archimedean point can never be situated outside history. We are always within history. In forcing our way through to that which lies before, or athwart, or after all history, into that which comprehends everything, into Being itself, we are seeking in our existence and in transcendence, what this Archimedean point would be if it were capable of assuming the form of objective knowledge.

(1) We overstep history by addressing ourselves to nature. Face to face with the ocean, in the mountains, in the tempest, in the radiance of sunrise, in the iridescence of the elements, in the lifeless polar world of snow and ice, in the primeval forest, wherever nature that is alien to man speaks to us, we may experience a feeling of liberation. A homecoming into unconscious life, a still deeper homecoming into the clarity of the inanimate elements, can sweep us along into stillness, into exultation, into painless unity. But all this is a deception if it is more than the transient experience of the mystery of natural Being, which maintains a total silence, this Being beyond everything that we call good and evil, beautiful and ugly, true and false, this Being that leaves us in the lurch without heart and without compassion. If we really find sanctuary there, we have run away from men and from ourselves. But if we take these momentarily overwhelming experiences of nature as mute signs, pointing to that which is above all history but which they do not make manifest, then they remain true in that they impel us forward and do not hold us back with ourselves.

(2) We overstep history into that which is timelessly valid, into the truth that is independent of all history, into mathematics and into all cogent knowledge, into every form of the universal and universally valid, which remains unaffected by all mutation, whether recognised or unrecognised. We may be seized with fervour at the apprehension of this clarity of the valid. We have a fixed point, a Being which persists. Again, however, we are misled if we attach ourselves to this. This validity too is a sign, but it does not bear the import of Being. It leaves us singularly unconcerned, it is disclosed in the continuous advance of its discovery. It is essentially the form of validity, whereas its content coincides with the endless plurality of the existent, never with Being itself. Only our understanding here enjoys the peace of something that persists. Not we ourselves. The fact that this validity exists, however, independently and freed from all history, is once again a pointer to the supra-temporal.

(3) We overstep history into the matrix of historicity, that is, to historicity in the entirety of the world's being. From the history of mankind a road leads into the matrix out of which the whole of nature—unhistorical in itself—moves into the light of an historicity. But only to the speculation—for which it becomes a language—that something in his own biological scaffolding, in landscapes and natural events, comes

from nature to meet the historicity of man. To begin with these are all alien in meaning and inconclusive, catastrophes or the indifferently existent; they are then, as it were, invested by history with a soul, as though they were correspondences springing from a common root.

(4) It is the historicity of our own existence that leads us into this matrix of historicity. From the point at which, in the unconditionality of our adoption and choice of the way we find ourselves in the world, of our bestowal upon ourselves in love itself, we become Being athwart time as historicity; from this point, light falls upon the historicity of history through the agency of our communication, which, passing through the knowable data of history, comes upon existence. Here we overstep history to the everlasting present; as historical existence in history we are above and beyond history.

(5) We overcome history by entering into the unconscious. The spirit of man is conscious. Consciousness is the medium without which there is for us neither knowledge nor experience, neither humanity nor relationship to transcendence. That which is not conscious is called unconscious. Unconscious is a negative concept, endlessly ambiguous in its implications.

Our consciousness is directed toward that which is unconscious, that is, toward everything we encounter in the world from which nothing inward communicates itself to us. And our consciousness is borne by the unconscious, it is a continual growth out of the unconscious and sliding back into the unconscious. But we can gain experience of the unconscious only through consciousness. In every conscious step of our lives, especially in every creative act of the spirit, we are aided by an unconscious within us. Pure consciousness is incapable of doing anything. Consciousness is like the crest of a wave, a peak above a broad and deep subsoil.

This unconscious that bears us has a dual meaning. The unconscious that is nature, per se and for ever enigmatic—and the unconscious that is the germ of the spirit, that strives to become manifest.

If we overcome history by entering into the unconscious as the existent which becomes manifest in the phenomenon of consciousness, this unconscious is never nature, but that which is revealed in the outcrop of symbols in language, poetry, representation and self-representation, in reflection. We live not only from out of it, but also toward it. The more lucidly consciousness renders it manifest, the more substantially, profoundly and comprehensively it becomes actual itself. For within it that germ is awakened whose wakefulness heightens and widens consciousness itself. The passage of the spirit through history not only consumes a pre-existent unconscious, but also produces a new unconscious. Both modes of expressions are fallacious, however, in relation to the one unconscious, to penetrate which is not only the process of the history of the spirit, but which is Being, above, before and after all history.

As the unconscious, its characteristics are purely negative, however. No cryptograph of Being is to be gained with this concept, as Eduard von Hartmann vainly sought to do in a world of positivist thinking. The unconscious is of value only to the extent to which it takes shape in consciousness, and thereby ceases to be unconscious. Consciousness is the real and true. Heightened consciousness, not the unconscious, is our goal. We overcome history by entering into the unconscious in order, rather, to attain heightened consciousness.

The urge to unconsciousness, which takes hold of us humans at all times of adversity, is illusory. Whether a Babylonian god seeks to put an end to the uproar of the world with the words 'I want to sleep', or whether Western man longs to be back in the Garden of Eden, before he ate of the Tree of Knowledge, whether he considers it best he had never been born, whether he strives to find his way back to a state of nature prior to all culture, whether he deems consciousness a calamity and looks upon the whole of history as a false trail and desires to bring it to an end—it is for ever the same thing in manifold guises. It is not an overcoming of history, but an evasion of history and one's own existence in it.

(6) We overstep history when man becomes present to us in his most exalted works, through which he has been able, as it were, to catch Being in motion, and has rendered it communicable. What has here been done by men, who allowed themselves to be absorbed by the eternal truth which became language through them, although it wears an historical garb, is above and beyond history and leads us along the route that passes over the world of history into that which is prior to all history and becomes language through history. In this realm there is no longer any question of whence and whither, of future and progress, but in time there is something which is no longer solely time and which comes to us, above all time, as Being itself.

History itself becomes the road to the supra-historical. In the contemplation of the great—in the provinces of creation, action and thought—history shines forth as the everlasting present. It no longer satisfies curiosity, but becomes an invigorating force. The great things of history, as objects of veneration, bind us to the matrix above all history.

(7) The apprehension of history as a whole leads beyond history. The unity of history is itself no longer history. To grasp this unity means to pass above and beyond history into the matrix of this unity, through which that unity is which enables history to become a whole. But this ascent above history to the unity of history remains itself a task within history. We do not live in the knowledge of history; in so far, however, as we live by unity we live supra-historically in history.

Every ascent above history becomes an illusion if we abandon history. The fundamental paradox of our existence, the fact that it is only within the world that we can live above and beyond the world, is repeated in the historical consciousness that rises above history. There is no way round the world, no way round history, but only a way through history.

(8) A glance at the long ages of prehistory and the short span of history, gives rise to the question: Is history not a transitory phenomenon, in view of the hundreds of thousands of years of prehistory? At bottom, there is no other answer save the general proposition: that which has a beginning also has an end—even if it lasts for millions or billions of years.

But the answer—which is impossible to our empirical knowledge—is superfluous to our consciousness of Being. For even if our view of history may be considerably modified according to whether we see unending progress, or the shadow of the end, the essential thing is that historical knowledge as a whole is not the ultimate knowledge. What matters is the demand for presentness as eternity in time. History is encompassed by the broader horizon, in which presentness counts as abode, verification, decision, fulfilment. That which is eternal appears as decision in time. To the transcendent consciousness of existence, history vanishes in the everlasting present.

Within history itself, however, there remains the perspective of time: perhaps the history of mankind will continue for a long, a very long time on the earth that has now become unitary. Within this perspective then, the question for everyone is: where he will stand, for what he will work.

OTHER WORKS BY KARL JASPERS

Allgemeine Psychopathologie. 1913. Fifth edition 1948. 748 pages. Springer-Verlag, Heidelberg and Berlin.

Psychologie der Weltanschauungen. 1919. Third edition 1925. 486 pages. Springer-Verlag, Heidelberg and Berlin.

Strindberg und van Gogh. 1922. 131 pages. Third edition Joh. Storm-Verlag, Bremen.

Max Weber: Rede bei der Trauerfeier. 1920. 30 pages. Second edition 1926. Verlag Siebeck, Tübingen.

Die geistige Situation der Zeit, 1931. 191 pages. Seventh edition Verlag W. de Gruyter & Co., Berlin. (English translation by Eden and Cedar Paul: *Man in the Modern Age,* Routledge & Kegan Paul, London, 1951.)

Max Weber: Politiker, Forscher, Philosoph. 1932. Second edition 1946. 58 pages. Joh. Storm-Verlag, Bremen.

Philosophie. 3 vols. 1932. Second edition in one vol. 1948. 913 pages. Springer-Verlag, Heidelberg and Berlin.

Vernunft und Existenz. 1935. New edition 1947. 124 pages. Joh. Storm-Verlag, Bremen.

Nietzsche: Einführung in das Verständnis seines Philosophierens. 1936. Second edition 1947. 487 pages. Third edition Verlag W. de Gruyter & Co., Berlin.

Descartes und die Philosophie. 1937. Second edition 1948. 104 pages. Verlag W. de Gruyter & Co., Berlin.

Nietzsche und das Christentum. 1946. 85 pages. Verlag der Bücherstube Fritz Seifert, Hamelin.

Die Idee der Universität. 1946. 132 pages. Springer-Verlag, Heidelberg and Berlin.

Vom lebendigen Geist der Universität. 40 pages. Verlag Lambert Schneider, Heidelberg.

Die Schuldfrage. 1946. 106 pages. Verlag Lambert Schneider, Heidelberg, and at the Artemis-Verlag, Zurich, 96 pages.

Antwort an Sigrid Undset u. a. Aufsätze. 1947. 31 pages. Südverlag, Constance.

Vom europäischen Geist, 1947. 31 pages. R. Piper & Co. Verlag, Munich. L'Esprit Européen, pub. Les Editions de la Baconnière, Boudry. (English translation by Ronald Gregor Smith: *European Spirit,* SCM Press, London.)

Der philosophische Glaube. 1947. 136 pages. Second edition 1948. R. Piper & Co., Verlag, Munich, and at the Artemis-Verlag, Zurich. 158 pages. (English translation by Ralph Mannheim: *The Perennial Scope of Philosophy,* Routledge & Kegan Paul, London, 1950.)

Von der Wahrheit. 1947. XXIV, 1103 pages. R. Piper & Co. Verlag, Munich.

Unsere Zukunft und Goethe. 1948. 43 pages. Artemis-Verlag, Zurich, and at the Joh. Storm-Verlag, Bremen.

Philosophie und Wissenschaft. 1949. 16 pages. Artemis-Verlag, Zurich.

Einführung in die Philosophie. 1950. Artemis-Verlag, Zurich. (English translation by Ralph Mannheim: *Way to Wisdom: An Introduction to Philosophy,* Victor Gollancz, London, 1951.)

INDEX

Note: Page number followed by "n" refer to endnotes.